THE ROUTLEDGE INTRODUCTION TO AMERICAN MODERNISM

The modernist period was crucial for American literature as it gave writers the chance to be truly innovative and create their own distinct identities. Starting earlier than many guides to Modernism, this lucid and comprehensive guide introduces the reader to the essential history of the period including technology, religion, economy, class, gender, and immigration. These contexts are woven into discussions of many significant authors and texts from the period. Wagner-Martin brings her years of writing about American modernism to explicate poetry and drama as well as fiction and life-writing. Among those authors emphasized are Ernest Hemingway, William Faulkner, Zora Neale Hurston, Langston Hughes, F. Scott Fitzgerald, Gertrude Stein, Willa Cather, John Dos Passos, William Carlos Williams, Mike Gold, James T. Farrell, Clifford Odets, John Steinbeck, and countless others.

A clear and engaging introduction to an exciting period of literature, this is the ultimate guide for those seeking an overview of American modernism.

Linda Wagner–Martin is Frank Borden and Barbara Lasater Hanes Professor of English Emerita at the University of North Carolina, Chapel Hill, USA. She has recently been awarded the Hubbell Medal for her lifetime of work in American literature.

ROUTLEDGE INTRODUCTIONS TO AMERICAN LITERATURE

Series Editors: D. Quentin Miller and Wendy Martin

Routledge Introductions to American Literature provide a comprehensive overview of the most important topics in American Literature in its historical, cultural, and intellectual contexts. They present the most up-to-date trends, debates, and exciting new directions in the field, opening the way for further study.

The volumes in the series examine the ways in which both canonical and lesser known writers from diverse cultural backgrounds have shaped American literary traditions. In addition to providing insight into contemporary and theoretical debates and giving attention to a range of voices and experiences as a vital part of American life, these comprehensive volumes offer clear, cohesive narratives of the development of American Literature.

The American literary tradition has always been flexible and mutable. Every attempt to define American literature as a static body has been thwarted by the nature of its subject, which is—like its nation's ideals—pluralistic, diverse, democratic, and inventive. Our goal in this series is to provide fresh perspectives on many dimensions of the American literary tradition while offering a solid overview for readers encountering it for the first time.

D. Quentin Miller and Wendy Martin

Available in this series:

The Routledge Introduction to African American Literature
D. Quentin Miller

The Routledge Introduction to American Modernism
Linda Wagner-Martin

The Routledge Introduction to American Women Writers
Wendy Martin and Sharone Williams

THE ROUTLEDGE INTRODUCTION TO AMERICAN MODERNISM

Linda Wagner-Martin

Routledge
Taylor & Francis Group

LONDON AND NEW YORK

First published 2016
by Routledge
2 Park Square, Milton Park, Abingdon, Oxon OX14 4RN

and by Routledge
711 Third Avenue, New York, NY 10017

Routledge is an imprint of the Taylor & Francis Group, an informa business

British Library Cataloguing-in-Publication Data
A catalogue record for this book is available from the British Library

Library of Congress Cataloging-in-Publication Data
A catalog record for this title has been requested

ISBN: 978-1-138-84739-2 (hbk)
ISBN: 978-1-138-84740-8 (pbk)
ISBN: 978-1-315-72683-0 (ebk)

Typeset in Bembo
by Book Now Ltd, London

Printed and bound in the United States of America by
Edwards Brothers Malloy on sustainably sourced paper

For Paul, Carly, and Jessica Wagner

CONTENTS

ACKNOWLEDGMENTS

Because this study is wide-ranging, discussing literature from more than sixty years, I have systematized references to excerpts of poetry and fiction so that several accessible anthologies serve as key sources. (The books listed here also appear in the Bibliography under the lead author's name.) These are the anthologies:

The New Anthology of American Poetry, Vol. 2. Ed. Steven Gould Axelrod, Camille Roman, and Thomas J. Travisano. (Rutgers UP).
The Heath Anthology of American Literature, Vol. C, D. Ed. Paul Lauter *et al*. (Houghton Mifflin).
Anthology of Modern American Poetry. Ed. Cary Nelson. (Oxford UP, 2000).
Chief Modern Poets of England and America, Vol. 2. Ed. Gerald DeWitt Sanders, John Herbert Nelson, M. L. Rosenthal. (Macmillan).
Within the text, the books will be abbreviated A (Axelrod), L (Lauter), N (Nelson), and S (Sanders), followed by page number. In the case of the Heath, excerpts from Volume C will be noted L C, page number and from Volume D, L D, page number.

This book would not exist were it not for the encouragement of the series editors, Professors Wendy Miller and D. Quentin Miller. My thanks to them and to Polly Dodson, Senior Editor at Routledge.

1

SOME ORIGINS OF MODERNISM

Modernism began with an energetic ambition to tell America's twentieth century story. Leaving behind four hundred years of acclaimed British letters (and another hundred and fifty years of United States literary efforts), writers who saw new impulses generating texts wanted to join the clamor. Truth could not be imitative, nor could it be conventional.

> Hog *Butcher* for the world,
> Tool Maker, Stacker of Wheat,
> Player with Railroads and the Nation's Freight Handler;
> Stormy, husky, brawling,
> City of the Big Shoulders . . .
>
> N 107

When in 1916 Carl Sandburg stormed the defenses of poetry readers in the United States, introducing all the blunt—and often distasteful—elements he found in "Chicago," he was asserting the power of common language. Cutting through a mystique about the country's second largest city, Sandburg's Chicago was studded with the bloody killing floors of the slaughter houses and workers amazed at the sheer quantity of meat packed into railroad cars for transport. Off in the distance sounded the clanging of hammers on metal. Further away the lush wheat fields softened the cacophony of the sounds of brutal work. The Midwest, its population growing by thousands of immigrants almost monthly, was known for its crude ("stormy, husky, brawling") power to achieve:

> Come and show me another city with lifted head singing so proud to be alive and coarse and strong and cunning.

If subtlety was the mark of effective poetry, Sandburg failed miserably in his evocative "Chicago."

A Swede, a folklorist, a musician, a biographer of his beloved Lincoln, a man sensitive to the sometimes disguised grandeur of urban life on the shores of Lake Michigan, the largest inland body of American water, Sandburg pounded out surging lines that seemed to breathe the essence of *work*. Hearing Whitman's long-lined rhythms as well as seafaring chants and Native American drum-accompanied hymns, Sandburg loved the "tall bold slugger" of the city.

He also loved the force of an image that borrowed from the world of nature:

> The fog comes
> on little cat feet . . . .
> *N 112*

Voracious for the new, Sandburg made choices in language and metaphor unlike those of any other United States poet except William Carlos Williams, who relied even less on metaphor and placed all his faith in replicating the rhythmic beauty of spoken words:

> As the cat
> climbed over
> the top of
>
> the jamcloset
> first the right
> forefoot
>
> carefully . . .
> Collected *352*

New and newly imaged, Williams' cat in his "Poem" and Sandburg's cat feet in his "Fog" represent the unapologetically *common* in the world of American modernist letters.

British literature tended to focus on the noble, the royal, as had Greek and Roman and Old Norse and African poems and stories for thousands of years. Part of the American tendency to break with tradition was this impetus to draw the *real*. The power of the common—in language and idiom, in narrative structures, in characterization, in belief systems and morality—became one root of the modernist aesthetic. If few patterns in literature existed for elevating the common, for making the exploration of the common a gripping endeavor, so much the better: writers in the United States were searching for ways to innovate. They did not intend to trace old patterns because they saw *themselves* as pattern makers, the most creative chroniclers of experience the world had ever seen.

A great many modernist writers became known, first, for their innovation. It was as if they were jousting with the heavily ingrained principles of established "literature." The shockingly non-poetic principles of *vers libre* (greeted by floods of ridicule in the journalistic and literary press) served initially as a base of operations for would-be contemporary writers. Whether T. S. Eliot or e. e. cummings or Carl Sandburg, American poets were defining and shaping the next century of poetics. Many of the poets who were key theorists of Modernism—Ezra Pound, Vachel Lindsay, Langston Hughes, H.D., Gertrude Stein, Robert Frost, Wallace Stevens— and most importantly, Eliot himself, eventually moved out of the United States, at least temporarily, finding Europe a more congenial atmosphere for their work in both art and theory.

American modernism could seldom be divided by genre, however: modernist writers wrote what they chose. Although today's readers think of Gertrude Stein with her plays, prose, and poems—and particularly her "portraits"—other examples are e. e. cummings, whose World War I novel (*The Enormous Room*) is still cherished; John Dos Passos, the master of bringing aesthetic forms into immense collective wholes (in his *U.S.A.* trilogy but also in *Manhattan Transfer, One Man's Initiation,* and other fictions, poems, and plays); William Carlos Williams, a veritable fountain of publications from plays to stories to histories to poems in configurations both streamlined and complicated (like the six books of *Paterson*); Marianne Moore, whose compelling work in language rivaled that of Laura Riding; Edna St. Vincent Millay's plays as well as her poetry; Jean Toomer with his virtuoso performance of all genres within *Cane*; and of course T. S. Eliot himself, whose poetry surfaced in his drama as well as in various poetic forms.

United States writers illustrated the high modernist theories with publication after publication. William Faulkner still thought of himself as a poet, which he was for the first fifteen years of his life as writer, almost to the time of his winning the Nobel Prize for Literature—that prize given for his immensely innovative novels. So too did Ernest Hemingway, who valued his non-fiction prose such as *Green Hills of Africa* as much as he did some of his novels and stories. Hemingway, who began as a "young Chicago poet," according to Harriet Monroe's *Poetry*, was reared on the didactic commentaries of Ezra Pound, Sherwood Anderson, and Stein. He also revered the writing of James Joyce, Virginia Woolf, Richard Aldington, and D. H. Lawrence. American modernist writers were much more cosmopolitan than some readers have noticed; they were also much more intrigued with the aesthetic worlds of painting, sculpture, photography, and music than some literary people of the past had been.

American modernism, eventually, made its mark on the world of literature through its fiction. (The power of plays by both Eugene O'Neill and Susan Glaspell, followed by Dos Passos, Edna St. Vincent Millay, John Howard Lawson, Elmer Rice, Thornton Wilder, Lillian Hellman, Clifford Odets, William Inge, DuBose Heyward, as well as Tennessee Williams and Arthur Miller, carried their own impressionistic force worldwide.) Sinclair Lewis, Willa Cather, and Edith Wharton were read around the globe, though at the time of their first publications, none of them was considered strikingly "modern." The influential French critics grouped Faulkner, Dos Passos, and Hemingway into a world-acclaimed triumvirate of greatness: the essence of one popular conception of American modernism is based on the work of these novelists. As the canon of frequently-studied American literature expands, these writers have at times been eclipsed—but they repeatedly resurface. New dimensions of their writing come to the fore: with the posthumous publication of Hemingway's *The Garden of Eden*, for example, he has become an author useful for the study of sexual preferences; and while John Dos Passos's stacks of writing are rarely studied in themselves—primarily because of his novels' length—contemporary writers still read, and borrow from, his expertise. In the case of Faulkner, his prominence—including his accurate if understated portraits of African American characters—has given rise to an entire field of literary and cultural critique: *Southern studies*, as well as to his seminal influence in the work of other now-classic American writers such as Toni Morrison and Cormac McCarthy.

Drawn by their writerly interests in creating new forms, new languages, and, accordingly, new insights and meanings, these several thousand American modernists were linked thematically by their focus on the intrinsic Americanness of twentieth century life: the common. The real. They aimed to find readers among the uneducated as well as the trained, among the amoral and immoral as well as the conventionally principled. These writers were collectively interested in the randomness of time and its measurement, as well as in the questioning of the human mind and its capacities: what *is* knowledge? what *is* meaning?

Much of the literary conviction of Modernism stemmed from the nineteenth century, but rather than this historical emphasis, observers instead saw that "Modernism" was an attitude more than a single style. Turning to the aesthetics of art in lieu of stable religious beliefs, writers (and painters, sculptors, architects, musicians) privileged dedication to craft combined with philosophical skepticism. The role of literature became less the traditional one of confirming social vision than of questioning it. The shape of literature changed to reflect its purpose: instead of predictable structures and rhymes, modern writing was chaotic and its structure was ironic, whimsical, and digressive. When Ezra Pound walked the streets of Paris, wearing his flamboyant scarf with its legend, "Make It New," people understood the importance of innovation—along with the eccentricity of Americans.

Modernist artists and writers were leaving behind the comfort of Robert Browning's well-known refrain, "God's in his heaven. All's right with the world." Rather than the largely Protestant belief systems that helped the higher classes run the United States, the new emphasis on inner, personal choice—drawing from the ideas of Nietzsche, Hobbes, Hegel, Marx, Darwin, T. E. Hulme, F. H. Bradley, William James, John Dewey, Henri Bergson, and Sigmund Freud—gave all people rights that social norms had previously forbidden. Current thinking recognized the animal (the primitive, the sexual) in the human; it also saw that people were responsible for their acts. In America, individuals were no longer shaped by the circumstances of their birth and by the trappings of social stratification. Like Horatio Alger, Americans believed they could become whatever they chose. Even as "the American dream" had already proved itself a fantasy, thousands of United States citizens—as well as the thousands of immigrants pouring into the country—saw themselves as *exceptional* persons. No matter the circumstances, in the United States, *they* would succeed. To use an even more positive emphasis, they *would* succeed.

What such immense philosophical change meant for literature was that both subject matter and form became obviously "new." As John Dos Passos recalled in one of his memoirs, "Currents of energy seemed breaking out everywhere . . . . Americans were groggy with new things in theatre and painting and music." It was what he called a "creative tidal wave":

> Under various tags: futurism, cubism, vorticism, modernism, most of the best work in the arts in our time has been the direct product of this explosion, that had an influence in its sphere comparable with that of the October revolution in social organization and politics and the Einstein formula in physics. Cendrars and Apollinaire, poets, were on the first cubist barricades with the group that influenced Picasso, Modigliani, Marinetti, Chagall; that profoundly influenced Mayakovsky, Meyerhold, Eisenstein; whose ideas carom through Joyce, Gertrude Stein, T. S. Eliot.
>
> *Dos Passos* Occasions *5*

As Paul de Man had summarized, a movement such as Modernism required a certain type of forgetting: all the impetus to create modern art stemmed from "a desire to wipe out whatever came earlier, in the hope of reaching at last a point that would be called a true present, a point of origin that masks a new departure. This combined interplay of deliberate forgetting with an action that is also a new origin reaches the full power of the idea of modernism" (Connerton 64).

When the first wave of descriptions of Modernism appeared in the annals of literary history, led by Richard Ellmann and Charles Feidelson, Jr., Maurice Beebe, Hugh Kenner, and others, the focus stayed on the vicissitudes of style. Beebe pointed out that the movement was formalist, and that such writing often created myths, set in an ironic context. Another characteristic was the author's objectivity, a technique probably drawn from the pervasiveness of journalism (and inherently connected with the appearance of photography, often integral to the impact of that journalism). Beebe also saw that what he called "solipsism," the author's self-consciousness, an equation between the work and the self, dominated literature created by James Joyce, Gertrude Stein, and, later, Ernest Hemingway (Beebe 1065). Used repeatedly as illustration for this theorizing were such books as William Faulkner's *The Sound and the Fury* and *As I Lay Dying*, Gertrude Stein's *Tender Buttons*, and John Dos Passos's *U.S.A.*—along with James Joyce's *Ulysses* and the Sitwells' poetry. (Because Joyce loomed so large, and because much of the theorizing contemporary with his publications was done by Ford Madox Ford, Ezra Pound, and particularly T. S. Eliot, the national line between British modernism and American was blurred for several decades.)

Perhaps the strongest link between Joyce and the bevy of American writers who eventually created "Modernism" as an American obsession was the content of their writing. The world-weary angst, the pervasive disillusion, affected nearly every modernist writer, and could be seen in nearly every modernist work. (The incipient threat of World War I already hovered . . . . even though that conflict remained in the future.) What connected these modernist writers was the very absence of religious certainty—and the resulting questions about established principles of belief. The twentieth century seemed to be the epitome of chaos, of an individualism of spirit and mode that was not necessarily admirable. The language of modern literature was chosen not so much because it could be a way of reaching the common reader, but rather as a means of protecting the writers themselves from the frustration of incomplete and probably faulty knowledge.

Content (when the reader could find it to summarize) seemed to be less significant than the structures authors chose to hold and express that content: the dominance of what writers and painters and musicians achieved wholistically took center stage. Implicitly, readers were crediting artists with intentionality: the changes in expected literary forms occurred for a reason. The reader or observer, then, was left with the intellectual problem of ferreting out those reasons. The various rationales that occurred from this quasi-exercise made up the principles of much modernist writing.

Modernist art was to be shaped according to its one primary aim: all language should feed into that single effect (no word should call attention to itself), as should all rhythmic patterns. No unnecessary words should appear. (The most famous illustration of this principle is Ezra Pound's reducing his two-line Imagist poem, "In a Station of the Metro," down from its original fifty lines.) Few adjectives should be used (because these are weaker, palliative words, without the direct strength of nouns or verbs). The use of any omniscient narrator should be curtailed: rather, the author should choose either a first-person storyteller or none at all. By adopting such methodology, the author frees himself/herself from hundreds of descriptive words, flat and sometimes predictable words.

Because time occurred largely in the author's consciousness, the linear "plot" for a story became unnecessary. A good reader could use the clues provided and re-create an accurate narrative. Henri Bergson's use of the concept of *durée* as a subjective measurement of time set the rational world on its heels: Bergson's emphasis was on looking past what he termed the arranged construct of time. Instead, people must pay attention to "the deep-seated self which ponders and decides, which heats and blazes up . . . whose states and changes permeate one another" (Bergson 125). Bringing human psychology into what had earlier been a somewhat mechanical concept, Bergson paved the way for later essays by Freud, and then by Jung, so that the interest in both consciousness—however defined—and psychology flowered in America. As Matei Calinescu later insisted, the modernists saw time as "the personal, subjective, imaginative *durée*, the private time created by the unfolding of the self" (Calinescu 53).

Because of the need to re-think time and linearity, for modernist writers (and other artists), the structural method of choice became juxtaposition, placing one story against another just as a painter might locate one block of color against another, so that the viewer (or the reader) could create those background explanations individually.

Sometimes authors chose to use a concentric pattern, lines of story spinning out from a center (or, in Pound's language, a *vortex*). Sometimes they used unidentified narrators and juxtaposed segments of story so that reading a text (such as Faulkner's *The Sound and the Fury*) became the *reader's* puzzle to work out. Often, any single text might have several narrators, so that the previously all-powerful concept of "point of view" became relatively unhelpful. Part of the fascination with fiction, then, was aligning the reader with the voice—the scene—and the time frame—which the author had chosen. Reading much modernist fiction (for example, John Dos Passos's *One Man's Initiation*) required familiarity with the idea of Modernism itself, as well as with the likelihood that this author or that might choose to use this technique or that. Responsibility for comprehension, then, lay with the reader.

Understanding Modernism became a means of whetting skills that were largely avant garde. Simple literacy might well be adequate; perhaps the college educated reader would even, in effect, be handicapped. (If college English courses stressed the existence of such tropes as the epic, the sonnet, the psychological novel, then finding none of these traditional characteristics in a piece of writing might send the reader away from the process of reading it well.) In this regard, the use of idiomatic (and thoroughly American) language helped readers. When William Carlos Williams wrote, "A big young bareheaded woman/in an apron/Her hair slicked back standing/on the street ... " (N 192), he was not being coy. He was not creating any kind of riddle. He was reaching his readers, the people of small New Jersey towns—largely of the working class, largely his patients—and his words, like the subjects of many of his poems, were common. In Modernism, being common took on a privileged status.

Pre-modern writing

Before the term "modern" was a currency useful in aesthetic discussion, American writers had already found new principles for their expression. The notion that literature was a kind of democratic exchange of ideas, of knowledge, had been in play during the last decades of the nineteenth century. Rather than outlining the literary terms *realism* and *naturalism*—and placing writing by William Dean Howells, Henry James, Sarah Orne Jewett, Frank Norris, and others within these divisions, I have chosen to discuss a handful of key American books that, in retrospect, can be seen to have connections with the modern. This is the list:

> Stephen Crane's *The Red Badge of Courage* (1895)
> Kate Chopin's *The Awakening* (1899)
> Theodore Dreiser's *Sister Carrie* (1900, then withdrawn; re-published in 1907)
> Jack London's *The Sea Wolf* (1904)
> Edith Wharton's *The House of Mirth* (1905)
> Upton Sinclair's *The Jungle* (1906)

And, as a bridge into Modernism itself, Gertrude Stein's *Three Lives* (1909).

In critic June Howard's description of realism—drawing from Charles Child Walcutt and to some extent expanding his insights—the changes in theme and presentation stemmed from what observers saw as "a perilous time, a period of change and uncertainty, of dislocations and disorders." War and the coveting of additional lands, the growing inequity between factory owners and workers, attitudes toward not only religious belief and language choices but toward class and race differences—not to forget the continuing dissension over states' rights and the outcome of the Civil War: a great many worries shrouded the United States psyche (Howard ix).

Uppermost in considerations of class was the privileging of literacy: how far could public schooling reach? How dependent on education were jobs? Without education, how savage would human beings become? The primordial fear of the uncouth, a kind of jungle fetish, underlay concerns about both education and housing, about work and achieving the "American dream." Accordingly, writers tended to make their products less effete, less well-made, and perhaps more related to journalism and popular writing of the time. Literature had no business excluding any reader (Howard xi). To illustrate the immense storm of change, this critic notes that the changes due to manufacturing and other ways of centralizing physical work, changes that unfortunately were often dehumanizing, were illustrated by "the growing cities, concentrating both unparalleled wealth and the tremendous influx of immigrants, [which] provided an even more impressive demonstration of the radical changes" (Howard 30).

Beset by recurrent depressions, by the struggles between capital and labor (and the publicity of strikes and their outcomes), and challenges to social and political authority, American citizens felt comfortable reading "clinical, panoramic, slice-of-life, stream of consciousness, and chronicle of despair" works (Howard 21). The documentary, with its reliance on photos, was an ideal mode to represent the country's psychological unease.

Howard points out that similar aesthetic conventions were changing in both anthropology (especially its interest in the criminal) and politics, where progressivism seemed less foreign than some had earlier thought. According to Eric Aronoff, defining literature without using the plural word, *cultures*, is misleading. He sees parallels between the changes in literature and history, anthropology and American studies—stressing the interdisciplinarity of the latter—and notes that such activity did not come only with Modernism. To describe his view, he chooses the "Mobius strip, that closed three-dimensional loop in which one might begin traveling along one side of the strip but end up seamlessly on the other," and then back again, as "what seemed like two sides are revealed to be one" (Aronoff 186).

Programmatic as critics might want to be as they penetrate definitions of such large concepts as realism and naturalism, readers must keep in mind Aronoff's preference for the Mobius strip, not a linear site (or sight) but a means of confounding linearity. What Howard comes to take as her stance, even amid the complexities she recognizes, is a mixture of stylistic tropes, characters germane to predictable narrative plots, and ways of authorial revelation of what was seldom optimistic writing. She emphasizes the authors' aims at getting at the truth—and the truth often leads to "the plot of decline or fatality, which structures a narrative as the anatomy of a progressive deterioration" (Howard 142). Set against one manifestation of the American dream—which she defines as "freedom through knowledge"—is the overwhelming plot of "determinism, survival, violence, and taboo" (Howard 12, 20). Detail, observable fact, a set of visual and audible "proofs" fed into the practice of realistic/naturalistic writing; as Howard points out, however, the distinction between fact and fiction is more than a simple literary marker. It has a great deal to do with, first, tone and then, ultimately, with meaning (Howard 172–3).

Dominant in June Howard's discussion of this mode is the work of both Stephen Crane and Jack London, particularly of Crane's *Maggie, A Girl of the Streets* (which was originally only privately published) and London's *The Sea Wolf*. Linked by the characteristic repetition of unbearable detail, and pushed from severely neutral opening scenes into a chill downward slide into the terror of both powerlessness and then death, these works illustrate the symmetry that realism in the early twentieth century suggested.

Stephen Crane's The Red Badge of Courage

Famed as being the first, and best, psychological study of a soldier in war, Crane's 1895 novella was written without its author having been to war. Crane was a journalist—an investigative journalist—and he drew on oral histories, written accounts, and Matthew Brady's photographs of the Civil War to infuse his fiction with the circumstances that would convince readers. Perhaps he wrote more accurately as a realist in his earlier *Maggie, A Girl of the Streets* and in his short pieces for the New York papers (such as "An Experiment in Misery"). In *The Red Badge of Courage*, however, he used realistic details in a form that was swift and streamlined, thoughtful and impassioned. In 1941, Ernest Hemingway said it was a perfect work (he was planning to use an excerpt from the book in his anthology of writing about war, but he found it impossible to separate passages out of Crane's writing). His praise was, "It is all as much of one piece as a great poem is."

EXCERPT FROM STEPHEN CRANE'S "A NEWSPAPER IS A COLLECTION OF HALF-INJUSTICES"

A newspaper is a collection of half-injustices
Which, bawled by boys from mile to mile,
Spreads its curious opinion
To a million merciful and sneering men,
While families cuddle the joys of the fireside
When spurred by tale of dire lone agony.
A newspaper is a court
Where every one is kindly and unfairly tried
By a squalor of honest men . . . .

Startling as Crane's reliance on the fear of the naïve young soldier, during a reign of patriotic literature that would never admit to uneasiness, lack of courage, or the possibility of death, *The Red Badge of Courage* yet played on middle-class values. Family was crucial, and as Henry Fleming left his mother alone on their farm, he realized that his selfish desire to see the world (along with the war) was doing great harm to her, and to their livelihood. In an apparently direct line from Henry James' great prolegomena about writing fiction, published in 1884, Crane chose a focus that was unrelieved: as Fleming learned about the terrors of war, he enacted a day-by-day set of choices that he thought might keep him alive. Interior narrative conveyed the tenor of war itself, but Henry Fleming remained the young naïf who could not believe the truth about war—that it was less about beliefs than it was about men killing brothers, hour by hour, feigning wounding to escape actual wounding.

Even for the ardent journalist, such treatment was unusual—Henry Fleming was the poor and uneducated child of a poor farming family. Just as writers tried to focus on a range of America's people, they consistently found themselves drawing characters from the financial elite. (Who in the United States became a journalist without some sort of family backing? Many writers—Crane included—had gone to college, or were from families with both educations and professions, as were Crane's parents.) Trying to understand the social layers below the middle class was difficult. Crane had first attempted that kind of portraiture in *Maggie*, his 1893 novel that was so graphic and so unpleasant that no commercial publisher would take it on: Crane's accounts of "the city, its poverty, and social problems" were both unusual and off-putting (Dow 59).

Crane also insisted on the legitimacy of journalism, defending this kind of writing against negative comparisons with "literature." But in his focus on members of the lower classes and their regrettable lives, he stressed repeatedly that "the problem of class difference was a problem of social justice." Readers from the middle class were not used to having to deal with sermonizing as they read journalism—why spend so much ink on the plight of the urban poor? It was Crane's "working and underclass sympathies" that made him a different kind of 1890s writer, one that the public found puzzling, if not shocking (Dow 56, 66, 70).

Crane's style (precise, intent, and often poetic) separated his writing from most of the fiction by William Dean Howells and Frank Norris (who tended to include much description and many repetitious scenes of dialogue in their long novels), but the crucial difference lay in his obviously deep sympathy for his characters. In *Virtual Modernism*, a 2013 book by Katherine Biers, in fact, she attributes Crane's distinctiveness to his philosophical ties to psychologists/philosophers William James and C. S. Peirce—drawing what he presented about his fictional characters from his actual experience with such people, or the models for them. She also termed his writerly abilities "a poetics of the virtual," as he chose to use stylistic moves that have much in common with technological changes at the end of the nineteenth century, as well as with the practices of both photography and film (Biers 35).

For this critic and for such other commentators on realism as June Howard, Leslie Fiedler, and Bill Brown, Crane's work that surpasses even *The Red Badge of Courage* is his long story, "The Open Boat," written after Crane's life-threatening fifty hours adrift when *The Commodore* was sunk returning from Cuba. This 1897 story tries to avoid its autobiographical truth—Crane had earlier written a journalistic account of the experience. He avoids his own celebrity, and names the four characters by their occupations: "cook," "captain," "oiler," "correspondent" (Biers 67). To create the essential story, he uses a scaffolding of color symbolism, suggesting that the men may die but drawing the reader's attention away from that doom and onto the larger significance of the experience. The story opens,

> None of them knew the color of the sky. Their eyes glanced level, and were fastened upon the waves that swept toward them. These waves were of the hue of slate, save for the tops, which were of foaming white, and all of the men knew the colors of the sea . . . .
>
> *L C, 497*

While this opening might well lead to representations of a philosophical nature— faith, skepticism, religion—in Crane's hands abstract values disappear: what counts are the actions of the four stranded (and commonplace) men—specifically their rowing (Biers 64). What seems to fascinate Crane most is his awareness of "a mediated nature of perception and of the shocks administered by war." For this critic, and particularly in this story, seeing Crane as an incipient modernist is not difficult (Biers 35).

The abrasive nature of Crane's fiction (and poetry), privileging as the author does the truly common American, was seldom mentioned in earlier literary critique: the United States prided itself on differences from England, and one of the most visible differences was the American allegiance to democracy and the plethora of democratic principles that such a philosophy entailed. For all its cant about respecting difference, however, the writers of the United States were still enamored of using white men as protagonists for literature. Immigrants (even if white in skin color), the poor (even if white in skin color), women (no matter where they stood socially), Americans of color (African Americans, Asian Americans, Latino/a characters, Native Americans), Jewish and Middle Eastern people as separate from Christian believers— and the distinction between Protestants and Catholics remained marked in the late nineteenth century: all such subjects would have been seen as unusual or even exotic in one way or another. Stephen Crane, then, wrote about the poor, especially the urban poor; as well as about the common soldier, the common farmer, the common prostitute, and even about himself in "The Open Boat," that character sharing what could have been a common fate of death with the sailors from *The Commodore*.

Kate Chopin's The Awakening

For women writers during the later nineteenth century, literary critics created the category of "regional writers." Rather than incorporate poetry and fiction by women into mainstream literary considerations, a way of both isolating and praising their work—always keeping it separate from the writing which readers, and influential critics, were really interested in—such a designation allowed them to publish and, perhaps, to earn a living, without admitting their work into the sacred canons of "literature." Kate Chopin, writing steadily after she is widowed in Louisiana, moving back to her native St. Louis and there publishing her stories and her several novels (to help support her six children), did not object to being called a "Southern writer."

One of the first of America's fiction writers to draw accurate portraits of women characters, Chopin broke with the more apparent traditional women seen in the stories and novels of Sarah Orne Jewett, Mary E. Wilkins Freeman, Alice Cary, Constance Fenimore Woolson, Harriet Prescott Spofford, Rose Terry Cooke, Rebecca Harding Davis, and others. Instead, Chopin's women figures were pacific, comforting, drawn with subtlety and metaphoric detail. Her nineteenth century American women characters may have been radical in some of their beliefs (and even in their behaviors), but the handling of their narratives by the gifted Chopin allowed readers to find uplift, and a reaffirmation of middle-class values, in the presentation. At heart, Chopin was more interested in drawing what some called "the new woman," the audacious and self-determined woman of the late 1890s. Imperious about her ideas, her sexuality, and her desires about profession as well as women's roles, the American new woman showed off her mental and physical strengths as she frequently decided against taking on "traditional" womanly activities. Writers who focused on this character sometimes drew the handicaps of race and class in full development, and at other times used sociology and psychology to explain a character's failures or successes.

Although women readers appeared ready for almost any theme in women's fiction, Chopin's 1899 novel *The Awakening* found those readers' limits. When Edna Pontellier chose death by drowning rather than life with either her husband and children, or with her lover, Chopin's readers were incensed—at least her *male* readers and critics. They did not approve of the sexual and emotional freedom Edna demanded for herself (and they decided that they had been misdirected from the start of the novel in that Edna was well-placed, married to a seemingly responsible man who loved her. In this novel, economics was not the problem, nor was fidelity). The most offensive plot development in *The Awakening* appeared to be the fact that Edna was willing to stop mothering her two little boys: there had never been so cavalier a mother figure in the stream of American letters. Edna's behavior, from the time of her somewhat adolescent love for Robert to the time of her assignation with Arobin, was—some readers said—inexplicable. Who had ever heard of such a character (except perhaps in Flaubert's *Madame Bovary*, years back in 1857).

An early sign of trouble in the Pontelliers' relationship occurs when Edna decides to sleep outside all night, alone: "'Leonce, go to bed,' she said. 'I mean to stay out here. I don't wish to go in, and I don't intend to. Don't speak to me like that again; I shall not answer you'" (L C, 386). From the various games of power that the spouses play, to Edna's recognizing her desire for the young neighbor Robert, tracking him down in his travels through friendships with other women; to her deciding to become an artist, and finally moving from her husband's house into a rented cottage of her own, the stages of Chopin's accuracy in drawing Edna's disaffiliation with marriage and children are vivid. In those terms, Edna's behavior, leading to her suicide (her merging with the great power of the waves) so contrasts with the expected outcome that readers knew only shock. Any fiction about a woman character was supposed to follow the romance narrative: it would end with marriage. If the woman protagonist would not, or could not, marry, she probably died—but that death should be unhappy, not freely chosen, as was Edna's outcome. Women writers learned from the reaction to Chopin's novel: the author came to be seen as something of a scandal herself, and she lived only a few years longer. Active women writers such as Ellen Glasgow and Edith Wharton learned to script traditional narratives, but to do so at times tongue-in-cheek and with occasional heavy irony.

A different kind of irony was inherent within Chopin's *The Awakening*. Edna's seemingly unself-conscious choice to drown, even though she had finally learned to swim, might well have been read as Edna's joining herself to nature. Since Henry David Thoreau's *Walden*, little attention had been given to characters in relation to the natural world—and with the increased urbanization of United States culture, finding spiritual solace in nature was becoming difficult. The prominence of both Chicago and New York as urban centers made readers aware of the impersonality of any city location, and people (both readers and writers) were becoming conscious of the value of place.

Theodore Dreiser's Sister Carrie

Dreiser chose to place Carrie Meeber, a lower class representative of the New Woman, in Chicago. The reaction to Dreiser's first novel was so negative that in 1900 his publisher withdrew the book (it reappeared in 1907, when cultural mores began to change). Ineffably confident, Carrie came from a poor Midwestern farm culture; she met Drouet, the man who would become her first lover, on the train into Chicago. Without proselytizing about sexuality (or, more appropriately in this case, virginity), Dreiser arranged his narrative so that readers saw Carrie as a woman who attempted to do work. First as a typist, then as a minor actress, Carrie took the talents she recognized in herself and made the effort to succeed financially.

EXCERPT FROM MELVYN DUBOFSKY'S *INDUSTRIALISM AND THE AMERICAN WORKER, 1865–1920* (p. 24)

When American-born elites thought of industrial workers in the late nineteenth century, especially of recent immigrants, they often projected onto workers images of untamed brutishness and potential violence. Lacking the well developed superego of the good bourgeois citizen, the immigrant worker, it was thought, easily succumbed to alcohol, sex, crime, and violence. In short, the middle class perhaps projected its own anxieties about sex, drink, and violence onto the working class at the same time that it sometimes perceived lower-class life as more human, natural, and perhaps, happier.

Dreiser wrote an unusual "seduction" narrative. The emphasis in this novel is not on Carrie's sexuality so much as it is on the character's power over men—on the way society regards her activities. Unlike Crane's Maggie or Chopin's Edna, Carrie does not commit suicide (although Dreiser strongly suggests that death will be the choice of her second lover, Hurstwood). Carrie sits in her rocking chair, with dissatisfaction, and gives herself over to a kind of wonder—that she has made her life something of a success, that she has not had to return to her family's home in defeat or shame (as stereotypical "fallen" women, pregnant, conventionally retrace their earlier paths). As Leslie Fiedler said decades ago, Dreiser wrote with a sympathy born of watching his own poor, middle western sisters fling themselves against the social boundaries that kept them defeated (Fiedler pointed out then that when Dreiser chose a title, his adding "Sister" to Carrie's name, in effect, was his autobiographical testimony (Fiedler 245).)

Fiedler quotes from a typical rejection slip Dreiser sent to would-be contributors when he edited the journal *The Delineator*: "We like realism, but it must be tinged with sufficient idealism to make it all of a truly uplifting character . . . . The fine side of things—the idealistic—is the answer for us" (Fiedler 246). In June Howard's assessment of the centrality Dreiser's *Sister Carrie* holds in any discussion of American realism, she thinks Carrie is more than superficially bold.

> Carrie is simultaneously hopeful and fearful. She vaguely expects new pleasures, yet is almost overwhelmed at finding herself suddenly adrift in this immense "sea of life and endeavor"; the mysterious city both allures with "the gleam of a thousand lights" and threatens "the grimness of shift and toil." This equivocal panorama, with the figure of the desirous and vulnerable Carrie set against it, is already the terrain of Dreiser's concepts as well as his story.
>
> *Howard 41*

Setting *Sister Carrie* in Chicago (and then in New York) makes the seduction story new; it becomes a part of the country's progressive ambition, a saga of materialism that could never have existed in the small town environs Carrie Meeber knew. Nor could it have been spoken of in connection with a *woman's* dreams. But the urban settings only add to the strange absence of morality: in the city, no one knows Carrie; no one knows Drouet; no one sees them living together as any kind of impropriety. No one has enough information to judge. In Dreiser's picture of city life, that life becomes synonymous with anonymity.

Charles Child Walcutt emphasized the point:

> Nowhere is a moral pointed. There is no inevitable punishment for transgression, no suggestion that there ought to be. In one passage Dreiser even appeals to nature as against conventional moral standards and intimates that the only evil in what is ordinarily considered sinful comes from the codes which call it evil, because they introduce elements of guilt and hypocrisy into conduct.
>
> *Walcutt 189*

The rampaging power of human sexuality, as well as the drive to succeed, justifies breaking agreed-upon moral codes: realism/naturalism was to thrive on such a belief.

Like other readers, Walcutt is much saddened by Hurstwood's fall after his accidental theft of funds (not to mention his taking Carrie out of state for his own romantic purposes). He states,

> Structurally the novel consists of the two life cycles which are opposed to each other in studied balance. What *Sister Carrie* exhibits that is most characteristically naturalistic is the complete absence of ethical plot complication. The movement of the novel does not depend upon acts of will by the central figures. There is no suspense waiting to be resolved by a decision which will be judged in terms of absolute ethical standards. The movement is the movement of life—skillfully selected and represented by the artist, to be sure, but still a movement which has little resemblance to the typical plot that begins with a choice or a crucial action and ends with the satisfaction of the forces and the passions set in motion by that choice. The difference is fundamental.
>
> *Walcutt 191*

Echoed in critic June Howard's description of Dreiser's calling Carrie, "a waif amid forces" and "a wisp in the wind," the absence of blame is one of *Sister Carrie*'s most striking effects. The novel, whether in 1900 or 1907, was responsible for feeding the literary world's sense that the United States—and its letters—had undergone an "abrupt contemporary mongrelization" of its traditional history (Klein 15).

Jack London's The Sea Wolf

In the long view of twenty-first century readers, Jack London himself seems to be the epitome of that mongrel impact—and not only in his writing. Born into true poverty in California, his mother abandoned by his father and later married to the London who adopted him, Jack London was the first American writer to create the genuine tramp or hobo in his fiction, partly because he had himself led that life. A high-school drop out, London did a range of work, including crew on a sealing vessel and become an oyster pirate; he apprenticed himself to an electrician; he marched with Coxey's Army to Washington and later spent 30 days in jail in Buffalo, New York. He finally decided to work hard in journalism—his early Alaskan stories gave him entry to this profession. To assess his accuracy of choosing a profession, the critic might begin with his 1902 work, *The People of the Abyss*, his survey of the way poverty impacted the London lower classes. 1902 also saw the publication of his *The Call of the Wild*, as forceful as were his stories "To Build a Fire" and "South of the Slot." London's fiction showed a kind of ferocity in life's circumstances unlike anything previously done in United States writing: Walcutt called him "an arresting storyteller and a writer of tremendous vigor." Considered along with other writers of his mode, London "stands like a colossus, rugged but precarious . . . . He fought with his background, his environment, and finally he fought his way through self-education to become famous" (Walcutt 87–8).

In his 1906 essay "What Life Means to Me," London the writer explained that he had thought that writing could give him a profession: "I was not afraid of work. I loved hard work." Eventually disillusioned with the sheer politics of working so hard—for little pay—he left the workforce and lived off his wits. This period was the bottom for London, "I fled from work. I became a tramp, begging my way from door to door, wandering over the United States and sweating bloody sweats in slums and prisons." Leaving what he called "the cellar of society," he then crafted his writing during his stay in Alaska. When the reader submerges himself/herself in the details of London's most famous Alaskan story, "To Build a Fire," absorbing the narrator's bad choices as he travels—alone—through sub-zero temperatures, the fiction becomes a hegira of impending death. Thoughtless and puny man, striving against the forces of nature, loses. London's effective telling of the simple story made him one of the United States' most famous writers.

Better known because it is a traditional fiction, *The Sea Wolf*, published in 1903, shows London working through immense quantities of detail (as he serves as the ultimate reporter) while he focuses on a male character who is proud of being little more than a brute. (There is a range of fairly recent criticism that links the strength and power of the *brute* with the gendered concept of the masculine; in Jack London's day, such a connection was implicit.) Contrasting with the protagonist, Wolf Larsen, captain of the ship *Ghost*, "a magnificent avatism" and a notoriously "unmoral" man, London's narrator for this novel is the somewhat effete poet and book reviewer Humphrey Van Wayden. At thirty-five, the educated critic has been turned into a cabin boy after the crew of the *Ghost* rescues him from a sinking ferry. The stories told by the crew about both Wolf and his brother, *Death* Larsen, make Humphrey (called "Hump" by the crew—because of his slow and feminized pace) aware of what he has become: a slave to the illiterate crew, and to Wolf.

Hump has no allies among the crew, so he tries to please Wolf and does his menial work as best as his comparatively fragile body allows. When the cook who is caring for him after his rescue takes after him ("'Look 'ere, 'Ump,' he began, a malicious light in his eyes and a snarl in his throat; 'd'ye want yer nose punched? If you think I'm a thief, just keep it to yourself, or you'll fine 'ow bloody well mistyken you are. Strike me blind if this ayn't gratitude for yer!'") To which phonetically spelled threat London adds clearly for his reader, Van Weyden's words, "I cowered away from the blow and ran out the galley door. What else was I to do? Force, nothing but force obtained on this brute-ship. Moral suasion was a thing unknown" (*Wolf* 34). A few hours later, Van Weyden makes a mistake and then the captain Wolf Larsen "kicked me, violently, as a cur is kicked. I had not realized there could be so much pain in a kick. I reeled away from him and leaned against the cabin in a half-fainting condition" (*Wolf* 36). The narrator is lucky; later he watches the captain kill one of his crew and be responsible for the deaths of other men.

The suddenness of the reader's opinion of the captain pivots on the rescue of the beautiful poetess, Maud Brewster—a woman whose books had once been reviewed by Van Weyden. Tied to the fact that when Van Weyden had cleaned Wolf's cabin, he had found a number of classic English works, with underlinings in the poetry: how could an educated man behave as did the captain? With Maud Brewster on board, some of Wolf's erudition comes into play and soon four men and the poetess, rescued after the mail steamer they were taking from San Francisco to Japan was capsized in a typhoon, had become his crew. *The Sea Wolf* becomes a predictable romance: Van Weyden watches Wolf's attraction to Maud Brewster grow. Finally, he acts to save her when he sees the captain forcing himself against her. Van Weyden knows he and Maud must escape the ship. Then, fate helps: the mysterious headaches the captain experienced lost him control of his ship. Though still violent and murderous, he becomes blind.

The *Robinson Crusoe* secondary plot shows Van Weyden growing stronger, compelled by his love for Maud to become a more physical man. What London privileged was his belief in "class equality, fervent nationalism, and Anglo-Saxon supremacy"—although in *The Sea Wolf* he refused to give the sealing ship's crew and captain, as well as the seal hunters, any kind of equality. In the words of critic William Dow, who quotes London's saying "Civilization must be compelled to better the lot of the average man," at times in his fiction London makes the feral character more impressive than the middle-class person (Dow 93; Brown 36).

It is Dow who critiques the prominence Jack London gives the male body in his various characterizations. London, says Dow, makes his readers conscious of "how the (provisionally) suffering body becomes a supreme form of 'authentic' knowledge. Through a discursive system that tends to define a proletarian body (grotesque, undisciplined, dirty) in opposition to the bourgeois body (sublimated, neutralized, classical), London had to objectify its felt-characteristics and make them steadily visible. To achieve such an effect he resorted to a "modernism" that included not only his inclination "to move 'inside' and to eliminate the distance between subject and object . . . but also one which takes on a 'bodily' form, embedding the class conflicts it encounters" (Dow 82–3). Readers who found London's fiction unpleasant in its frankness (as well as its normal background of brutality) were probably reacting as well to what they personally demanded from "literature." As Dreiser had insisted, any realism "must be tinged with sufficient idealism to make it all of a truly uplifting character."

Without reference to any specific period or aesthetic, "literature" was to serve a moral purpose; reading good literature was the privilege of the middle and upper classes, who could claim literacy whether or not they had attended college, to decide what publishers printed. The immense popularity of Jack London's fiction (and journalism) was in some ways an insult to what the literary critics had conceived as their value in life.

Edith Wharton's **The House of Mirth**

As Edith Newbold Jones, Mrs. Wharton was the daughter of those *Joneses* New York society was trying to keep up with. Wealthy and well educated (at home, with tutors for specialized subjects), Edith Wharton had also had a European childhood; she knew what the heights of civilization meant, she had seen the world's famous art in place, and she had learned to speak all the civilized languages. As a writer, she felt that one of her roles was to educate her readers in this mass of carefully-acquired knowledge. But she also knew that social position and economic substance did not change the nature of the human heart.

Wharton's fiction was frequently compared with that of Henry James, who was a dominant realist from years before Stephen Crane, Theodore Dreiser, and Jack London. James wrote about the privileged classes. To do so he created a distinctive and subtle prose that some people questioned: Ezra Pound later said that James wrote no unnecessary words. Wharton herself did not agree with either Pound's comment or the initial comparison, but she wanted to change the notion that all women who wrote were "regional," intent on creating "local color." If following in James's footsteps meant being taken seriously as an accomplished writer, Wharton was willing to accept the comparison. Although she wrote with more humor, and gave her readers characters so trapped in their social mores they could not think for themselves, she did—like James—create upper and middle class cultures, in all their social propriety, cultures that were recognizable to her avid readers. It was usually said that Wharton wrote social novels, the twentieth century version of the novel of manners, as if her catalogues of society were the most impressive quality of her work.

The catalogues were not. What was pervasively impressive was the way Wharton drew her characters. By the time of the 1905 publication of her novel *The House of Mirth*, what was most impressive was the psychological and social journey Lily Bart attempted. In Lily Bart, Wharton had created one of America's most beloved heroes—although she did so through layers of irony. It is possible for readers to see the novel as traditional romance, with the foolish woman—Lily—losing everything because she does not follow society's rules and marry an appropriate rich man. But it is also possible to read the book as ironic, with nothing but condemnation for those people who manage to succeed within the hypocritical culture, Lawrence Selden included. In that context, Lily's death becomes a severe indictment of both her culture and her would-be lover.

Some readers found in Lily Bart the epitome of the unwise virgin, the woman whose role in society was to marry well but whose sense of self and independence kept her from doing so. (As economic changes made the United States more and more often a divided country—prosperity ranging from the extreme wealth of the Rockefellers and other capitalists to a much lower class of people who lived an existence by barter, the relentless poverty of Jack London's tramps and America's workers, readers came to follow the adventures of the wealthy as a new kind of *celebrity*.) Most of Wharton's readers, and *The House of Mirth* was—like most of her novels to come—a best-seller, envied the classes she described. They knew as well as did Lily Bart how to play the role of the virginal naïf, how to capture a man of wealth and breeding—a man who was himself white, Protestant, and probably descended from bloodlines in either England, the United States, or Western

Europe. Yet, one of the reasons for Lily Bart's defiance is that she has fallen in love with a man who is professional but not wealthy. In creating Lawrence Selden (her "anti-hero," in Wharton's words), the author made the stilted upper class society real. Had Selden been less concerned with the social forms that restricted him as much as they did Lily Bart, he could have proposed and ended her torture as she watches her best friends turn against her, gossip about trivialities in order to gain power themselves, and in one case actually set Lily up to take blame that should have been theirs. Selden himself, however, did not want to give up his dreams of succeeding in this effete New York culture.

Although Wharton shows clearly that Selden is ineffectual, a talker who never acts, he still appears to be a good man: he believed in a woman's right to choose her own life. But his belief was unsupported in that he never realized how little income Lily Bart had. To compare her with his cousin Gerty—who worked to earn her own living—was anathema to him as he created fantasies about his helping Lily. When Wharton added the final chapter, the brilliant scene of Selden's mourning over Lily's body—when all the book's readers understood that he could have prevented her death, whether it was accidental or intentional—the author played the final card of her ironic scaffolding.

The creation of Simon Rosedale, the upstart Jew who fights hard to enter society, is a mixed blessing for the novel. Accurate in that people of this moneyed class would not accept a man who had earned his own fortune, particularly in the miasma of anti-Semitism, when Rosedale later has the chance to rescue Lily (given that he has achieved wealth, whereas Selden would never make that kind of money), he turns her down because she has been damaged because of her erstwhile friends' gossip. The character of the Jew that at first appears to be cleverly and ambiguously drawn drops into stereotype in the last scenes between Rosedale and Lily.

Wharton's ironic tapestry of Lily's choices, set against those of her aunt, her friends, Rosedale, and Selden, provokes readers to assess not only the United States Victorian belief system, but the humanity professed by these upper class characters. By showing the different strategies Lily tries in order to regain both her reputation and her finances, Wharton plays upon a quotient of disbelief in her readers: once placed as high as Lily Bart was, would her financial ruin be so quick—and so apparent? With the downward progression of this protagonist, Wharton moves her novel from social realism into a kind of fantasy, a romantic saga that her readers would find less than painful. *The House of Mirth*, then, becomes a readable novel, and not reality.

Upton Sinclair's **The Jungle**

Even in 1906, it was obvious that the scope of the novel as form had broadened tremendously. What Sinclair accomplished in *The Jungle* might well have been left to long essays in the journals and magazines associated with muckraking. (*McClure's Magazine* encouraged the investigative reporting of such progressive writers as Ida Tarbell, Lincoln Steffens, Finley Peter Dunne, R. S. Baker, S. S. McClure, Floyd Dell, Charlotte Perkins Gilman and others.) When Sinclair investigated the meat-packing industry, focusing on Chicago, and found such unclean and brutal conditions, he felt compelled to expose the unappealing truth. (Because of the outcry that *The Jungle* created, the federal government passed legislation aimed at correcting abuses in this industry. Later, F. D. Roosevelt brought into being the Beef Inspection Act and the first Pure Food and Drug Act.)

One of the widest read novels written by an American, *The Jungle* was socialist in intention. Following the hard life of Jurgis Rudkus, the Lithuanian peasant who came to Chicago with his family to work in Packingtown, the novel shows the inevitable destruction of the family, worn into oblivion through relentless work, horrible living circumstances, and alcohol's poison. (True of the best journalists, Sinclair had lived for seven weeks in Chicago's Packingtown; he knew what the conditions were.) He also understood that recent immigrants were susceptible to the supposed "easy money" of the packing houses, and much of *The Jungle* necessarily describes the bewilderment of hard-working and often language-challenged immigrants.

By the end of his long life, Upton Sinclair had published over fifty novels, had joined and then resigned from the Socialist party, and had served as America's conscience in myriad areas. What he found in *The Jungle* was that characters could serve as argumentative voices for political causes: they might be termed "didactic" but readers were as interested in their causes as they were in their presentation. (*What America Read, Taste, Class, and the Novel*, a recent study by Gordon Hutner, states that there was little predicting which novels would become best-sellers, which books would prick readers' interest. With the Pulitzer Prize in Fiction usually going to the book that offered the most clear moral statement, judging "value" was often dependent on qualities other than style and structure (Hutner 76).)

EXCERPT FROM UPTON SINCLAIR'S *THE JUNGLE*

They knew that one word, Chicago—and that was all they needed to know, at least, until they reached the city. Then, tumbled out of the cars without ceremony, they were no better off than before; they stood staring down the vista of Dearborn Street, with its big black buildings towering in the distance, unable to realize that they had arrived . . . . They were pitiable in their helplessness; above all things they stood in deadly terror of any sort of person in official uniform, and so whenever they saw a policeman they would cross the street and hurry by. For the whole of the first day they wandered about in the midst of deafening confusion, utterly lost; and it was only at night that, cowering in the doorway of a house, they were finally discovered and taken by a policeman to the station. In the morning an interpreter was found, and they were taken and put upon a car, and taught a new word—"stockyards."

Sinclair's term for his kind of fiction was "the contemporary historical novel": *Oil* told the story of the Teapot Dome scandal; *Boston*, that of the Sacco and Vanzetti trial and executions; and the "Lanny Budd" novels, Sinclair's accounts of both world wars.

When Sinclair introduces Jurgis in *The Jungle*, he compares him to "a boy from the country." He does not remark about the European culture from which he and his family come. Instead he makes the character recognizable to American readers: eager, muscled and proud of his unusual strength, Jurgis "would stand round fidgeting, dancing, with the overflow of energy that was in him. If he were working in a line of men, the line always moved too slowly for him, and you could pick him out by his impatience and restlessness." Back in Lithuania, he had heard the stories of great American wealth, and he had convinced his beloved Ona to travel with him to the States.

> He would go to America and marry, and be a rich man in the bargain. In that country, rich or poor, a man was free, it was said; he did not have to go into the army, he did not have to pay out his money to rascally officials—he might do as he pleased, and count himself as good as any other man.
>
> *L C, 608–9*

The American dream writ large led to the protagonist's eventual loss of work, his injuries keeping him from supporting and protecting his family. What he learned then was that in America, families such as his could literally starve to death. The novel's closing scene announced the tragedy:

> They were beaten; they had lost the game; they were swept aside. It was not less tragic because it was so sordid, because . . . it had to do with wages and grocery bills and rents. They had dreamed of freedom; of a chance to look about them and learn something; to be decent and clean, to see their child grow up to be strong. And now it was all gone—it would never be! They had played the game and they had lost. Six years more of toil they had to face before they could expect the last respite, the cessation of the payments upon the house; and how cruelly certain it was that they could never stand six years of such a life as they were living! They were lost, they were going down—and there was no deliverance for them, no hope; for all the help it gave them the vast city in which they lived might have been an ocean waste, a wilderness, a desert, a tomb.
>
> *L C, 621*

Readers knew the story all too well. They knew that Sinclair's journalistic stance, his repetition (as above) of the *facts* not mattering, not alleviating the conditions, drove home the unpleasant truths of inadequate payment for hard work. They did not mind uncomplicated plots or unchanging qualities. They did not read Sinclair the same way they read Edith Wharton, nor would Sinclair have wanted them to make him an elite literary figure. Given the kind of upper-class society that Wharton chose to write about, and the kind of context Kate Chopin had provided for her novel about her "awakening" woman character, the sense among most readers was that women writers still cherished the truths about polite, and privileged, society. That attitude was to change with the publication in 1909 of Gertrude Stein's *Three Lives*.

Gertrude Stein's **Three Lives**

Stein had first titled her three-part set of novellas "Three Histories." As unusual a focus as Upton Sinclair's shaping a novel around the horrors of Chicago's meat-packing industry, Stein's attention to two lower-class German serving maids ("The Good Anna," "The Gentle Lena") and to one African American woman ("Melanctha") was strikingly unpredictable.

Gertrude Stein wrote as a Jewish woman, highly educated at the Harvard Annex (Radcliffe) under the tutelage of William James, and then as a medical student at Johns Hopkins Medical School. After 1903 she had lived abroad in France, often with her older brothers Leo and, in separate households, Michael and his wife Sally. All collected the art that surrounded them (Pablo Picasso's portrait of Gertrude, represented on the cover of this book, dates from 1909). She had written other fiction and she thought of herself as a poet (when *Tender Buttons*, her poem collection, appeared in 1914, she became a comparatively well-known modernist). By the time of her finishing *Three Lives*, she had lived as a lesbian with Alice B. Toklas, the American from Seattle who was to be her lifetime companion. Neither of their families' Jewish households would accept their romance.

Stein's choice of common American characters—women she might have known as housemaids in the Stein households of Baltimore, Maryland, and various California towns, as well as her observing black women in Europe—marked her as an *experimentalist*. *Three Lives* was reviewed, albeit grudgingly. In the *Washington Herald*, an anonymous reviewer used the condescending description: "a rather peculiar exposition of the art of character delineation, in which is shown the constant repetition of ideas in minds of low caliber and meager cultivation." Class-identified, this reviewer sees no rationale for Stein's drawing such low-born women. He accordingly advises her, for her next effort, to work with "minds of a higher caliber." *The Nation* reviewer also stumbles about having to consider the lives of "three humble souls wittingly or unwittingly at odds with life. Whoever can adjust himself to the repetitions, false starts, and general circularity of the manner will find himself very near real people. Too near, possibly." Again, a relatively low social status is equated with impaired mental acuity, and even the distinctiveness of Stein's somewhat cubist style is seen to reflect the faulty minds of the characters. Class trumps race here, as both reviewers fail to mention that "Melanctha" is black—and obviously the most intelligent of the three characters Stein chose to draw.[1]

The Nation reviewer also comments on Stein's "extraordinary vitality conveyed in a most eccentric and difficult form": William James called her writing in this book "a fine new kind of realism."

It was never going to make her any money, Stein's *Three Lives*, and because she lived on a small stipend from her family trust, income was significant to her. (None of her writing, until *The Autobiography of Alice B. Toklas*—a book about herself told through the narrative lens of her partner, a book that continued to break all the rules common to accepted autobiography—in the mid 1930s, did that. And the fame of that single text brought her, with Alice, back to the United States for the first time in thirty years, fearful of the prohibitive cost of living in America and equally fearful of being ostracized because of their lesbianism.) Throughout her productive writing life, Stein conveyed the power of language, always used idiosyncratically even if effectively, as well as the aural prominence of United States talk. Even in France, she lived—and spoke—as an American; and she continuously read and wrote about American history. Whereas in *Three Lives* she elevated the common to literature, in *Four in America* (1932) she profiled in detail Ulysses S. Grant, Henry James, Wilbur Wright, and George Washington. Occupied with the qualities that led to a person's being noticed—whether as a political force, as an inventor, or as a writer—Stein again drew away from the concept of what any "literature" *ought* to be about.

Three Lives gave readers the awkwardness of language—its inefficiency. The character of Anna died after being worn out from her generous, giving life. Known as "good," always self-abnegating, repressing her tendency toward love of another woman in order to, in effect, put herself into a kind of servitude to the accomplished men who employed her for meager wages, Anna lived a joyless life in human terms. Praise from the society around her was all that she had. Similarly, Lena's death occurred after yet another child is born to her life of servitude, hers in wedlock. As Stein describes these existences, being "gentle" is probably a worse indictment than being "good." That "Melanctha" does not bear an adjective that limits her is positive, but she is so enthralled by the argumentative discourse with Jeff, a man who professes to be her superior in knowledge and social position, that she cannot act on her own terms. All three of Stein's common women in her carefully worked-through histories are dead by the end of their stories. Accordingly, the title *Three Lives*–applied as it is to dead characters—conveys the sharpest and most pervasive irony of all Stein's effects.

Pre-modern history (a glimpse)

Major events in American history tend to coalesce around wars. It is often said, for example, that World War I prompted the emergence of the modern movement. Considering that rationale, this brief and focused chronology should no doubt begin with the years of the Spanish-American war, 1898–1899. But because so many of these texts of pre-modernism dealt with either women's lives or the economics of men's lives as wage-earners, this list is much later than that conflict. Starting in 1905 with the founding of the Industrial Workers of the World (IWW), the labor group called "the Wobblies," this chronology emphasizes events from 1908 through 1910, giving a cultural context to the literary production then.

1908: Exhibit in New York of paintings by the Revolutionary Black Gang (called "apostles of ugliness.")

1909: 20,000 women shirtwaist workers strike in New York, protesting long working hours, poor pay, and bad working conditions. (The 1912 Triangle Shirtwaist fire, with its numerous deaths, resulted from these conditions.)

1909: The founding of the NAACP (the National Association for the Advancement of Colored People, originally The Negro National Committee).

1909: Stein's *Three Lives* published.

1910: An estimated eight million women work outside the home.

1910: An estimated eight million immigrants come to the United States.

1910: The first "woman suffrage" parade held in the United States, in New York City.

1910: The White Slave Traffic act (the Mann Act), prohibiting the transportation of women across state lines "for immoral purposes," is passed.

1910: The Independent Artists Exhibition in New York (riot police helped control the thousands of people trying to enter the warehouse to see the exhibit; the 1913 Armory Show of largely European painters followed this initiation).

1910: The Mexican Revolution.

It goes without explicitly saying that writers write out of the circumstances of their own lives—and the lives that surround them. Without writing slavishly about historical circumstances, United States literary figures had to recognize that urban centers were taking over the provinces of the country, and that all too often the freedoms that had accrued from the earlier existence of a westward frontier were diminishing. As Frederick Jackson Turner had said in 1910, "A new national development is before us, without the former safety valve of abundant resources open to him who would take. Classes are becoming alarmingly distinct . . ." (Rauchway 2).

Note

1 James Smethurst explains that many writers and critics looked on "Melanctha" as "the seminal document of United States modernist fiction," even though "it is marked by openly racist statements of biological essentialism." This critic points out that Stein seemed unselfconscious about any such racism, and "sent copies of *Three Lives* to Booker T. Washington and W. E. B. Du Bois" (Smethurst 170).

Suggested further reading

Matei Calinescu, *Five Faces of Modernity: Modernism, Avant-Garde, Decadence, Kitsch, Postmodernism.* Duke UP, 1987.

Marianne DeKoven. *Rich and Strange: Gender, History, Modernism.* Princeton UP, 1991.

Richard Ellmann and Charles Feidelson, Jr., eds. *The Modern Tradition: Backgrounds of Modern Literature.* Oxford UP, 1965.

Andreas Huyssen. *After the Great Divide: Modernism, Mass Culture, Postmodernism.* Indiana UP, 1986.

2
THE "FOREIGN" IN AMERICAN MODERNISM

American literature, like the geographic construct of the United States itself, is sometimes considered to be smaller than it, in reality, is—especially during the early twentieth century, when American literature was setting readers the world over agog. It seemed somehow appropriate that the newest branch of the long-established British language had become the most prominent. Rather than being denigrated for its informality, its reliance on the commonest of idioms, American English had somehow given rise to works that were, simply, unique.

As Werner Sollors pointed out,

> In 1910, American literature was still of marginal significance outside of the borders of the United States. More American publishers were engaged in disseminating British authors than European houses were in reprinting the Americans. American literary culture lived from importing, not exporting, works . . . . From 1910 to 1950, the United States shifted from a country of consumers of European culture—"gondola guzzlers," as David Quixano, the hero of Israel Zangwill's play *The Melting-Pot* (1908), put it disparagingly—to a near-universal global "content provider" for all media, old and new.
>
> *Sollors 362*

The power of what came to be known as *American* modernist writing eventually sent historians and critics back to reconsidering the definition of *America* itself. As literary theoretician Wai-Chee Dimock put it, what we call "American" is often a short hand, a "simplified name for a much more complex tangle of relations" (Dimock *Deep Time* 3). Emphasizing phrases such as "double threaded," Dimock sees the countless connective tissues that link the United States to the rest of the world, a world that grows smaller every year in its global, transnational, and post-national characteristics. She also privileges the use of the phrase "deep time," indicating what she terms a set of longitudinal frames that may help readers understand patterns of intersection (Dimock *Deep Time* 73).

Greil Marcus and Werner Sollors, in their introduction to *A New Literary History of America* (2009), comment on the tendency of all historians, including literary ones, to avoid bifurcating the streams of "history." They point to a parallel set of information tracks: historical story, that of "discovery and founding," set alongside an "underbelly" narrative of "crime, sin, and . . . violation, a rebuke to its own professed ideals." They continue, "From the first appearance of the word 'America' on a map to Jimi Hendrix's rewrite of the national anthem . . . the cultural history is a matrix" (Marcus and Sollors xxiii, xxv).

There were problems in America as the twentieth century opened. Some of the dissension in the United States came from the movement of farmers into cities. Susan Hegeman describes those inherent conflicts: such spatial divisions between industrial and agrarian regions, or between urban centers and rural provinces, were seen as cultural as well, such that "never before (or since) were issues of taste and cultural value articulated in such geographic terms" (Hegeman 20–7). Increasingly, the eventual overcrowding of those cities was blamed on the pressures of housing millions of immigrants, but the fact that those people came from such diverse backgrounds and ethnic origins, and spoke so many different languages, led to further kinds of differences. As linguistics theorist Joshua L. Miller recently explained, the political stance in the United States was to denigrate *non-English* languages. He explained that while racial and ethnic prejudice was frowned upon, keeping direct offensive comments to a minimum,

> linguistic discrimination was permissible . . . . When Latina/os, Jews, or Asian Americans were not explicitly restricted from professions or from participating in public debates, language restrictions were invoked or implied as a way of preventing or diminishing their civic participations. Denigration of African American, Native American, German, Italian, and Irish speech forms operated in much the same paralyzing and humiliating manner through epithets, vaudeville performance, dialect stories, and, later, radio, film, and television.
>
> *Miller 17*

Critic Katherine Biers adds to the discussion by pointing out that black speech (like African American music) was never associated with "uplift." In fact, "blackness has . . . often been featured in the American national imaginary as a *failure* of speech—an inarticulacy that can't, or won't, 'tell.' . . . Psychoanalysis, semiotics, and critical theory have attached significant importance to this inarticulate zone between speech and silence" (Biers 113).

To place African American language, music and literature within what Marcus Klein calls the "foreign" is to make the "outsider" group much larger than some earlier observers have recognized. Klein sees United States cities as "ghetto conglomerates," and by doing so he gives new dimensions to the various kinds of difficulties the country's population growth (either with or without

---

**EXCERPT FROM HERBERT G. GUTMAN'S *WORK,
CULTURE AND SOCIETY IN INDUSTRIALIZING AMERICA:
ESSAYS IN AMERICAN WORKING-CLASS AND SOCIAL
HISTORY*, pp. 71–2**

Immigrant groups and the working population had changed in composition over time, but the rhetoric of influential nineteenth-and early twentieth-century elite observers remained constant. Disorders among the Jersey City Irish seeking wages due them from the Erie Railroad in 1859 led the Jersey City *American Standard* to call them "imported beggars" and "animals," "a mongrel mass of ignorance and crime and superstition, as utterly unfit for its duties, as they are for the common courtesies and decencies of civilized life." . . . In 1869 *Scientific American* welcomed the "ruder" laborers of Europe but urged them to "assimilate" quickly or face "a quiet but sure extermination." Those who retained their alien ways, it insisted, "will share the fate of the native Indian."

---

exclusionary political tactics) created. One economic distinction is that during this time, cities of a million or more people "were made up of persons two-thirds of whom were either foreign born or first-generation native born" (Klein 14). Statistics show that 25,000,000 immigrants came to the United States between 1880 and 1930. In the tentative assessment of Andrzej Gasiorek, "It has been suggested that this modernist ferment was motivated by fears about the impact on culture and society of the increasingly literate lower-middle and working class." Those who wrote and painted and composed wanted to keep "high" art away from "mass culture." Gasiorek continues, "Anglo–American modernists were guilty of appalling snobberies" (Gasiorek 180).

Living in any ghetto forced immigrants to re-think their purpose in coming to the United States. "The ghetto obliged honor to the old ways, the traditional ways." Even the act of writing in English could be seen as subversive. To write in *English* "was an act of emigration, and therefore an act of hostility directed against a most peculiarly sensitive and imposing society" (Klein 20–1). What led to even a little praise for such immigrant writers as Mary Antin and Abraham Cahan was their choice to work in the genre of memoir. Antin wrote *From Plotzk to Boston* in 1899, when she was just eighteen; her *The Promised Land* appeared in 1912. In each she discusses her journey from Russia through Germany to the United States, but in the latter she dwells on the mixed and contrasting feelings an immigrant experiences in America.

The Promised Land, then, conveys irony as well as the protagonist's feeling of blessedness. When she describes her first day of school in Boston, an experience her older sister Frieda is never to have because their father cannot make enough money to support his family alone, she exudes the joy of the child who has been told that education will mean everything to her life:

Education was free. That subject my father had written about repeatedly, as comprising his chief hope for us children, the essence of American opportunity, the treasure that no thief could touch, not even misfortune or poverty. It was the one thing that he was able to promise us when he sent for us; surer, safer than bread or shelter.

L C, 824

Antin creates a poignant scene as her father—willingly leaving Frieda to earn wages doing hard work rather than coming to school—conducts the three younger children into the Boston school. She describes his pride: "This foreigner, who brought his children to school as if it were an act of consecration, who regarded the teacher of the primer class with reverence, who spoke of visions, like a man inspired . . . ." (L C, 829), and then she subtly appropriates, and emphasizes, the man's acceptance of the fact that his oldest child, Frieda, will never be educated.

Abraham Cahan, who wrote five volumes of his memoirs (*Leaves from My Life*), was better known in United States literature for his fiction, *Yekl, A Tale of the New York Ghetto* (1896), his stories in *The Imported Bridegroom* and elsewhere, and *The Rise of David Levinsky* (1917). A newspaper editor and journalist, this Russian émigré brought to America both Yiddish and English intellectualism. Well-educated in Russia, Cahan taught there until his radicalism brought his life under threat; in 1882 he came to Philadelphia, and then to New York. From 1903 to 1946 he edited the *Daily Forward*, expanding it from a Jewish newspaper into a widely-read and less sectarian one: Cahan was at the center of life on New York's Lower East Side for much of the first half of the twentieth century.

Several films were made from his fiction (*Hester Street* in 1975, for one). The accuracy of his descriptions of sweatshop life keeps his writing useful even now; yet he draws scenes that are more than sociologically interesting. Usually there is a romance plot to be worked through. In *Yekl*, Jake (a thoroughly Americanized Jew) decides to leave his Russian wife, from whom he has been separated for three years, to marry a more Americanized Jewish woman. In many of Cahan's stories, heterosexual romance may be an ingredient but the language play among the immigrant workers—made more humorous because of the characters' unease with English—often creates comedy.

The irony of the Statue of Liberty implicitly expressing such welcoming sentiments, even as immigrants from around the world found treatment in the United States much worse than they had expected, was not lost on literate migrants. Because being a literary success was so difficult (even for native English speakers, educated white Americans with family financial backing), it is not surprising that few immigrant writers became household names. About the same time as Cahan's later novel, *The Rise of David Levinsky*, Anzia Yezierska began publishing her stories. Fleeing from Plotzk, as had Mary Antin, the Yezierska family settled in New York's Lower East Side. Because her father was a Talmudic scholar, Anzia tried to support her family—selling, doing sweatshop work, going to school nights, and finally attending Columbia Teacher's College. John Dewey befriended her; she was so intent on becoming a writer that she turned her daughter over to the child's father after her second marriage ended in divorce.

EXCERPT FROM EMMA LAZARUS'S "THE NEW COLOSSUS" AND NOTE

. . ."Keep, ancient lands, your storied pomp!" cries she [Statue of Liberty]
With silent lips. "Give me your tired, your poor,
Your huddled masses yearning to breathe free,
The wretched refuse of your teeming shore.
Send these, the homeless tempest-tost to me,
I lift my lamp besides the golden door!"

A gift from the French people, the statue by Frederic-August Batholdi was brought to the U.S. by money raised by Joseph Pulitzer; the hand of liberty holding the torch was on display during the 1870s so that Americans could see how colossal the statue would be, 305 feet from ground to tip of torch. In 1903 the poem by Lazarus was engraved on a bronze tablet on the interior wall of the pedestal.

In 1920 her story collection, *Hungry Hearts*, was published; it was followed by the novels *Salome of the Tenements*, 1922; *Children of Loneliness*, 1923; *Bread Givers*, 1925; *Arrogant Beggar*, 1927; *All I Could Never Be*, 1932, and later works. Optioned by Hollywood, *Hungry Hearts* led to Yezierska's being offered a screen writing position in California. Few writers from the twentieth century made such an impact on the reading public. Important for creating the lives and voices of women immigrants, Yezierska used dialogue and plot sensitively and effectively. She had learned her craft well; she earned the success that she found.

Usual thematic emphases in writing by immigrants are the conflicts between assimilation and accommodation: how does a person new to the United States adjust to circumstances, customs, and situations that are not only new but foreign? While this set of controversies occurs in Mary Antin's writing, it is less visible in the work of either Cahan or Yezierska. Sui Sin Far (Edith Maud Eaton) and Onoto Watanna (Winnifred Eaton) were two Eurasian women who were also sisters, (born of a Chinese mother and a British father, immigrating to America and living first in Canada and then in the Pacific Northwest). When they began publishing, their stories were so well crafted that readers did not expect such finesse. In 1899, Onoto Watanna published the first Asian American novel, *Miss Nume of Japan*; it was followed by almost a dozen similarly exotic novels about Japanese women. In 1915, anonymously, she brought out *Me: A Book of Remembrance*. This autobiographical novel criticized the attitudes of white supremacy, and the roles people of color, especially women, were forced to assume in order to survive in the United States.

The writers did not use customary themes; in fact, Far often produced fiction that centered on a character's lack of surety, even ambivalence. Critics commented on the ways she created a "shifting sense of identity." *Mrs. Spring Fragrance*, her collected stories and essays, appeared in 1912; critical of the United States in its treatment of immigrants from China, the book remains in print.

First known for her political essays, Emma Goldman was also a Lithuanian Jew who immigrated to the United States in 1885 and worked in a Rochester, New York, garment factory. When she moved to New York City in 1889 and met Alexander Berkman, she was groomed by Johann Most to speak for the anarchist cause. Goldman was arrested with Berkman when his plot to assassinate Henry Clay Frick failed (Frick had brutally oppressed the strikers in the Homestead steel mill strike); Berkman was sentenced to twenty-two years in prison. Goldman continued her career speaking for union causes and, later, for the rights of women—birth control in particular. She was jailed several times for that activity.

Associated with Leon Czolgosz's assassination of President McKinley in 1901, Goldman disappeared for several years. When she came back in 1906, she founded the journal *Mother Earth* and began lecturing again. In 1911 she published *Anarchism and Other Essays*; in 1914, *The Social Significance of the Modern Drama* (discussing Ibsen, Strindberg, and Shaw, among other playwrights). In 1931, after living for some time in Russia and, becoming disillusioned, returning to America, then she published her autobiography, *Living My Life*.

Considerable activity by women poets, many of them immigrants to the States, has often gone unrecognized. When Lola Ridge's *The Ghetto and Other Poems*, her first poem collection, appeared in 1918, she was already forty-five, and had long been active in publishing. Born in Ireland, Ridge spent much of her childhood in New Zealand before being brought to America. One of the leading radical poets of this time, she brought convincing sentiments about labor abuses, and other miscarriages of justice, into her poems; in fact, she seldom wrote personal poems at all. A cadre of strong women poets occupied a more than marginal space in the evolution of a poetry that foreshadowed work to be strikingly visible during the 1930s—Ruth Lechlitner, Muriel Rukeyser, Joy Davidman (an early winner of the Yale Younger Poets prize), Genevieve Taggard, and coming at the far end of this incipient period, Margaret Walker, whose long poem "For My People" was first published in *Poetry* in 1937. (Walker was also to win the Yale Younger Poets prize.)

Anticipating a feminist movement yet to come, these women poets were much more focused on class inequities than on gender. Except for Ruth Lechlitner's much-anthologized "Lines for an Abortionist's Office" poem, and Ridge's central "The Ghetto," the work of women poets during the 1920s and the 1930s scruti-nized social and political events—they, in effect, created a kind of subversive history. Speaking to the difference, both generationally and philosophically, of the three, critic Nancy Berke notes that

> Ridge, Taggard, and Walker thought differently as radicals: they also perceived women's position vis-à-vis a world that needed to be turned upside down from their respective experiences as women: Irish immigrant anarchist, WASP communist, and Black Christian radical. None believed that a special

women's language could bring about social change; neither did each believe that women's voices could be ignored altogether.

Berke 27

One of Ridge's provocative poems from *The Ghetto*, for example, traced the abomination of the lynching of Frank Little ("Frank Little at Calvary"[1] depicts the death of the union leader at the hands of hired killers at the Anaconda Copper Mine in Montana). Part Native American, this World War I organizer had led strike efforts after several hundred mine workers burned to death at the Butte Speculation Mine, June 8, 1917. This poem, along with her often anthologized "Electrocution," first published in *The Double Dealer* in 1921, marked hers as an effective voice of protest. In both "Electrocution" and the Frank Little poem, Ridge describes the martyred man through his vision:

I know he looked once at America
Quiescent, with her great flanks on the globe
And once at the skies whirling above him . . . .
Then all that he had spoken against
And struck against and thrust against
Over the frail barricade of his life
Rushed between him and the stars.

in *Berke 43*

A month after the Little lynching in Montana, East St. Louis broke into an unprecedented race riot, in which white workers maimed and killed black workers. This internal class race war was memorialized by Ridge's poem "Lullaby," in which the sonority of the song is twisted to be about the white attackers, yet spoken in a quasi-black idiom. Mockery adds to the savage indictment of the closing quatrain:

Rock-a-by baby, woolly and brown . . . .
(There's a shout at the door an' a big red light . . . .)
Lil' coon baby, mammy is down . . . .
Han's that hold yuh are steady an' white.

White women, mothers themselves, have thrown this African American baby into a blazing fire: told in the black woman's voice from beyond her grave, "the woman's murderers speak in her place, appropriating her dialect, as they throw her child into a fire they have set with the aid of their husbands and children. The real shock is that the white women rock the baby and sing to it before they kill it" (Berke 47). In this comparatively long poem, Ridge includes a number of incriminating details: she describes "the singin' flame an' the gleeful crowd," she marks the death of the mother ("Mammy's in a heap/ By her own fron' door in the blazin' heat"), and she seemingly praises the stability and control of the white women's hands:

Hans that are wonderful, steady an' white!
To toss up a lil' babe, blinkin' an' brown

in *Berke 47*

In Ridge's later collections (1920, *Sun-Up*; 1927, *Red Flag*; 1929, *Firehead*; 1935, *Dance of Fire*), she similarly reflects on and images history—her famous poems about the executions of Sacco and Vanzetti, for example, are "Two in the Death House" and "Three Men Die." Ridge was the only woman contributor to the journal *Left*, just as, a few years later, Muriel Rukeyser would be the only female contributor to *Dynamo*.

Although not foreign born, Genevieve Taggard was apparently more readily accepted—particularly by Mike Gold and Joseph Freeman as they published *New Masses*.[2] After her first poem collection—*The Eager Lovers*—appeared in 1922, Taggard published more than eighteen books (some edited); she was the editor of *Measure*; known for her leftist politics, she married a second spouse who worked for TASS, the American office of the Russian News Agency. Some of her earliest poems were more feminist than political but she was known for writing strong poems throughout the twenties and the thirties. Her most famous collection is *Calling Western Union*, 1936, where many of her poems—"At Last the Women Are Moving," "Feeding the Children," "Up State—Depression Summer," "Mill Town"—illustrate her poetic aim, to create "a social narrative." From "Up State" come the memorable lines about the sick (and one presumes malnourished) child,

> And it was weeks along and still she lay.
> The doctor came and went and wanted medicine
> No one could buy . . . .
>   Then poor Tom
> Blundered about the porch and milked a little
> And pumped some water and went in, afraid.
> And the kid died as slowly as she could . . . .

The power of Taggard's poetry is that it cannot be easily summarized. In this poem, for example, the child's death is followed by more than a dozen lines, focused on the farmer's struggle to keep his land. That poem ends, "They sold the calf. That fall the bank took over" (N 337–8).

Taggard's more political poems like "At Last the Women Are Moving" and "Feeding the Children" are single-themed, and show occasional humor; the immense quantity of her poetry has seldom been properly evaluated, for all its countless translations into languages other than English. Considering both Ridge and Taggard, Berke concludes, "Lola Ridge's antideath penalty, antilynching, pro-worker lyrics of the 1920s suggest that women still actively engaged in public discourses. Similarly, by 1925, Taggard had become an active participant in left cultural debates about transforming society" (Berke 86–7).

If not "foreign," something "Other"

Writers who represented something other than a middle or upper-class, educated white society brought into literary consciousness new dimensions of character, new plots, new metaphors, and new strategies for teaching—or at least intriguing—readers.

Such a tactic was visible in 1912 when James Weldon Johnson published his long prose work, *The Autobiography of an Ex-Colored Man.* As we have seen, early twentieth century American literature had become the home of many immigrant fiction writers and autobiographers: some of their readers shared ethnic interests with the writers, others were hungry for different life experiences, still others were simply curious. When the first critiques of Johnson's novel appeared, the book was taken as genuine autobiography, and speculation was that the author had himself "passed" as white. To change the terms of a literary genre was not uncommon: many African American writers had long nourished an instinct for irony.

Years later, in 1925, when Paul Robeson made his concert debut at the Greenwich Village Theatre in New York, he sang only Negro spirituals; he repeated that performance other times. The line between traditional concert fare and spirituals was the ironic subject (Spencer 52). But in the years before that concert, American cultural gate-keepers were consistently disparaging African American music of all kinds (including the spirituals that were often regularly sung in white churches). The fear was the "sexuality" inherent in the blues and the increasingly popular jazz: many young American white women were not allowed to go to jazz joints. Katherine Biers points out that everybody wanted to avoid "the vulgarity of ragtime .... By keeping black music inadmissible to the cultural origins of American national expression, these origins were preserved from the taint of slavery" (Biers 116).

Rare was the appearance of African American writing in mainstream publishing channels: much African American writing appeared in newspapers and magazines published for and circulated among those readers, usually separated out from more mainstream venues. Late in the 1890s, it was estimated that more than 200 black newspapers were in circulation; the most prominent of these were the Detroit *Plaindealer*, the *New York Age*, the Chicago *Defender*, and the Indianapolis *Freeman*. The most famous was probably Ida B. Wells-Barnett's *Free Speech* in Memphis, Tennessee.

Critic Charles Scruggs in his influential study *Sweet Home* says repeatedly that black American writing was never considered mainstream: "the recognition of linguistic kinship never meant that white modernists saw Afro-Americans as equals in any sense" (Scruggs 212). He continues,

> High modernism as a cultural event helped confirm all Afro-Americans, not necessarily only Afro-American *writers*, in their continued invisibility. Migrants to the cities themselves, blacks barely participated in the high modernist literature created primarily by white urban immigrants between 1910 and 1940, and their absence is another paradigm of high and low, of a difference that modernity does not melt down.
>
> *Scruggs 211*

Even after the flood of African American workers from the South hit United States cities (several million during and after the war years, and nearly all headed to cities), publishing circumstances did not change. Biers points to this visible difference as she discusses Johnson's autobiography: "black culture as such was barely on the national radar. Instead, cultural gatekeepers were absorbed in a project of national (not racial) uplift that aimed to elevate popular tastes and establish a distinctively American [musical] culture" (Biers 109).

What Johnson achieves in *The Autobiography of an Ex-Colored Man* is, in many ways, highly articulate satire. His work here is less directly aimed at African American readers than was W. E. B. Du Bois's earlier *The Souls of Black Folk*. That 1903 treatise on African American life and music quickly was seen as gospel: people quoted from it; they also sang from it. Less didactic than it might have been, given that Du Bois's earlier works were sociological studies (he had the Ph.D. in history from Harvard), *The Souls of Black Folk* charted a path for African Americans in the twentieth century. The author gave his readers such concepts as "double-consciousness," "this sense of always looking at one's self through the eyes of others." According to Du Bois, the African American "ever feels his two-ness—an American, a Negro: two souls, two thoughts, two unreconciled strivings; two warring ideals in one dark body." From this peculiar position, however, grows the ability to have second sight, to understand all the non-black comments made within his hearing, even as it may lead to a disabling ambivalence as the African American must take action that sometimes hurts his people.

Johnson's approach in *The Autobiography of an Ex-Colored Man* is to reach the underbelly of that African American sensibility. One long screed of ironic subterfuge masquerades as "true" life experience. Published anonymously, the book was not attributed to Johnson as author till 1927; by that time it had become a classic that repeated the wisdom of *The Souls of Black Folk*. Johnson's protagonist, son of a black mother and a white father, is caught throughout the narrative in the discomfort of being an intellectual, yet having to be cautious (Johnson's choice of dialogues among several different speakers works to show those cautions). By using a picaresque structure, Johnson can take his character into parts of the United States that are less or more racist. Written in first person, the book gives readers a protagonist who is not always admirable. As Richard Gray describes it,

> The subjects of earlier black autobiographies had tended towards the sensitive, the sympathetic, even the noble. The 'ex-colored man' is not that at all: on the contrary, he is proud and rendered unattractive by his pride. And pride comes here before a fall. In the end, he has to recognize his error: that, as he puts it, 'I have sold my birthright for a mess of pottage.' Sometimes, he reflects bitterly in the final chapter, 'it seems to be that I have never really been a Negro, that I have been only a privileged spectator of their inner life.' At other times, he adds, 'I feel that I have been a coward and a deserter, and I am possessed by a strong longing for my mother's people.' But such feelings come too late. Trapped in the white world now, with two children who are to all appearances white, the 'ex-colored man' cannot escape, and he can only reveal his 'secret' covertly, anonymously, in the pages of this book.

Gray 162

EXCERPT FROM PAUL LAURENCE DUNBAR'S "WE WEAR THE MASK"

We wear the mask that grins and lies,
It hides our cheeks and shades our eyes,—
This debt we pay to human guile;
With torn and bleeding hearts we smile,
And mouth with myriad subtleties . . . .

Without investigating the power of the long tradition of slave narrative as a genre, and the existing but newer tradition of African American writers who found mainstream publishers (such as Booker T. Washington, Charles Chesnutt, Pauline Hopkins, Countee Cullen, Frances Ellen Harper, Angelina Weld Grimke, Georgia Douglas Johnson, Anne Spencer, Claude McKay, Alice Dunbar-Nelson, and Paul Laurence Dunbar, whose 1896 poem collection *Lyrics of Lowly Life* quickly became a classic), the reader of the incipient history of Modernism must recognize how much activity there was in groups of Americans who remained only marginally visible to the literary world. Latino-a culture had its spokesperson in Jose Marti; Native American culture privileged the writing of Mary Austin and Gertrude Bonnin, who wrote under her tribal name of Zitkala-Sa. Literature that spoke for the voiceless immigrant and segregated cultures was available though the interested reader had to know where to look for it. As Thomas Strychacz argues in *Modernism, Mass Culture, and Professionalism*, one kind of shorthand to describe what Marcus Klein called "the foreign" is to emphasize "mass culture" and contrast it with high brow literary production. Strychacz groups ethnic and immigrant writing into one category, that of mass culture, and notes that it's possible to see the power of Modernism in the ways "various writing strategies articulate a history of exclusions and acts of silencing; an account of works in which an historical engagement with a consumer-driven mass culture has disappeared underground" (Strychacz 9).

The Masses, Mother Earth, *the* Liberator, *et al.*

Just as African American writing had newspapers and magazines specific to it and its readers, as did Spanish language outlets, so the left-of-center intellectuals early in the twentieth century created their journals. Emma Goldman's *Mother Earth* was one of the first to be formed and funded; the *Masses* was one of the longest-lasting (and came to have a second life during the 1930s as *The New Masses*). Associated with the *Masses* was a group of leftist young men, largely immigrant, largely socialist—among them Van Wyck Brooks, Paul Rosenfeld, Max Eastman, Floyd Dell, Waldo Frank, Lewis Mumford, Joseph Freeman, Randolph Bourne, Don Freeman, John Reed, Alfred Stieglitz, and others. Lola Ridge, with Kay Boyle as her assistant editor, served as the American editor for *Broom*. Except for Ridge and Boyle, Taggard, Mary Heaton

Vorse, Tillie Lerner (Olsen), and Emma Goldman, most of the editors and contributors were men. Occasionally Sherwood Anderson and Sinclair Lewis are grouped here, as are—a bit later—William Carlos Williams, Carl Rakosi, Louis Zukofsky, Charles Reznikoff, Kenneth Fearing and others.

The commitment in these journals was to creating a tradition of *American* empathy and history (rather than including all of Western culture in that tradition). The politics expressed in these journals were not strident (and sometimes far from orderly); as Marcus Klein said,

> The *Masses*, especially, comprehended a latitude in which impertinence became polemical and polemics were fun. What it lacked in theoretical strictness, it made up for in an ebullience which served better as an organizing principle. The magazine had been founded in 1911 by a man named Piet Vlag, a Greenwich Village restaurant owner who had ideas about consumers' cooperatives. It had quickly run out of money, and Vlag had left for Florida. Eastman had just left his teaching job in the philosophy department at Columbia University, and so was available to revive the magazine.
>
> *Klein 48*

David Minter emphasizes that these writers were "self-consciously cosmopolitan," and even as they proselytized about creating "Americanness," they also looked for ways to explore what Randolph Bourne called "transnationality"—"a weaving back and forth, with other lands, of many threads of all sizes and colors." (They were not particularly cognizant of, or impressed by, the power of the British.) Eclectic in their reading, they kept returning to Walt Whitman, and to the Imagists they added Robert Frost, Edgar Lee Masters, Vachel Lindsay, James Oppenheim and Carl Sandburg (Minter 69).

Minter, however, sees the group as innocent of real political strength. They were searching for what Floyd Dell called a "new spirit abroad, generated by the search for new values in life and art." They assumed Socialist sentiments, but their activities were more aesthetic than political. For the years that Max Eastman edited *Masses*, 1913–1917, it spoke for radicalism. Minter calls it

> both commodious and evasive. It brought politics cheek by jowl with the early love poems of e. e. cummings. Through its pages, as a faithfully uncritical [Don] Freeman put it, the winds of change "released by Omar Khayyam, Friedrich Nietzsche, Edward Carpenter, Walt Whitman and finally Sigmund Freud blew across America . . . to rescue us from the crushing oppression of puritanism, from the implacable sense of guilt."

Reading *Masses*, one could find "the irreverent cartoons of Art Young, the iconoclastic essays of Dell, the proclamations of labor agitator Arturo Giovannitti, the exposes of Mary Heaton Vorse, and the travel reports of John Reed." Even before the 1918 passage of the Alien and Sedition Act, the federal government banned using the U.S. mails to send *Masses* to subscribers. Then in 1918 the government prosecuted Eastman, Dell, and Young—unsuccessfully—for "conspiracy against the government" (Minter 70, 75).

Werner Sollors builds his monograph, *Ethnic Modernism*, around the premise shared by this discussion.

> African Americans, European immigrants, and members of other minority groups were, *as* immigrants and ethnics, part of modernity, as they lived through experiences of migration, ethnic identification, and often, alienation. In many ways, they also participated in, and significantly advanced, the course of Modernism in the United States; Afro-American artists, including Fletcher Henderson, Louis Armstrong, Duke Ellington and Charlie Parker, were central to the development of the new American music; modern composers Arnold Schonberg and Kurt Weill escaped to America from fascist Europe; immigrant and émigré artists like Joseph Stella, Max Weber, Ben Shahn, Man Ray, and Marcel Duchamp helped to establish modernist art; European exiles like Josef Albers were prominently active in such institutions as Black Mountain College while Hans Hoffmann taught the principles of modernist art and 'abstract expressionism' in New York.
>
> *Sollors 364*

Notes

1 An even more often anthologized poem by Ridge is her 1935 "Stone Face," which protests the incarceration of labor leader Tom Mooney; finally convinced that his accusation of murder and his conviction stemmed from his role as union leader, President Woodrow Wilson commuted his death sentence to a lifetime in prison.
2 Born in Washington state, Taggard grew up in Hawaii where her parents, both Christian missionaries, had been sent to open and run a public school. She was educated at University of California at Berkeley and then moved to Greenwich Village, bringing her socialist beliefs cross country.

Suggested further reading

Philip Gleason. *Speaking of Diversity: Language and Ethnicity in Twentieth-Century America*. Johns Hopkins UP, 1992.
Matthew Jacobson. *Whiteness of a Different Color*. Harvard UP, 1998.
Marcus Klein. *Foreigners: The Making of American Literature, 1900–1940*. U of Chicago P, 1981.
Werner Sollors. *Ethnic Modernism, The Cambridge History of American Literature VI*. Ed. Sacvan Bercovitch. Harvard UP, 2008.

3

POETRY AS ORIGIN

Discussions of American modernism within the twenty-first century have increasingly emphasized that to be modern was to be affiliated with the highest social classes, the writers and readers who were well educated (or at least differently educated), the increasingly numerous publishers and gallery owners who understood the aesthetic changes emanating from Europe. In critic John T. Matthews' recent discussion, he prefaces his comments by pointing out that all critics, all cultural observers, share "a common inclination to present the history of artistic periods as a succession of styles, aesthetic convictions, and quests for imaginative originality." His attribution of stylistic changes to the British tradition moves to his more central point, that the artists and writers who wanted to be identified with the *modern* established "a rich tradition of artists speaking to one another through acts of fierce concentration on the work of art itself" (Matthews 283).

The political sensibility of Modernism, continues Matthews, was aimed at *offending* "bourgeois society." Modernists wanted to "strip away habitual beliefs and values, and to demand acts of self-scrutiny and metaphysical exploration . . . ." They did this by creating works that prided themselves on "being difficult, by deliberately being hard to understand." These traits of Modernism—its "formal inventiveness and inscrutability—constituted a revolt against the recipients' familiar expectations, against comfortable habits of art consumption." In short, artists identified with Modernism wanted to separate art from "social, political, and economic contexts: and tried to avoid contamination by 'popular' taste, as well as by 'mass' culture, monopoly capitalism, political and scientific discourse, [and] technological production of goods" (Matthews 283–4).

Making Modernism more of a class statement, and aligning its visible creators—Ezra Pound, Ford Madox Ford, Gertrude Stein, and T. S. Eliot—with unquestionable elitism, Matthews (perhaps unintentionally) defines the movement by what Andrew Ross early on termed its "failure." Critics late in the twentieth century seemed to agree that the idea of "Modernism" remained conservative, tied by its difficulties in form and content to readers well versed in established traditions, and—in Klein's words—those who aimed at "fabricating a past from random oddments of history." Modernism "was not quite officially hostile" to the American dream of all those immigrants, and lower class readers, who believed in that concept fervently (Klein 20, 39). It did, however, privilege the aesthetics of the *placement* of words—whether in poems or fiction—instead of emphasizing the rallying content of those words. In fact, if any piece of modernist writing became a call to action, the work would have been judged a failure.

The English-speaking literary world early in the twentieth century could be identified with such little magazines and journals as *Poetry* (Chicago), the *Criterion*, the *Dial*, the *Little Review*, the *Double Dealer*, *Reedy's Mirror* and others that used reviews. (*Mother Earth* and the *Masses* were not mentioned in the usual lists.) Eliot, Pound, F. S. Flint, and Ford Madox Ford wrote hundreds of critical pieces between 1910 and 1930. Critic John McCormick notes that "The unquestioned veracity and propriety of poetic experiment," combined with all the poetic theory available, "conspired to urge" fiction writers as well as poets to experiment (McCormick 88). John Dos Passos, who began his publishing career as a poet, reified that comment: "Poetry was more important than submarines or war guilt or brave little Belgium or the big board on the New York stock exchange" (Dos Passos *Best* 24).

Once World War I began, it was natural for literary critics to include those expectations and tragedies in their current discourse (even though the United States would delay entering the conflict for several more years). But America maintained its hungry quest for culture: not uncommon were remarks about Futurism, Impressionism, Imagism, Surrealism, and other language experimentation in published works, such as Stein's *Three Lives*. The result of notice by critics was to change the artistic experience of United States writers—to enrich it, to free it, and in some cases to destroy it; but always to emphasize its existence. For the first time in American history, public attention was pointed toward painting and poetry, even if some of that attention aimed to ridicule these arts.

New ideas, new currents in art were coming from all directions. The French Symbolist poets, popularized by F. S. Flint, brought new life to a waning formal poetry, just as realism and its resulting naturalism invigorated the popular novel. Soon after the turn of the century, some private and as yet undescribed experimentation was occurring: Pound had written some free-form poems by 1908 when he first met Ford Madox Hueffer (later Ford Madox Ford). Pound was well aware of the 1905 Fauves; the Autumn Salon; the 1908 Cubist exhibition in Paris, the same year as New York's Revolutionary Black Gang exhibition; Picasso and Braque's 1911–12 collages. While the graphic arts seemed to have found some new direction, between 1908 and 1912 literature was filled with experimentation, but observers saw less sense of purposeful direction.

It was 1913 when Ezra Pound began coining terms. He chose to publish his first statements about what he called *Imagism* in the young Chicago journal, *Poetry*.

EXCERPT FROM EZRA POUND'S "A RETROSPECT"

In the spring or early summer of 1912, H.D., Richard Aldington and myself decided that we were agreed upon the three principles following:

1 Direct treatment of the "thing" whether subjective or objective.
2 To use absolutely no word that does not contribute to the presentation.
3 As regarding rhythm: to compose in the sequence of the musical phrase, not in sequence of a metronome . . . .

Dividing his comments between himself and "F. S. Flint," to accrue some British prominence, Pound created a prolegomenon that would influence the writing of poetry for at least a decade (until Amy Lowell took over the yearly anthologies, and the movement became known as "Amygism"). Later Pound moved on to what he termed "Vorticism" so that poems could become longer, spinning away from a single image into cascades of splintering images and metaphors. It was a key decade for the changing impulses of the modern.

Pound himself wrote few imagistic poems, but he was drawing heavily on the writing his former fiancé, Hilda Doolittle, had created. (Pound also named this poet "H.D.," a change which gave this woman's poetry and its aesthetics both prominence and intentionality. Already living in London, H.D. was about to marry the British writer Richard Aldington; she had published widely in the various collections given over to "Imagist" writing.)

Many of H.D.'s early poems are written in one stanza, focused by one image, without rhyme or obvious rhythm: "Oread," "The Pool," "Heat," "The Helmsman," "Orchard," "Evening," "Lethe," "Helen," and "Sea Rose" are classic Imagist poems. The latter poem opens,

> Rose, harsh rose,
> marred and with stint of petals,
> meager flower, thin,
> sparse of leaf . . .
>
> *N 234*

and continues for another twelve lines, always reflecting the speaker's voice, always elaborating on the ways this "stunted" rose maintains its beauty. A 1916 poem, "Sea Rose" serves to illustrate those Imagist principles Pound listed in 1913.

Pound's essay defined the Image as "that which presents an intellectual and emotional complex in an instant of time." By stressing the inclusive power of the image, he strengthened the Imagist principle; and his emphasis on *speed* gave new life to the post-Victorian poem that was sometimes buried in detail. Pound's definition owed something as well to James Joyce's concept of "epiphany." As

Pound continues, "It is the presentation of such a 'complex' instantaneously which gives the sense of sudden liberation; that sense of *sudden growth*, which we experience in the presence of the greatest works of art . . . ." ("A Few Don'ts," 200).

Pound emphasized that words used sparingly were effective, and he explained about *vers libre* that such practice was one means of attaining the more germane if elusive structure, which he called *organic form*, a shape consonant with the mood and content being expressed. He expanded on this notion by discussing the unity of tone and mood that the best poems illustrate: "The term harmony is misapplied to poetry; it refers to simultaneous sounds of different pitch. There is, however, in the best verse a sort of residue of sound which remains in the ear of the hearer and acts more or less as an organ-base."

The aim of the Imagists—at least of Pound, Flint, and H.D., then spreading to Amy Lowell, William Carlos Williams, T. S. Eliot—seems to have been a freedom to let the poem achieve its own unity, a wholeness of effect unmarred by artificial and probably traditional literary contrivances. In this aim, they were only echoing the great principles of literature, but they discounted the shock value of the poems they published. Pound said important things about concision, drawing from Ernest Fenollosa the wisdom that verbs are the active parts of speech (he also learned through his work with the scholar of Chinese that the Chinese ideogram was the perfect image). As Pound said later in 1914, "The point of Imagisme is that it does not use images as ornaments. The image is itself the speech" ("Vorticism" 469; see Coffman, Eckman).

"Go in fear of abstractions," Pound warns. "Use either no ornament or good ornament." "Don't be descriptive"—instead, "Present." Such axioms demanded that the poet constantly choose, whether or not to include this word, or, indeed, any word at all. The modern poet was to become a polisher of gems.

John Dos Passos, who published his poems along with those of his Harvard friend e. e. cummings, built "Winter in Castile" around several images:

> The weazened old woman without teeth
> who shivers on the windy street corner
> displays her roasted chestnuts invitingly
> like marriageable daughters . . . .
>> *Dos Passos* Pushcart *43*

In cummings' own early work are such now-famous poems as "in Just-" (his poems are titled by their first lines) which opens

> in Just-
>
> spring when the world is mud-
> luscious the little
> lame balloonman
>
> whistles far and wee . . .
>> *N 344*

Typography and its experimental possibilities, the uses and misuses of capitalization, arranging lines and words within lines to replicate breath rhythms—as he did in the spelling of his name with all lower-case letters, cummings pounced on the principles of Modernism and kept them at his side until his death in 1962.

Amy Lowell's poems made another kind of Imagist statement. Always longer lined, and seemingly less modern in appearance, her poetry made more use of irony, in both word choice and line arrangement. In "September, 1918," for example, she follows a deft quatrain within the poem with a single but emphatic war-related line:

> . . . Under a tree in the park,
> Two little boys, lying flat on their faces,
> Were carefully gathering red berries
> To put in a pasteboard box.
> Some day there will be no war . . . .
> *N 44*

Similarly, in his 1915 poem "Buttons," Carl Sandburg combines the image of moving buttons on a war map to show defeat and victory, with a juxtaposed image of the physical deaths occurring:

> (Ten thousand men and boys twist on their bodies in a red soak
> along a river edge,
> Gasping of wounds, calling for water, some rattling death in their
> throats)
> *N 109*

One of Wallace Stevens' earliest published poems, "The Death of a Soldier," 1918, opens effectively with a stark image:

> Life contracts and death is expected,
> As in a season of autumn.
> The soldier falls . . . .
> *N 138*

EXCERPT FROM MICHAEL LEVENSON'S "INTRODUCTION," *THE CAMBRIDGE COMPANION TO MODERNISM*

So much of the artistic passion of the period was stirred by questions of technique, where "technique" should not suggest attention to "form" as opposed to "content," but should imply rather the recognition that every element of the work is an instrument of its effect and is open to technical revision. Nothing was beyond the reach of technical concern: not the frame of a picture, not the shape of a stage, not the choice of a subject, not the status of a rhyme . . . .

T. S. Eliot's early poems, though generally longer than much Imagist verse, shared the prominence of the image:

The winter evening settles down
With smell of steaks in passageways.
Six o'clock.
The burnt-out ends of smoky days . . . .

L D, 1284

Although William Carlos Williams began his career as poet writing more formally, once he met both H.D. and Pound during his days at the University of Pennsylvania Medical School, he quickly converted to Imagism ("the red wheelbarrow," "The Young Sycamore," "The Great Figure"). By the 1920s, however, he was creating a matrix of obvious prose with poems interposed:

I will make a big, serious portrait of my time. The brown and creamwhite block of Mexican onyx has a poorly executed replica of the Aztec calendar on one of its dicefacets the central circle being a broad-nosed face . . .
What chance have the old?
There are no duties for them
no places where they may sit
their knowledge is laughed at
they cannot see, they cannot hear . . . .

N 173–4

Just as Pound was to use all aspects of Imagism within his long poem *The Cantos*, so Williams would perfect this product of poetic prose and poem within his six-volume *Paterson*. In the case of H.D., she continued to write poems, often very long poems, but she also (like Williams and John Dos Passos) wrote a great deal of fiction. The same can be said of nearly all these modernist, Imagist poets, because, clearly, the ability to publish successfully (and earn money) meant their giving more attention to prose in the form of fiction.

For the American writer more interested in fiction than in the poem, Pound's principles about Imagism could easily be translated. For "image," read "scene." As philosopher Henri Bergson wrote in his *An Introduction to Metaphysics*, "the image has at least this advantage, that it keeps us in the concrete . . . . [M]any diverse images, borrowed from different orders of things, may, by the convergence of their action, direct consciousness to the precise point where there is a certain intuition to be seized" (Bergson 27–8).

To bring fiction writers into the company of these Imagist poets, one may consider the work of Sherwood Anderson. One of the powerful effects Anderson was able to create in his unusually effective short stories (published singly and then as a part of his 1919 book, *Winesburg, Ohio*) was that of the unforgettable scene. Few stories presented their happenings as concretely as Anderson's glimpse of his protagonist George Willard saying goodbye to Helen White in "Sophistication":

The boy's voice failed and in silence the two came back into town and went along the street to Helen White's house. At the gate he tried to say something impressive. Speeches he had thought out came into his head, but they seemed utterly pointless. 'I thought—I used to think—I had it in my mind you would marry Seth Richmond. Now I know you won't' was all he could find to say as she went through the gate and toward the door of her house.

Anderson Winesburg *290*

Each of his "Winesburg" stories illustrates the use of both concrete description andmetaphor. Each involves the reader in an empathy with diverse characters— usually through the association between metaphor and person. Wing Biddlebaum's ineffectual hands, Enoch Robinson's room, Reverend Hartman's window, Kate Swift's anger, Elizabeth Willard's makeup—by presenting the key to lives graphically and visually instead of rhetorically, Anderson creates both sharp impact and swift pace. The *poetic* fictional method allows condensation.

Anderson's images also create *tone* for the stories. Many stories begin with the snow that serves both to muffle and to beautify.

Snow lay deep in the streets of Winesburg. It had begun to snow about ten o'clock in the morning and a wind sprang up and blew the snow in clouds along Main Street . . . . "Snow will bring the people into town on Saturday . . . . Snow will be good for the wheat"

Anderson Winesburg *184*

In "The Teacher," he creates a snow-bound isolation to parallel the isolation of both George Willard and Kate Swift, the teacher of the title. All the action occurs on the snowy night; all the emotions are bleak, and remain so: contact is never made. The central image—for the emotions of the characters as well as the story proper—occurs early:

By nine o'clock of that evening snow lay deep in the streets and the weather had become bitter cold. It was difficult to walk about. The stores were dark and the people crawled away to their houses.

Anderson Winesburg *158*

Similarly, in "Death in the Woods," one of his later and often anthologized stories, he sets the narrative of the nearly invisible Mrs. Grimes in the midst of her life of sheer toil—again in the bitter cold.

She was an old woman and lived on a farm near the town in which I lived. All country and small-town people have such old women, but no one knows much about them. Such an old woman comes into town driving an old worn-out horse or she comes afoot carrying a basket. She may own a few hens and have eggs to sell. She brings them in a basket and takes them to a grocer. There she trades them in. She gets some salt pork and some beans. Then she gets a pound or two of sugar and some flour.

Portable *533*

Here the metaphor becomes the refrain: "Well, things had to be fed. Men had to be fed, and the horses that weren't any good but maybe could be traded off, and the poor thin cow that hadn't given any milk for three months.//Horses, cows, pigs, dogs, men" (ibid. 539).

Anderson came to writing after a business career; he drew from what he read and heard, and saw the way writers contemporary with him worked. After his brother had given him a copy of Gertrude Stein's *Tender Buttons* in 1914, he unearthed her 1909 *Three Lives*: much of his structuring of scene, his pointed use of dialogue, his paragraphing based on the way his sentences divided, and most obviously his use of very common characters echoed her example. Anderson originally called *Winesburg* "the book of the grotesque," and his choice of people who could—or would—not have existed comfortably outside of their small community was a kind of homage to Stein's three women characters.

Thinking of each aesthetic work as a whole meant that writers needed to justify the structures they chose. To meld separate short stories into one structure was an innovative approach to the formalist "novel"—but more to the point was Anderson's acute finesse in writing shorter pieces. Aligning the single story, or the single scene, with other parts of the work often led to juxtaposition, a technique that placed one image against another, sometimes without explanation. Laying one square of color against another, in a montage almost Cubist, the stark positioning of one character's language or presence against another's—and doing so without the help of an omniscient narrative voice—was a technique that demanded more knowledge from the reader than most fiction would have required. Anderson was often criticized for his seemingly off-handed arrangements of structure.[1]

When H.D. began writing her fiction—well after she was a successful Imagist poet but much earlier than the actual publication dates of her novels would suggest, she knew all about images, and how to weave them into paragraphs of fluid prose. She preferred juxtaposition as her structural practice, with the divisions between paragraphs—the white space—signaling the change in both action and idea. *HERmione* is the narrative of her early bisexual relationships, beginning with her accepting Ezra Pound's offer of marriage. Its emotional tone is her vast feeling of personal defeat once she has left college because she could not do the mathematical work she knew her father and brother would have expected from her (both men were astronomers). Personal failure and the metaphor of death, if not suicide, colors the novel.

Gart Grange wilted like a butterfly put under a glass case, like a leaf, suffocating . . .
[...]
A boy was shooting in the Farrand forest and caught his leg in a trap that the Farrand coachman or caretaker had had arranged there for trespassers. Hermione heard him howling, ran into the Gart woods to find him half-way

down their woodpath dragging the trap on an ankle. The woodpath was splashed with raw blood almost to the Werby cross-field . . .
[...]

"'Ain't this here heat too suffocating? Ah always say this September heat is worse than real mid-summer.' 'Yes, Mrs. Rennenstocker.' 'Did you say your mama didn't like that new Nora that you've got now?' 'No. I didn't say mama didn't like Nora. I said it was hard not having Mandy.'"

H.D. HERmione 114–15

The heat that suffuses Gart Grange, the absence of Hermione's beloved maid Mandy, and the incipient threat of physical harm that the neighbor boy's blood represents create context for the acts that separate Hermione from both the Pound character and her family members. The mélange of emotions that H.D. builds reminds the reader of Pound's principle which he called a work's "organ base," a tone or mood that connects even seemingly random segments of any writing.

Writers were to rely on the strength of the image and on the necessity for a recognizable organ base of mood and tone, which created the rhythms of the poem. Pound continued to emphasize juxtaposition as a structural device. He also warned against choosing a narrative voice that was overly emotional: his use of the word *objective* was sometimes misunderstood. Either do without an involved narrative voice or choose one that might mimic journalistic objectivity. Above all, aim for simplicity, a quality that stems from directness and avoiding traditional poetic diction. Such simplicity is to be subtle and sophisticated. Pound explained further:

There are various kinds of clarity. There is the clarity of the request: Send me four pounds of ten-penny nails. And there is the syntactical simplicity of the request: Buy me the kind of Rembrandt I like. This last is an utter cryptogram. It presupposes a more complex and intimate understanding of the speaker than most of us ever acquire of anyone. It has as many meanings, almost, as there are persons who might speak it . . . . It is the almost constant labor of the prose artist to translate this latter kind of clarity into the former; to say "Send me the kind of Rembrandt I like" in the terms of "Send me four pounds of ten-penny nails."

Pound Literary 50

In the case of H.D.'s work, though the emotive segments might be partially submerged under the speaker's self-consciousness, these elements from her life illustrate, too, one of Sigmund Freud's principal ideas, that a person's "unconscious" may remain hidden. According to Freud, large portions of any person's life are "unorganized" ("timeless") and therefore cannot be controlled rationally. He also believed that part of this "chaos" could, and often would, "discharge instinctual impulses" which would be unexpected, impulses that might cause "pleasure" in some people and "unpleasure" in others (Freud *Reader* 573–4). After the 1913 publication of the English translation of Freud's *The Interpretation of Dreams*, much of the English-speaking world read Freud. (At Freud's invitation, H.D. became an analysand, and after working with him, wrote *Tribute to Freud*.)

Modernism as a style also worked frequently with the enumeration of objects (it was not only William Carlos Williams who said that there were "no ideas but in things"). To provide a more substantial statement of this implicit principle, critic Douglas Mao recently stated that Modernism shares "the feeling of regard for the physical object as object—as not-self, as not-subject, as most helpless and will-less of intentions, but also as fragment of Being, as solidity, as otherness in its most resilient opacity . . . . the open acknowledgement of such a feeling seems one of the minor trademarks of the writing of this period" (Mao 4).

Pound was one of the earliest to include prose in his discussion of the poetic principles he called Imagism, doing so here and in several 1913 essays in both *Poetry* and *The New Age*, as well as in his 1914 essay on Vorticism. In 1915 he praised "prose that gives us pleasure paragraph by paragraph"; in 1917, prose "that one can enjoy sentence by sentence and reread with pleasure." His move to Flaubert's *le mot juste* is soon to come. By 1922 when *Ulysses* (as well as *The Waste Land*) appeared, Pound saw both as the logical fusion of the epic poem tradition and the nineteenth-century novel, and began in earnest his own long poem, *The Cantos*. As he was to muse decades later, "the most important critical act of the half-century was in the limpidity of natural speech, driven toward the just word" (Pound *Confucius* 327).

The work of T. S. Eliot and *The Waste Land*

One writer who moved into longer forms—of poetry and drama rather than prose—even before Imagism was an accepted mode was Thomas Stearns Eliot. When he first met Ezra Pound in London, as he traveled on fellowship when he was a doctoral candidate at Harvard, Eliot had already written "Prufrock" and other poems, but he had decided they were then unpublishable. In 1914 Pound convinced Harriet Monroe to print them in *Poetry*. When *Prufrock and Other Observations*, Eliot's first collection of poems, was published in 1917, Pound's review was ecstatic. He pointed out that Eliot had come to Modernism "on his own." He stated that Eliot's work "interests me more than that of any other poet now writing in English." He claimed a kind of universalism for these poems, saying that Eliot's characters "are the stuff of our modern world and true of more countries than one. I would praise the work for its fine tone, its humanity, and its realism; for all good art is realism of one sort or another." Pound also defends Eliot's use of *vers libre*, noting that his poetry—in its sparseness—is not impersonal; it still conveys his voice; he has "given a personal rhythm, an identifiable quality of sound as well as of style." (*Literary Essays*.)

From his associations with Pound and the artistic community of London (including his marriage to Vivienne Haigh-Wood), Eliot chose not to return to Harvard to defend his dissertation; he also began writing the essays and reviews that were themselves influential to the development of Modernism. While it is clear that Eliot was becoming one of the shapers of the late modernist movement, it is not clear why critics have been so focused on his 1922 poem, *The Waste Land*, unless the fact that James Joyce's novel *Ulysses* was also a 1922 publication makes the fusion of British modernism and American modernism convenient.

What Eliot was achieving in "The Love Song of J. Alfred Prufrock" (first published in 1915) did not change dramatically as he composed his 1922 *The Waste Land*. The juxtaposition of sections, which varied by line length and tone, was the structural model for the latter poem; it also had governed the arrangement of the speaker's voice in "Prufrock." Following in the patterns established by Robert Browning, Eliot here constructed Prufrock's dramatic monologue. But he also drew on the ideas of Henri Bergson, whose lectures at the College de France he had attended during 1910 in Paris. Even more influential than William James, Bergson assumed the importance of the fluidity of time, and the effectiveness of representing what he called "stream of consciousness" in new aesthetic ways.

Whereas Browning's dramatic monologues usually ran in sequential lines from start to end, maintaining voice and language he found essential to his chosen speaker, Eliot's "Prufrock" was a montage of juxtaposed images—many not spoken by the male voice but associated with him and his life through images. Images became refrains in a manner that was more lyric than narrative:

> In the room the women come and go
> Talking of Michelangelo.

As pause and punctuation, this couplet divides the speaker's metaphoric soliloquy, which opens "Let us go then, you and I,/When the evening is spread out against the sky . . . ." Charting the ineffectiveness of the male speaker, a man who delays all things in his life that might bring pleasure, Prufrock's "love song" is the opening irony of the waste of human life. Marked by the politely apathetic phrase, "indeed there will be time," the remarked stanzas trace "a hundred indecisions," some "for a hundred visions and revisions."

As the poem modulates, Eliot uses the word "dare" repeatedly. Prufrock is obviously NOT a man who dares, or who even *thinks* of daring. Another key verb in the second half of the poem is "presume" . . . . "And should I then presume?/And how should I begin?" Quickly moving to references to both Lazarus and to Hamlet, with his famed indecision, Eliot then uses these references as refrains, compounding the comparatively sedate pace of the early stanzas with more and more frequent interjections, many single, some seemingly random:

> I should have been a pair of ragged claws
> Scuttling across the floors of silent seas . . . .

The poignance is imaged toward the end of the poem in the personally distraught couplet,

> I grow old . . . I grow old . . .
> I shall wear the bottoms of my trousers rolled. . .
> *N 278–82*

As the poem ends with the poet's declaration that he/we will "drown," the malaise that has created Prufrock's malady—whether physical or psychological—becomes more real than its language. The tone Eliot achieves at the conclusion of "The Love Song of J. Alfred Prufrock" leads seamlessly into the opening segments of his very long poem, *The Waste Land*. He remains in this emotional place, but this time he chooses an assortment of legends, images, languages, and historical periods, as well as the contemporary fittings of war, gender issues, sexuality, abortion, poverty, and institutionalization: the wildly veering and unpredictably changing moods and tones of the work are uncharacteristic for the seemingly stable Eliot.

Events in Eliot's own life had—somewhat disguised—fed into this mélange: problems in his marriage, his own physical and mental collapse in 1921, the acclaim for his first collection of poems and his subsequent essays (including the important 1919 "Tradition and the Individual Talent"), and the financial problems of maintaining a London life for two. When he had finished *The Waste Land*, under the close scrutiny of both his wife and Pound (to whom he dedicated the poem as his being *il miglior fabbro*, the better maker), it appeared in the United States in the *Dial* and simultaneously in London in his own journal, the *Criterion*. In 1923 it appeared in book form, there accompanied by the extensive notes that are usually published with it. The notes translate the foreign languages, give readings from Jessie Weston's book on the Grail Legend, *From Ritual to Romance*, as well as from James G. Frazier's *The Golden Bough*, and other sources. They gloss the references to Shakespeare, to Thomas Middleton, to John Milton, to Dante, to Baudelaire, to Elizabethan poetry, to Spenser, to the Bible, to Buddha's *Fire Sermon*, to St. Augustine's *Confessions*, to Andrew Marvell, to Verlaine, to Tiresias and Oedipus, to Goldsmith, to Queen Elizabeth, and to sites in London as well as India. Striking hard against the concept that American Imagism drew from the common language and used common people as characters, Eliot's masterful poem seemed to discount most of Pound's principles.

The Waste Land was structured as a montage of separate scenes (the speaker in the poem says near its end, "These fragments I have shored against my ruin," explaining the method as if it were a theme), and it evoked the sense of journey. Archetypal in many of its themes, the poem echoed what was to be known as the mythic method, used to the fullest extent in Joyce's *Ulysses*. Much modernist literature traced a search or journey, drew on life-giving water or sunlight and darkness, and made clear the significance of Freud, Jung, Frazier, and other accounts of both archetypes and myth.

In Eliot's long poem, the Fisher King attempts to save his country from drought, searching for water to transform the wasted land into a fruitful one. The distancing of grief and anger that the poet conveys illustrated Eliot's notion of the objective correlative perfectly: the artist was to choose an object, a concrete image, to convey feelings rather than expressing those feelings directly to the reader. Irony was the mode for most of *The Waste Land*, and the numerous allusions reinforced the idea that language had become code. Only readers who had experienced the disillusion that modernist texts described could be accurate readers.

EXCERPT FROM T. S. ELIOT'S "TRADITION AND THE INDIVIDUAL TALENT"

. . . No poet, no artist of any art, has his complete meaning alone. His significance, his appreciation is the appreciation of his relation to the dead poets and artists. You cannot value him alone: you must set him, for contrast and comparison, among the dead. I mean this as a principle of aesthetic, not merely historical, criticism. The necessity that he shall conform, that he shall cohere, is not one-sided; what happens when a new work of art is created is something that happens simultaneously to all the works of art which preceded it. The existing monuments form an ideal order among themselves, which is modified by the introduction of the new (the really new) work of art among them . . . .

In a peculiar sense he [the new artist] will be aware also that he must inevitably be judged by the standards of the past. I say judged, not amputated, by them; not judged to be as good as, or worse or better than, the dead; and certainly not judged by the canons of dead critics . . . .

The poem became, like Joyce's *Ulysses*, a text that had to be taught. Explication was a good bit of discussion—what Eliot meant by these prayers in Hindu, what that section meant in relation to the rest of the poem. The teacher held the keys to understanding. Such a situation was not what Imagism and its first practitioners had thought to create. Even in Eliot's own essays, the importance of notes and reference systems was never mentioned. What Eliot did pronounce was the way even the newest art was still tangential, was still growing from ancient, and not so ancient, roots. Feeding into the concept that Modern art was not personal was Eliot's phrase about the aesthetic act being "a continual extinction of personality."

From this confluence of *The Waste Land* with Joyce's *Ulysses*, taking the year 1922 as more significant to ideas about Modernism than the year 1913, when Pound first wrote his rationale, literary criticism incorporated the idea of erudition—the writer must be schooled, must be learned. In terms of class, the writer has probably been a member of at least the middle class and has been formally educated. Again at odds from the earlier sense that the *common* was to provide the key, the *American* common, this shift in sentiment as well as definition left practitioners of Modernism open to the charge of elitism. In the work of critic Andreas Huyssen, for example, Modernism is set against any interest in mass culture, as well as against bourgeois principles. He sees that "modernist literature since Flaubert is a persistent exploration of . . . language." He recognizes its need to efface content, as well as subjectivity and authorial voice. Such literature is "self-referential, self-conscious, frequently ironic, ambiguous, and rigorously experimental" (Huyssen 53–4). While it is those latter things, no modernist writer would like to think his/her work needed "no content," or that any sense of the author's voice would be erased. Even as Eliot had himself paid great tribute to Ezra Pound, the primacy of Pound's role in creating and publicizing Imagism was being forgotten.

Robert Frost, Edgar Lee Masters, Others

Not all twentieth century American poets wanted to be considered modernist. Yet some, like Robert Frost, even though he worked in formal and traditional structures, benefited from Pound's diligence in finding, and supporting, the new. When Frost's first two poem collections were published in England—*A Boy's Will*, 1913, and *North of Boston*, 1914—Pound was one of the first reviewers to see that he chose speech rhythms that worked. He could forgive the iambic pentameter and the regular stanza divisions: he saw the new edge in Frost's thoroughly American prosody.

Born in California (and not in New England), Frost came east and tried to earn a living teaching and writing. Two of the Frosts' children died; supporting the others and themselves was difficult. That was the reason Frost took his family to England. Returning, flushed with his success as a published poet, Frost managed to support his family and his art through teaching, aided by his new-found fame. Among his *oeuvre* of poems are very few that might be considered Imagist. All are, however, perfectly fashioned works. Many seem to derive from the patterns set up by Robert Browning in his monologues: critics often used the word "masks" in discussing Frost's more speakerly poems.

Two poems from his first book, "Storm Fear" and "Mowing," show the finesse Frost achieved in his sometime unique formats. The first opens,

> When the wind works against us in the dark,
> And pelts with snow
> The lower chamber window on the east . . . .
> *S 71*

setting up an intricate internal rhyme and assonance pattern that manages not to destroy the sense of a voice reminiscing.

Contrastingly, the longer (and longer-lined) "Mowing" opens, in its casual sonnet form,

> There was never a sound beside the wood but one,
> And that was my long scythe whispering to the ground.
> What was it it whispered? I knew not well myself;
> Perhaps it was something about the heat of the sun . . . .
> *S 71*

As will become Frost's frequent practice, one of the poem lines will encapsulate—provide a mnemonic phrase—so that the work becomes quotable. In this poem, the reader remembers line nine: "Anything more than the truth would have seemed too weak."

For readers who loved the poem as a work to remember, memory enhanced by end rhyme or stanza rhythm, Frost's poems captured the efficiency of those qualities even in some of his writing that was less formally structured. Pound appreciated the quality of surprise that Frost achieved: if not humor, there was often irony. There was sometimes satire; more often there was the hint of anti-intellectualism. Always there was the surprising restraint, as the form of the poem transcribed its effects with perfect symmetry. And for all its intricate formal experiments, Frost's poetry created characters who could easily be believed as American commoners.

In this appeal, Frost was like E. A. Robinson, whose portraits of fictional characters had been captivating American readers since the late 1890s; and also like Edgar Lee Masters, whose 1915 *Spoon River Anthology* provided a more varied gallery of American characters. Masters' poems were focused on the limitations of the United States as a microcosm of small towns, and represented the prose movement called "the revolt from the village." Many of his poems presented what Sherwood Anderson later would term "grotesques." Robinson's work had a broader range, formally, taking his imagery from abstractions rather than physical details. When "Miniver Cheevy" rests his brief in highly accented quatrains, almost sing-song in effect, Robinson's 1910 elegy, "For a Dead Lady" moves with somnolent grace:

> No more with overflowing light
> Shall fill the eyes that now are faded,
> Nor shall another's fringe with night
> Their woman-hidden world as they did . . . .
> *S 41*

Again, as in "Tasker Norcross," the influence of Browning helps Robinson build a very long and detailed monologue, a poem that in its first stanza approaches the title subject:

> There were three kinds of men where I was born:
> The good, the not so good, and Tasker Norcross.
> Now there are two kinds . . . .
> *S 58*

Both Robinson and Masters influenced the so-called "Chicago poets," whose work was typified by Carl Sandburg in its wide-ranging effect, from short Imagist poems to the longer-lined, chant-based monologues and "Chicago" itself. A folklorist and musician, Sandburg brought numerous seemingly non-poetic techniques into his art. So too did Vachel Lindsay, one of the most popular poets of the early twentieth century. In a culture given to performance and choral reading, Lindsay's "General William Booth Enters Into Heaven" as well as his somewhat exotic "The Congo" could be heard throughout the United States. "The Congo," subtitled "A Study of the Negro Race," was published in 1914—Chicago had brought African American culture into the purview of the whole country. Less than politically correct, the poem is divided into three long segments, parts which vary rhythmically. The first, titled "Their Basic Savagery," incorporates the "BOOM" of the impulse to drum, with either "a silk umbrella" or "the handle of a broom," and takes the reader to jungles, cannibalism, and "hoo-doo." The second, titled "Their Irrepressible High Spirits," focuses on "wild crap-shooters" who "danced the juba in their gambling hall." This segment continues the "boomlay, boomlay, BOOM." So too does part three, titled "The Hope of Their Religion," which incorporates the twelve apostles into both hoo-doo lore and Protestant hymn stanzas. In other poems Lindsay chronicles "Nancy Hanks, Mother of Abraham Lincoln," "The Apple-Barrel of Johnny Appleseed," and the lengthy "Bryan, Bryan, Bryan, Bryan." Though perhaps more ephemeral than he would have wished, Lindsay brought a sense of lived American history into the realm of poetry.

Along with Marianne Moore, always a credible member of the Imagist school—though writing in much more complicated stanza forms—there were some excellent women poets who became known largely through Imagism. (Their presence is one of the reasons Amy Lowell took over the editing of what were then called Imagiste Anthologies.) Adelaide Crapsey practiced tanka and haiku to perfection, and created a five-line form called the *cinquain*; Sara Teasdale was given numerous accolades for her short poems, as was Elinor Wylie, who later turned to writing novels; Hazel Hall wrote about disability and work; Edna St. Vincent Millay was one of the twentieth century's most beloved—and most famous—poets, known especially for her sonnets and sonnet sequences. As Sonnet XXX from *Fatal Interview* opens,

> Love is not all; it is not meat nor drink
> Nor slumber nor a roof against the rain,
> Nor yet a floating spar to men that sink . . . .
> *S 320*

America was quoting her 1917 "God's World" for decades: "O World, I cannot hold thee close enough!/Thy winds, thy wide grey skies! . . . "(S 312).

Passive and pacific in most readings, these women writers were considered separate from the *radical* women poets—Genevieve Taggard and Lola Ridge— already discussed. Their work formed a separate strand of more political Modernism, along with the poems of Kenneth Fearing, Edwin Rolfe, Horace Gregory, and Joseph Kalar, among others.

Knowing history in order to protest its inequalities seems to lead readers to categorize writers as "radical." Yet the American modernist poet who made the most uses of the country's history—Hart Crane—was never so classified. Much of Crane's poetry is drawn from United States history. Following in Eliot's footsteps in that his poems showed his wide learning, Crane yet judged *The Waste Land* as too dour, too disingenuous. Not all of America was waste, and Crane was adamant about capturing the essence of a country with openings for ambition, for empathy. After he published his first collection in 1926, the well-reviewed *White Buildings*, he began to formalize the long poem he considered his magnum opus, *The Bridge*.

Based on his vision of the Brooklyn Bridge, the imaginary of the long poem included sections based on Columbus's return voyage home ("Ave Maria"), on traveling by train through the Mississippi River region ("The River"), and on a flight over the East coast ("Cape Hatteras"). In this poem as well as in shorter works, he sometimes used blank verse; sometimes rhymed stanzas; sometimes *vers libre*. His word choice might be ornate or powerful or obscure: he prided himself on having a wealth of resources at his command.

Living an openly gay life in New York, Crane worked to earn his living (in advertising, in menial labor, and occasionally in his wealthy father's businesses in Cleveland) but he seldom prospered. After being given a Guggenheim fellowship to travel to Mexico, and living there (for the first time in a heterosexual relationship), Crane committed suicide on the return trip by boat. It was April, 1927; he was thirty-three.

In one stanza from "Voyages," Crane created a kind of accidental epitaph:

Bind us in time, O Seasons clear, and awe.
O minstrel galleons of Carib fire,
Bequeath us to no earthly shore until
Is answered in the vortex of our grave
The seal's wide spindrift gaze toward paradise.

A 633

Note

1 In a comparatively unknown pair of reviews, both Hemingway and Stein praise Anderson's 1924 *A Story-Teller's Story*. Stein comments on the fact that Anderson *expresses* life (rather than describing or embroidering it). She places him in the company of Mark Twain, Fenimore Cooper, and William Dean Howells. For Hemingway, Anderson is *the* great American writer, especially here because he has written "in his own particular form, a series of short tales jointed up sometimes and sometimes quite disconnected." He is at his best writing short stories and, in all, "He is a very great writer" (*Ex Libris* 2.6, March 1925:176–77).

Suggested further reading

Glauco Cambon. *The Inclusive Flame: Studies in American Poetry*. Indiana UP, 1963.
Stanley K. Coffman, Jr. *Imagism: A Chapter for the History of Modern Poetry*. U of Oklahoma P, 1951.
Roy Harvey Pearce. *The Continuity of American Poetry*. Princeton UP, 1961.
M. L. Rosenthal. *The Modern Poets*. Oxford UP, 1960.

4

HEMINGWAY, DOS PASSOS, CATHER, LEWIS, AND THE AMERICAN STYLE

If the aesthetic streams that fed into American modernism were labeled—*Imagism, A*—a parallel and equally influential stream would be marked *The Psychological Novel, B*. Beginning in 1884 with novelist Henry James's important essay, "The Art of Fiction," ideas that are usually attributed to Sigmund Freud, Henri Bergson, and William James (the older brother of Henry James, who could be called the founder of the discipline of psychology) are given clear expression.

Part of Henry James's effectiveness as writer stemmed from his belief that human consciousness developed in nonlinear patterns. What a character knew depended not on how many years he or she had lived, but on how many "moments of being," how many epiphanies, had been experienced. These moments of recognition might take pages to describe—or to lead up to—but the resolution of many of James's characters' dilemmas, as well as their lives, occurred on the basis of these ephemeral turnings. For James, as for the later modernists, circularity, layers of metaphor, and repetition and nuance were more effective narrative devices than were linear plot lines.

No other American novelist in the last quarter of the nineteenth century created the kinds of books that James did—investing his considerable ability with language in the portrayal of nuance (as compared with the portrayal of detail) set him apart from the largely realist aims of many fiction writers. (James's realism was always that of character, not of place or context.) His readers respected the lengths to which he would go to present subtle but definitive characterization. His characters opened to the reader as if they were living people. In congruence with this ability, whatever narrators James chose to use did not explain personalities, or at least they did not *simply* explain personalities.

In the matrix of James's fiction, the reader had the opportunity to see the characters in so many situations that he or she was able to predict their choices and their actions. Focusing on apparently slight scenes, James worked with conviction

---

EXCERPT FROM HENRY JAMES'S "THE ART OF FICTION"

. . . the good health of an art which undertakes so immediately to reproduce life must demand that it be perfectly free. It lives upon exercise, and the very meaning of exercise is freedom. The only obligation to which in advance we may hold a novel, without incurring the accusation of being arbitrary, is that it be interesting . . . . A novel is in its broadest definition a personal, a direct impression of life: that, to begin with, constitutes its value, which is greater or less according to the intensity of the impression . . . .

We are discussing the art of fiction; questions of art are questions (in the widest sense) of execution . . . . A novel is a living thing, all one and continuous, like any other organism, and in proportion as it lives will it be found, I think, that in each of the parts there is something of each of the other parts . . . .

---

and authority through plots that consisted of these characters' various life choices. And because so many of the characters he drew were themselves slight, with little obvious dramatic interest, modernists learned what kinds of characters could be used in fiction that depended for its effect on *suggestion*, on the presentation of the epiphanic moment. They learned that a restrained narrative, properly handled, could become luminous.

The power of James's fiction rested partly on the reader's ability to understand character from oblique signs, almost in a kind of shorthand—a technique not far from poetic presentation. His fiction often operated through irony, much of it dramatic irony. (James was never far from writing a play, and sometimes—as in *The Other House*, published as a novel in 1896, he first wrote the play and then the novel and then the play script, drawn from the novel.) Some of James's characters seemed not to comprehend what was happening to them; because they did not know enough, they could not see the emerging life pattern. The reader, however—a love of sleuthing encouraged by James's fragmentary development of narrative—saw that some information was being withheld and that other information was designed to appear unpredictably. "Reading" James's fiction thus became an intriguing subjective act. The concept of fiction as labyrinth that Latin American writer Jorge Luis Borges was later to express was already developing in James's fiction. And by setting the *American* consciousness against that of the *European,* as he did in his novels *The American, Daisy Miller, The Portrait of a Lady,* and much of his last and greatest fiction, James made his American readers see that naiveté and innocence, which he considered integral to the new American vision, were positive.

James's influence on Modernism was greater than that of Stephen Crane or William Dean Howells because he consistently dealt with the most complex of subjects: how to live well and with honor in a civilized world, a world that was barely comprehensible and ultimately without much virtue. It was to become the modernists' primary theme. Characters such as Isabel Archer from James's *The Portrait of a Lady* and Lambert Strether from *The Ambassadors* were doomed by their own freedom of choice, and yet James's fiction admitted that choice was never free but rather influenced by machinations of the old order—both European and traditional American. In James's fiction, sexual betrayal often served as a metaphor for the more significant betrayal of honor.

James's critical writings also spoke for a flexibility that modernist writers respected and echoed. James believed that whatever convinced the reader was an effective method, that organic form—shape and voice suitable to effect and story—was the desired organization for any writing. He also was certain that the most workable approach to writing was through the writer's emotional understanding because any genuine interest a reader felt for a character should be on the basis of shared emotional experience. Modernism was to draw heavily from these principles. Ezra Pound showed his respect for James's work by editing a special Henry James number of the *Little Review* in 1918, and in his own essay there, stating that James had never written an unnecessary word. (Pound did critique the novelist for what he called James's "dam'd fuss about furniture," *Literary Essays* 308.)

Although James was a comparative failure as a dramatist, he wrote a great deal of criticism about plays and playwrights (collected first in 1908 and then more comprehensively in 1948 as *The Scenic Art*). The same search for the new that Pound had expressed in *Poetry* was already in process when American dramatists looked at the newly realistic stage. Would-be dramatists were congregating at both Provincetown (i.e. the Provincetown Players) and the Washington Square Theater in New York. Borrowing from German expressionism and French symbolism, playwrights in the United States knew well the works of Henrik Ibsen, George Bernard Shaw, August Strindberg, and Anton Chekhov—and were conversant with the American realistic writers for stage, James A. Herne, Edward Harrigan, Hamlin Garland, Brander Matthews, and William Gilette.[1] Critic Brenda Murphy describes late-nineteenth century and early twentieth-century playwriting in the United States,

> The realistic play disrupts the traditional patterns of tragedy and comedy precisely in order to express its skepticism . . . . The rhythm of life, these plays constantly suggest, is not a movement toward transcendence or harmony but a continual return to the mundane; not resolution or closure but irresolution and open-ended action; not spectacular, world-rending moments of truth but graduate processes of partial revelation, which may or may not effect some limited change in character or environment.

She continues, here making the forms of drama parallel the American poem and the fragmentary short story, "The distinguishing characteristic of realistic dramatic structure is lack of closure . . . . Realistic theoretic form in drama is precisely the refusal to reduce the complex rhythms of human life to the paradigm of a generically conventionalized action" (Murphy xii).

Many writers were attracted to the stage. Edith Wharton tried (and failed). Between 1903 and 1915, William Carlos Williams, with his *Others* friend Alfred Kreymborg, was fascinated with writing for the theater, as were Zoe Akins, Rachel Crothers and Alice Gerstenberg (whose 1911 play *Overtones* was produced in the States by the Washington Square Players and—even more startlingly—in England, with actress Lily Langtry starring in the work about the divided consciousness of two women characters, represented on stage as four speakers.) Similarly, the forceful feminist writing of Susan Glaspell, to be seen in such plays as *Trifles, Inheritors, The Verge,* and *Alison's House* (a play about the restricted life of poet Emily Dickinson, which won the 1931 Pulitzer Prize for Drama), set the tone for the successful Provincetown Players—again, the psychological impetus for action was paramount. In the case of *Trifles,* the division of worlds between male characters and female provided an unobstructed view of gendered, sexualized power.

Whether or not Eugene O'Neill was actually a protégé of Glaspell's, as is sometimes said, he wrote and wrote and wrote, trying to find the best strategies for using "realistic structure and deeply psychological characterization." Murphy discusses his "amazing array of dramatic compositions . . . in 1913–14 alone he wrote eleven plays that reflect a wide range of the dramatic types in the American theater of the time, from *A Wife for A Life,* a brief Western sketch intended for vaudeville, to *Bound East for Cardiff,* the experimental 'slice of life' that won him the support of the Provincetown players" (Murphy 113, 115). Beside O'Neill's productions, the

---

EXCERPT FROM GLASPELL'S *TRIFLES*

County Attorney:	[Looking around.] I guess we'll go upstairs first—and then out to the barn and around there. [To the Sheriff] You're convinced that there was nothing important here—nothing that would point to any motive.
Sheriff:	Nothing here but kitchen things. [The County Attorney, after again looking around the kitchen, opens the door of a cupboard closet. He gets upon a chair and looks on a shelf. Pulls his hand away, sticky.]
County Attorney:	Here's a nice mess. [The women draw nearer.]
Mrs. Peters:	[To the other woman.] Oh, her fruit; it did freeze. [To the County Attorney] She worried about that when it turned so cold. She said the fire'd go out and her jars would break.
Sheriff:	Well, can you beat the women! Held for murder and worryin' about her preserves.
County Attorney:	I guess before we're through she may have something more serious than preserves to worry about.
Hale:	Well, women are used to worrying over trifles . . . .

works of Robert Sherwood, Philip Barry, and S. N. Behrman seemed almost trivial. As observers of the American stage noted, by the time O'Neill's 1918 *Beyond the Horizon*, his 1920 *The Emperor Jones*, and his 1922 *The Hairy Ape* were being produced, viewers knew that traits of expressionism (as well as the probing tactics of psychological realism) would be included. No one was surprised that changes in the threatening forest would mirror changes in the mental state of the character, the Emperor Jones.

For all the literary interest in drama and writing, however, the most cataclysmic event of the early twentieth century was, obviously, the First World War—and its beginning among the European players in 1914 seems to contradict the rampant experimentation in American writing and arts. For Americans, and even for those who lived abroad, the conflicts with German powers remained "other": perhaps for German-American citizens living in the United States, the war seemed both threatening and intense because people who had immigrated from Germany, many of whom still used the German language, were often persecuted for their ethnicity.

When the United States joined the war in April, 1917, most aesthetic progress (or at least its most fervid experimentation) stalled. For the next year and a half, until the Allies defeated the Nazi forces and the Armistice was signed November 11, 1918, American attention and effort was dedicated to the fight for liberty—if not for the United States, for France, England, and the other Allied countries. Being patriotic replaced being an experimental modernist. Even though Teddy Roosevelt called going to war "The Great Adventure," World War I was more carnage than expedition—trench warfare alone was enough to put an end to further wars.

Once the United States declared war in 1917, two million soldiers served in the American Expeditionary Forces; of those, 49,000 were killed and more than 230,000 were injured. The slaughter of hundreds of thousands of civilians as well as military personnel from all Allied countries made writing about the war impossible. As Paul Fussell pointed out in his 1975 *The Great War and Modern Memory*, the war was an indescribable subject. Of the leading established modernist writers, none had been at the front. "Joyce, Eliot, Lawrence, Pound, Yeats . . . not being present, were inhibited by scruples of decency" (Fussell 174). It would be the task of the next generation of American writers—men such as Alan Seeger, John Dos Passos, Thomas Boyd, e. e. cummings, Ernest Hemingway—some who joined as Red Cross workers even before America had declared war, to take on the subject of war and its brutal horrors.

Of the established modernists, it was Pound who tried to capture the debacle and its various kinds of horror: his long fragmented poem, "Hugh Selwyn Mauberley," replete with juxtaposition, quotations from other languages, changes in tone and rhythm, and free-form scatterings of dialogue, could have become the most famous poem of World War I. Pound had, however, already passed the palm of being the quintessential modern poet on to his London friend and associate, T. S. Eliot. And during the months Pound was writing "Mauberley," he also was working with Eliot on the draft of his even longer poem, *The Waste Land*.

"Mauberley" was published in 1920, but it was little recognized as the great poetic distillation of World War I.

Pound's poem, however, was that. The character Mauberley understood "consciousness disjunct," the way the human mind learns to dissociate from the damages of seeing what war does, what war is. In Thomas Boyd's *Through the Wheat*, the novel's protagonist William Hicks finally goes insane, torn between what culture *thinks* war is like and what he *knows* it is. When Virginia Woolf two years later created that same kind of human damage in Septimus Smith (her returning war veteran in *Mrs. Dalloway*), "war nerves," later called post-traumatic stress syndrome, would be easily recognized. Using a similarly wounded character's point of view, Pound incorporated even more fragmentation into his narrative poem.

Disdaining Mauberley's American roots (describing the character as "born in a half-savage country"), Pound's speaker moves from various histories to World War I. Part IV of the poem opens with a litany of men's motives for volunteering:

> These fought in any case,
> and some believing,
>   pro domo, in any case . . .
> Some quick to arm,
> some for adventure,
> some from fear of weakness,
> some from fear of censure,
> some for love of slaughter, in imagination
> learning later . . .
> some in fear, learning love of slaughter.

All choices end with the men in question who eventually "walked eye-deep in hell/Believing in old men's lies, then unbelieving/came home, home to a lie . . . ." This segment ends with the harsh couplet:

> hysterias, trench confessions,
> laughter out of dead bellies.

Part V of the poem opens as if to conclude this litany:

> There died a myriad,
> And of the best, among them,
>
> For an old bitch gone in the teeth,
> For a botched civilization . . . .
>   *L D, 1116*

The forays Pound takes later into other aspects of civilization and culture are more flaccid, based often on references to Greek or Roman beliefs, so that the heart of the poem tends to rest with Parts IV and V. Robbed of what Pound saw as valuable contextualization, his criticism of the country's leaders (whom he pictured spouting propaganda about war) becomes something of a rant.

That there are no women characters in Pound's poem—only the expletive "bitch" applied to an abstraction for civilization—would not surprise Jane Marcus, whose pioneering criticism of the writings of women who were nurses and ambulance drivers in World War I created a complex paradigm of male writings and female. Isolated as a "male" genre, just as war itself was a male activity, writing about war was considered the province of men. Marcus's critique parallels the gendered position expressed most forcefully by Shari Benstock in her *Women of the Left Bank, Paris, 1900–1940*. In her discussions of the biographies and work of Margaret Anderson, Natalie Barney, Kay Boyle, H.D., Mina Loy, Edith Wharton, Gertrude Stein and others, Benstock notes

> Once women Modernists are placed beside their male colleagues, the hegemony of masculine heterosexual values that have for so long underwritten our definitions of Modernism is put into question. Modernism may then be seen to be a far more eclectic and richly diverse literary movement than has previously been assumed.
>
> *Benstock* Bank *6 and see Clark, Haytock, Hutner, Marcus, Friedman*

In a later essay, Benstock adds specifics to her definition of the modern. After illustrating the way a T. S. Eliot poem is customarily discussed, Benstock points to myriad contradictions, which she terms "grievous misconceptions and oversights," in assumptions about Modernism:

> It restricts the definition of literary Modernism to Anglo-American centrism, eliminating a crucial defining element of Modernism—its internationalism . . . It situates literary Modernism in a psychology of reaction *against* the reigning cultural-social-political-religious-economic practices of the day, eliminating altogether those aspects of Modernist practice that overtly or covertly supported the status quo: a Modernism of conservation such as was lived and practiced by Eliot, Pound, and Wyndham Lewis . . . .
>
> *Benstock in Broe 21*

She continues to argue against associating Modernism with the First World War, as well as with adopting too simple and too homogeneous a definition of the modern (so that many of the elements that characterize the period are obscured), and, by over-simplifying the term. Such critical attitudes disallow a

> range of literary practices that developed through the various stages of Modernism. This set of defining prerequisites to the Modernist experience eliminates women from the historical canvas because women's experiences differed from those of men in two crucial ways: women were often not directly

involved in the war; women usually did not have the classical education that provided them access to the Word in the Modernist sense—in the sense of knowing Latin and Greek.

Benstock in Broe 22

There are other commentaries and other poems, and varied readings of Eliot's *The Waste Land* attribute much of that work's power to its relation to war, but it remains to the next generation of modernists to make the war as vivid and as incisive—and as tragic—as it was. How did these younger writers set their fact-based impressions into print without contradicting what they probably saw as the government's blatant propaganda? The romanticism of going to war, of saving the world from fascism, was relentless: it was an early expert advertising campaign—to find recruits, to find finances, to earn the rest of the world's respect. In Europe, towns, seaports, cities, whole geographic areas were destroyed. Yet the United States military thought that they would win the war as soon as they entered the conflict. Yes, it was a noble cause. But it was still a somewhat mysterious undertaking. As David Minter said, "The United States entered the Great War reluctantly, it entered late, and it remained uncertain of its motives almost to the end" (Minter 75).

Ernest Hemingway and war

By the time Hemingway was crafting his *In Our Time* prose poems in 1923–24 and giving the readers sympathetic to Modernism such well-imaged phrases as "separate peace," he had himself been to war. The second child—and first son—of

---

EXCERPT FROM ERNEST HEMINGWAY'S *IN OUR TIME*, CHAPTER VI

Nick sat against the wall of the church where they had dragged him to be clear of machine-gun fire in the street. Both legs stuck out awkwardly. He had been hit in the spine. His face was sweaty and dirty. The sun shone on his face. The day was very hot. Rinaldi, big backed, his equipment sprawling, lay face downward against the wall. Nick looked straight ahead brilliantly. The pink wall of the house opposite had fallen out from the roof, and an iron bedstead hung twisted toward the street. Two Austrian dead lay in the rubble in the shade of the house. Up the street were other dead. Things were getting forward in the town. It was going well. Stretcher bearers would be along any time now. Nick turned his head carefully and looked at Rinaldi. "Senta Rinaldi. Senta. You and me we've made a separate peace." Rinaldi lay still in the sun breathing with difficulty. "Not patriots." Nick turned his head carefully away smiling sweatily. Rinaldi was a disappointing audience.

Grace and Clarence Hemingway, Ernest is named for Grace's powerful father, Ernest Hall. Born July 21, 1899, in Oak Park, Illinois, he is raised in some instances along with his older sister, Marcelline, as twins. (She is delayed in order to start school the same year as Ernest; by that time they are dressed differently.)

Eventually there are five Hemingway children. Grace continues giving music lessons; Clarence is a practicing family doctor. Oak Park is a bastion of social conservatism, and the children are raised with many *oughts* and *shoulds*. The bright Ernest reads everything in sight; he also plays football and learns to box. Even though his mother has used the inheritance from her father to build the family's new and imposing Kenilworth house, the essential Hemingway life for Ernest occurs during the summers when the family (usually without Clarence) moves to their cottage on Walloon Lake in mid Michigan, and the children run free. As Michael Reynolds pointed out, Hemingway's experiences with the summer people, friends from Horton Bay and Petoskey, and the last of the Ojibway Indians who lived in the woods close to Horton were life-changing. "Those summers of trout fishing, camping out, hiking, baseball games, and awakened sexuality were as important to the education of young Hemingway as were his school years in Oak Park" (Reynolds 20).

Clarence was something of a naturalist. He taught Ernest to see wild life and birds, and to learn the waters and forests of the Michigan area; he taught him to shoot game, and to clean and cook it. The Midwestern rural experience balanced the ultra civilized Oak Park months, and in both Hemingway learned to value perseverance and doing one's best. Finally, after graduating from Oak Park High School, Hemingway found a way to intern at the Kansas City *Star* rather than going to college. He had written for the school paper all through high school, doing humor pieces as well as covering athletics. He knew he wanted to become a writer in the mode of Stephen Crane, Jack London, Theodore Dreiser and Teddy Roosevelt. The power of journalistic work—plain spoken, unembellished, relatively objective—drew him to big-city newspapers. (His later version of his life was that his mother Grace had spent *his* "college" money on a second Michigan cottage, but by then he was angry about his mother's sending him away from the Michigan summer cottage, reproving him for being a bad influence on his younger siblings.)

When Hemingway left Kansas City and joined the Red Cross volunteer forces in Italy, the United States was still a non-combatant in World War I. Hemingway arrived in Italy in June of 1918 and volunteered to staff the Piave River front canteen. Wounded by a trench mortar shell on July 8, he was hospitalized for five months in Milan. 237 pieces of shrapnel were embedded in his legs and groin; he went through much physical therapy, and he observed fellow hospitalized soldiers. He also fell in love with his older American nurse, Agnes von Kurowsky.

Being returned home to Oak Park, Hemingway continued his recuperation. He stayed in a rented room in Petoskey, Michigan, that winter, writing, writing, and trying to write—better—about his war experiences. It would be nearly a decade before he mastered the direct simplicity that was his goal—he tried desperately to avoid romanticizing either the military or his wounding. Of the prose written during his convalescence, many sketches were of people (reminiscent of Sherwood Anderson's Ohio characters, but treated very briefly). Of his writing, he felt most satisfied with his poems, many about the war. Later published in *Poetry*, "Riparto D'Assalto" begins with the detailed description of soldiers riding in a cold truck—their physical pain and discomfort, their sex-oriented reveries, and then the ride itself,

> Damned cold, bitter, rotten ride,
> Winding road up the Grappa side . . . .

In keeping with the shock of the war's deaths, this poem ends with the reader's parallel shock. It ends with a single line, naming the place "where the truck-load died" (Hemingway *Collected Poems* 26).

With such Hemingway poems as "Ultimately," "The Age Demanded," "Captives," "Champs D'Honneur," "Mitraigliatrice," other effective works draw on the author's nostalgia for the past. "Along with Youth" seems to have been a personal favorite, its images steeped in the tone of near-reverence:

> A porcupine skin
> Stiff with bad tanning,
> It must have ended somewhere.

Making the speaker's memories of tanned game parallel his "Piles of old magazines," Hemingway ends the poem with a sharp image of destruction, comprised of several separate pieces: "the canoe that went to pieces on the beach," "the year of the big storm," and "the hotel burned down/At Seney, Michigan" (ibid.)

Recovered at least partly from his wounds, Hemingway worked at advertising jobs in Chicago, where he lived with Michigan friends. When Katy Smith invited Hadley Richardson, a friend from college, to visit, the older, talented Hadley—recovering from the death of her mother, for whom she had cared many years—prompted Hemingway into courtship. The letters between Chicago and St. Louis tell the love story, poignant in its effulgence (the pair sometimes writing more than a letter a day). By this time, Hemingway had received his "Dear John" letter from Agnes, in which she explained the differences in their ages and experiences; he had also been asked to leave the cottage because of his alleged bad influence: he could not forget either Agnes, his first love, or Grace, his mother. He had lost them both.[2] By courting Hadley, who was almost a decade older than he, Hemingway was refuting the implication that he was just a kid.

Married in the September that followed their meeting, 1921, Hadley and Ernest moved to Chicago but it was soon clear that they wanted to live abroad: Hadley's inheritance funded their travel to Paris. Scarcely twenty-two, Hemingway used letters of introduction which Sherwood Anderson had written for him, and met both Gertrude Stein, a particular friend of Anderson's, and Ezra Pound. From that time, Hemingway read everything available in Sylvia Beach's *Shakespeare and Company* bookshop, met everyone he could, and became the intimate of Modernism's great writers. He continued to write for the Toronto *Star*, covering such political events as the Genoa Economic conference and the Greco-Turkish War; with Hadley, he traveled to Switzerland, Austria, Italy, the Black Forest, and Chamby for winter sports. It is in 1922, when Hadley travels to join him on assignment in Switzerland, that she loses the suitcase containing all his stories and poems (as well as duplicates of everything).

Because Gertrude Stein did not make specific remarks about one's writing, the influence of Pound was paramount on Hemingway's carving out imagistic prose as well as poetry. Pound later wrote about his young disciple that Hemingway was an "Imagist," describing the younger man as

> accepting the principles of good writing that had been contained in the earliest imagist document, and applying the stricture against superfluous words to his prose, polishing, repolishing, and eliminating, as can be seen in the clear hard paragraphs of the first brief *In Our Time*, in *They All Made Peace*, in *The Torrents of Spring*, and in the best pages of his later novels.
>
> *Pound "Small Magazines" 700*

Meteoric as Hemingway's rise to prominence appeared to be, after his meeting Pound and Stein in 1922, in 1923 *Poetry* magazine published six of his poems and later that year Robert McAlmon published a limited edition of *Three Stories & Ten Poems*. In 1924 Bill Bird published the lower-case *in our time* (confused in Pound's comment with the full book of that title which appeared in 1925). *In our time* was a slim booklet of only the vignettes, prose poems pared down from what Hemingway viewed as real stories (Hemingway called these vignettes "unwritten stories") (Reynolds 27). Arranged differently from the 1924 book to the 1925, the vignettes of Hemingway's first accomplished work repeated the pattern of war as focus (see box above) and then incorporated a new set of dynamic portraits, those of the Spanish bullfights. The power, the seriousness, of *In Our Time* comes from the war vignettes. The exotic quality, the sense of romantic travel and customs, comes from those based on bullfighting. Hemingway had learned early that he could not write about his middle western small town. Nor could he be satiric about Oak Park's upper-class conservative values. What Hemingway had in his writer's kit was *remarkable* material: the war, deaths of friends, his own wounding (told eventually in his 1929 novel *A Farewell to Arms* as an out-of-the-body experience), as well as great love, extensive European travel, and equally extensive experience with the Pamplona bullfighters and their culture.

Many critics still think the 1925 *In Our Time* may be Hemingway's best piece of writing. Widely reviewed, catching the spirit of post-war euphoria in its keen attention to possibility, the book also spoke to levels of personal fear that readers found gripping. It filled in as illustration when a reviewer such as Edmund Wilson commented authoritatively that young writers wanted to create "something in which every word, every cadence, every detail, should perform a definite function in producing an intense effect" (Wilson *Shores* 15). John McCormick thought that Hemingway's prose vignettes were examples of "The unquestioned veracity and propriety of poetic experiment in the 1920s, together with the publication of a great variety of prose that seemed to derive from the same fountainhead as that of poetry" (McCormick *Middle* 88).

In David Seed's very recent view, Hemingway's *In Our Time* resembles H.D.'s prose as it "emerges from a matrix of modernist experimentation in which the nature of visual perception is explored . . . . [Particularly the *In Our Time* sketches] explore modes of visual representation" (Seed 68). Seed comments on the boxed excerpt above as being constructed as

> a sequence of images which, as in Cubism, slightly alter the perspective as we progress from one to the other. Nick's posture is given, then a close-up on his face. The shift to Rinaldi is effected through a general comment on heat, a descriptive equivalent to a brief dissolve as the focus moves. Rinaldi himself is lying face down, so cannot offer a point of view; hence the switch back to Nick. The final sentence in the passage has taken over his point of view to give us a symbolic image, of war damaging private life: a private interior has become transformed into a grotesque external image of debris.
>
> *Seed 71*

This critic finds the force of Hemingway's view in the fact that Nick as character, especially in the vignettes, "exemplifies the sights and experiences of war. He is both seen and seeing; object and subject" (ibid.)

Hemingway's personal experience gave him these avenues of perception. He had not only been "at war" and then, for a longer period of time, in convalescence; he had covered war and peace treaties throughout Europe. His subjective vision was forced to merge with the objectivity necessary for journalistic work; and throughout the process of the young writer's learning about war and its effects, he was reading—not only accounts of World War I but memoirs, fiction, battlefield maps, from not only this recent war but wars throughout history. Hemingway was creating himself as maestro of the battlefield. (Neither Pound nor Anderson could mentor him in these subjects, but Gertrude Stein's driving a Ford for the Red Cross during World War I qualified her to be a kind of expert observer about some war experiences. Hemingway would later deny any influence on her part.)

Less competitive than becoming a writer of war was the identity of Hemingway as writer of the bullfight. By the time of his publishing his companion volume to the bullfight, the 1932 *Death in the Afternoon*, Hemingway had thoroughly explored the lore and traditions of the ritual; he already knew many of the premier bullfighters, and he valued his friendships with them. His exacting vignettes in *in our time* and *In Our Time* introduced the world of readers in English to the serious religious ceremony of the bullfight.

As the manuscript collections of Hemingway materials show (the Lilly Library at Indiana University, the Ransom Archive at University of Texas, the Hemingway Room at the John F. Kennedy Library in Boston), Hemingway kept stacks of materials about both bullfighting and war—fragments, essays, photographs, and a few plays. These topics were his storehouse of valuables, and he had come to them almost from the start of his career as writer.

Part of Hemingway's strategy as he carefully used the vignettes that comprised all of *in our time* as interchapters within and between the short fictions that created the longer book, *In Our Time*, was to *disguise* the centrality of the themes of both war and the bullfight. An avid reader of book reviews, Hemingway knew that he could not appear to be monolithic: he did not want to be the "returning wounded soldier" who wrote repeatedly about himself and his wounds. He wanted to be the vibrant, perhaps even brilliant, young writer who knew how to create a story with a few well-chosen (and probably unexpected) words. He wanted the emphasis in the reviews of his *In Our Time* to be on *craft*.

Leaving too much to the taste of people who understood contemporary (i.e. modernist) writing was also a possible mistake. Accordingly, Hemingway chose the sonority of the phrase from the English *Book of Common Prayer* as his title. Not only did *In Our Time* echo a religious passage in itself; it made the book appealing to readers who respected the new, even the avant garde, couched in the envelope of formal religious ceremony. *In Our Time* intentionally echoed the tones of T. S. Eliot's *The Waste Land* and John Dos Passos's first war novel, *One Man's Initiation—1917.* Writing was, without question, serious business.

The key stories in *In Our Time* are, regardless of any attempts at disguise, war stories. The excitement of enlistment colors some of the vignettes, but most of the short pieces are somber, as are Hemingway's two superb and evocative stories. These share the trauma of a damaged man's returning home. Classically accurate in describing Harold Krebs' PTSD, "Soldier's Home" draws the troubled man—alienated from all family members except his sister—trying to locate himself in relation to social norms. Equating Krebs' mother with a superfluity of religious zeal, Hemingway chastises the mother for her utter stupidity about war, and more pointedly, about what her son had endured, lived through, and been damaged by. (The mother's comments about her understanding what her father had been through in the Civil War are often ridiculed—as well as chosen to illustrate the depths of the irony the various scenes of dialogue between Harold and his mother evoke.)

All the "war" details are blurred, caught as if in an aging photograph, to indicate that Harold's own reactions are similarly blurred. He is treading water/treading life as he tries to avoid irreparably hurting his family, particularly his overbearing mother, and probably irreparably hurting himself. What irony does exist spins outward from the story's title: "Soldier's Home" misleads the reader to believe that the man has been institutionalized in some impersonal veterans' "home." But the more despairing realization is that—had he been somewhere else besides his own family home he might have made some real recovery—gives the reader a second turn: the initial positive reading of *home* is changed to one of sadness. As the bacon fat hardens on Harold's plate, and the reader envisions his finding somebody who knows nothing about his experiences to take on some date in that prestigious family car, the sorrow the story has created leaves a miasma of gloom in its wake.

"Big Two-Hearted River" gives the returning veteran a second study. Going off alone (leaving that coercive family behind), the Nick Adams figure here conveys his decisions in meticulous detail—whether or not to carry the cans of beans, whether or not to bait the hook with this or that. Life-giving choices obscure the fact that the character has little "self" left to employ in making choices. The protagonist has no mentors—no family, no parents to set themselves at war over his behavior, no lover—but his psychological health does not allow for anything but careful concentration. To get through an hour, a day, a week—that is the task for the troubled young veteran. The unusually long story makes the reader attend to this tense concentration: this man cannot do more than he has already accomplished. One of the most diligent sections of Hemingway's objective description closes the story (laboring over this prose poem, he takes the reader step by step through the end of the day spent fishing):

> Nick cleaned them [the trout], slitting them from the vent to the tip of the jaw. All the insides and the gills and tongue came out in one piece. They were both males; long gray-white strips of milt, smooth and clean. All the insides clean and compact, coming out all together. Nick tossed the offal ashore for the minks to find.
>
> He washed the trout in the stream. When he held them back up in the water they looked like live fish. Their color was not gone yet. He washed his hands and dried them on the log. Then he laid the trout on the sack spread out on the log, rolled them up in it, tied the bundle and put it in the landing net . . . .

When the protagonist finishes his duties, taking every part of those tasks with great seriousness, he finds the elusive calm. The story closes, with sufficient information, with his realization that "There were plenty of days coming when he could fish the swamp" (Hemingway *In Our Time* 155–6).

Integral to the effect of separate stories is the impact of the book's arrangement. Nick's death occurs in the vignette that comes just before "Soldier's Home," for instance. The balance between this story holding the central position in *In Our Time*, with "Big Two-Hearted River" in its two parts concluding the book, creates meaningful emphasis. To open the book with the stories of a father's failing his son—"Indian Camp" and "The Doctor and the Doctor's Wife"—breaks into the reader's consciousness with the awareness of male lineage. Where do the sons of the military learn to be men? But much of the arrangement of *In Our Time* occurred because Hemingway had only a few stories that he knew were good—perfect, perfectly written for what he wanted to express. The underlying force of this 1925 book rested in the vignettes, coupled where they could be made to pair with the obvious war stories and with the love stories, themselves often speaking of losses and disappointments ("The End of Something," "Cat in the Rain," "A Very Short Story," "Cross-Country Snow," "Out of Season") .

When Hemingway published his second collection of short stories *Men Without Women* in 1927, the war emphasis continued. "In Another Country" is the briefest of commentaries on the harsh lives of the wounded, punctuated by the loss of love even in civilian times. One of Hemingway's masterpieces, "Now I Lay Me," pairs near the end of that collection with both "After the Storm" and "A Clean, Well-Lighted Place," signaling a reprise of "Big Two-Hearted River": endurance. "Now I Lay Me" meditates on isolation; "A Clean, Well-Lighted Place" brings together the aging depressive with others who care for him. Among the later stories the World War I stories continue, among these "A Way You'll Never Be." Perhaps because they were published distant from each other, these fictions about the damaged soldier have seldom been read as a group. The aesthetic versatility of Hemingway as writer makes them tonally fused, illustrating what Pound would have called their *organ base*, but the approach and the tactical strategies make them seem different.

More demanding to be considered as writing about war is Hemingway's 1926 novel, his first long fiction, *The Sun Also Rises*. Post-war, the characters in Pamplona (and, before that, in London) are pleasure seekers intent on forgetting. Each has—during the war—been wounded; lives are in disarray. Lady Brett, working during the war as a VAD, has seen plenty of sorrow (as well as having an abusive relationship in her marriage). Jake Barnes is unrelievedly the wounded survivor (one of Hemingway's classic images is Jake's looking at his lower body in the mirror: "Undressing, I looked at myself in the mirror of the big armoire beside the bed." The scene continues with comments about the way French rooms are furnished. Then Jake thinks to himself, "Of all the ways to be wounded. I suppose it was funny") (Hemingway *Sun Also Rises* 303). The war exists in a kind of repressed mood; the more visible tone is hedonism.

Rather than focusing on one or two characters, or one or two romances, Hemingway here uses a panoply of relationships. The men compete for not just Brett's affections, but for each other's friendships: at the center of the male wrangling stands Jake, apparently surrounded by disinterest and therefore withdrawn from all actual conflict. The women compete for the love of Pedro Romero, the young matador. The Spanish bullfights are located as arenas for conflict: buttressed by the religious underpinning of the bull-versus-human battle, "sport" a more appealing matrix than the carnage of war.

Running throughout the novel, whether Hemingway be drawing fishing scenes or bullfight; bedroom scenes or bar, is the set of steady classical analogies: Jake Barnes as surrogate for the patient and long-suffering Jacob, with some overtones of Roland, the great French warrior of the eleventh century (his book is *Chanson de Roland*). (The Rinaldi who appears in both the *In Our Time* vignettes and in the 1929 *A Farewell to Arms* is the second–in–command for Roland/Orlando in this epic account; the key battle occurs at Roncesvalles, the site of Bill and Jake's pilgrimage with their new friend Harris, and it is there that Jake finds and begins to absorb peace.) There are also the analogies between Brett and Circe. Throughout the religious scenes, Jake is comfortable; Brett would rather visit the gipsy camp (she is turned away from the Catholic Church because she wears no hat; she cannot even attempt to go to confession.)

Structurally, Hemingway increases the irony at the end of *The Sun Also Rises.* Admitting her love for Jake, expecting to be praised for having left Romero, Brett fails in using language to cement her bond with the Jake who has, of necessity, become her rescuer. She cajoles him and tries to keep him from drinking, "Oh, Jake . . . we could have had such a damned good time together." But he does not accept her easy solution. Instead he says, "Yes." And then he adds, "Isn't it pretty to think so?" (Hemingway *Sun Also Rises* 247). Largely on the basis of this closing scene, readers who discuss Modernism sometimes begin with the quality of irony.

It was only three short years later that Hemingway's war novel, *A Farewell to Arms*, appeared from Scribner's (and was soon made into a Hollywood movie). Abandoning disguise, Hemingway focused on the Italian battles—using as characters in the parallel romance plot the British VAD Catherine Barkley, and pairing together Rinaldi and Frederic Henry as competitors for Barkley's affection. *A Farewell to Arms* seemed to be the story of World War I, but for most of Hemingway's wide-ranging readers, it was a love story set during the conflict. Hardly cutting edge modern, this novel attempted to create hope: in Frederic Henry's great love for Catherine, a love reciprocated without question, emphasized because it is Henry's voice that tells the story, Hemingway used all the essentials of the great love stories of the world. Beside that narrative, war in the context of background seemed arbitrary. In the alternation of fear and disappointment set against the lyric moments of genuine, selfless love, readers found the romantic promise of hope.

Hemingway wrote a poem for Max Perkins, his editor at Scribner's, once it became clear that there was no limit to the sales that this novel might reach:

> There's more than
> War in
> A Farewell to Arms
> It is
> The Great Modern Love Story
> *Donaldson 148*

Like much of Hemingway's fiction, *A Farewell to Arms* was drawn from sources besides the autobiographical: the author was never a part of the retreat from Caporetto. Neither did he and a lover row across the impossibly wide lake to the safety of Switzerland. Severely wounded early in the summer of his duty as a Red Cross aide, Hemingway obviously did not desert from the Italian army; he had never been in service to that army at all.

So far as this novel is concerned, Frederic Henry needs to be involved in the war: how else can he be abroad and in peril, removed from family and friends, and in various kinds of dangers? Readers respond to the inherent dangerousness of Henry's situation. Even after that character deserts, an act which Hemingway makes justifiable in the execution scene during the Caporetto retreat, he and Catherine are still under military rule. Whereas initially Catherine was also in service, contributing her life to the care of the wounded after the death of her own fiancé, in order to accompany Frederic Henry, she also must leave her post. In effect, she deserts as well. No matter how involved the reader becomes in the story of the Henry-Barkley love, the shadow of the war (and Henry's possible court-martial, or worse) is omnipresent.

As part of that war novel structure, Hemingway includes scenes from battle, scenes from behind the lines, scenes in the officers' quarters. Although not many enlisted or drafted men are prominent in the narrative, the Italian ambulance drivers are treated as well-defined characters, and the officers, particularly the young priest and the Italian physician, Rinaldi, are significant figures. Hemingway convinces the reader that this is a genuine war; it does not exist merely in the minds of Frederic and Catherine. It is much more than an abstract worry for them. It brings the continuous threat of death.

A Farewell to Arms, as its ambiguous title hints, is also the story of Frederic Henry's great love—and loss. The arms that he loses are Catherine's, and the arms he never had can be said to be those of his son, the child who never lived even though he was, in fact, born. Autobiographically, Hemingway had divorced Hadley, who remained caring for their son Bumby; he was now married to Pauline Pfeiffer, and they were awaiting the birth of their first son. This is, however, not the novel's story. The circumstances lend some credibility to the mournful tone that dominates the book, since the narrative voice throughout belongs to Frederic Henry. What the reader hears is *bereavement*: the voice of the man who has been so damaged by both the war and the unexpected loss of his own separate peace remains a constant in the telling of the story.

In much of Hemingway's later writing, the reader can unearth the war, if only in the devastation of personal loss. He recreates the actual war in *For Whom the Bell Tolls*, of course, as well as in his short stories about the Spanish conflict. He draws the aging warrior in *Across the River and Into the Trees*, war there a kind of reminiscent but still vital context. Even in *The Old Man and the Sea*, he pits the bravest of men against the overwhelming forces of nature. Hemingway's emphasis on writing about war, however, comes through most strikingly in his fragile and earnest attempts to create fine, natural, understated poetry and prose. It is these early years, and these early works—all completed before Hemingway was thirty—that marked both his career and the sense of what American modernism was.

Dos Passos, Cather, and Lewis

In countless ways, the writing of John Dos Passos reflects many of Hemingway's aesthetic concerns. Given the years of publication of their early books, one might say Hemingway is creating a mirror image of Dos Passos's 1920s writing. Friends though they became, there is no suggestion during Hemingway's early years in Paris that he was avidly following Dos Passos's work. Yet their books show that each had formed very similar aesthetic views.

In 1917, Dos Passos published his poetry in a collection titled *Eight Harvard Poets*. By 1920 he had published his first war novel, *One Man's Initiation—1917*, which was followed quickly the next year by the better-received and more realistic *Three Soldiers*. In 1922 he brought out a full collection of his own poetry titled *A Pushcart at the Curb*. That same year saw the publication of travel writings, *Rosinante to the Road Again*. In 1923 he published a Boston/Harvard novel titled *Streets of Night*. But in 1925 came Dos Passos's modernist block-buster, a truly avant garde testimony to urban existence. In *Manhattan Transfer*, Dos Passos brought his own convictions about the poem into the novel. Much more radical than anything Hemingway had yet published, or would publish by 1926 with *The Sun Also Rises, Manhattan Transfer* impressed the literary world with excitement, gender distinction, and vivid prose. In draft, Dos Passos had used the title "Tess of 42nd Street," drawing on readers' familiarity with Thomas Hardy's *Tess of the d'Urbervilles: A Pure Woman* and placing his women characters in the cauldron of New York skyscraper living. Five years later, he kept that sense of location for the first book of his *U.S.A.* trilogy, *The 42nd Parallel*.

All Dos Passos's writing, however, began with his poetry. The manuscript of *A Pushcart at the Curb*, housed in the Dos Passos collection at the University of Virginia, is twice as long as the published book. There are, of course, the cryptic imagist poems, as here in XI:

> Beyond ruffled velvet hills
> the sky burns yellow like a candle-flame.
>
> Sudden a village
> roofs against the sky
> leaping buttresses . . .
> *Dos Passos* Pushcart *34*

A few poems move from ornate language into the simplicity more modern writers would choose, as when Dos Passos shifts gears in a poem that describes his ambition— to "build an Arc of words." Instead, he admits, the poet's pen betrays him:

> All I can write is the orange tinct with crimson
> of the beaks of the goose
> and of the wet webbed feet of the geese . . .
> *Dos Passos* Pushcart *99–100*

Some of Dos Passos's poems are experimental; others, relatively staid and orderly, as is one comprised of quatrains. "Phases of the Moon" ends with a kind of pro-legomenon that represents Dos Passos's eager attempts to recreate his own version of America:

Through all these years the walls have writhed
with shadow overlaid upon shadow.
I have bruised my fingers on the windowbars
so many lives cemented and made strong.

While the bars stand strong, outside
the great processions of men's lives go past.
Their shadows squirm distorted on my wall.

Tonight the new moon is in the sky.
            Dos Passos Pushcart *200–1*

Part of Dos Passos's fascination with World War I was that he had opportunity to watch these "great processions of men's lives"—to be, in fact, a part of them. "The fellows in my section are frightfully decent—all young men are frightfully decent. If we only governed the world instead of the swagbellied old foggies that do" (Dos Passos *Best* 44). Much of the plot of both *One Man's Initiation—1917* and *Three Soldiers* concerns the dichotomy between the author's optimistic acceptance of his fellow soldiers and his later awareness of their sometimes disappointing behavior under stress.

A greater part of Dos Passos's excitement about the war, however, seems to have been the accessibility of genuine experience as subject for his writing. As he recalled in his memoir, *The Best Times*, about his year in the ambulance corps, he was still "absorbed in the problem of how to write clearly," but his fascination lay in the war as subject: "War was the theme of the time. I was in a passion to put down everything, immediately as it happened, exactly as I saw it." As he explains his heightened perceptions, he turns to the increasing use of concrete images, juxtaposed one with another: "The chance of death sharpened the senses. The sweetness of the white roses, the shape and striping of a snail shell, the taste of an omelet, the most casual sight or sound appeared desperately intense against the background of the great massacres" (Dos Passos *Best* 44).

Dos Passos had graduated from Harvard, and had then traveled, writing the essays and poems that he occasionally published. He then joined the Red Cross ambulance corps—and remained in Europe for several years, until the Armistice. It is not surprising that his first two books were about the war. Both were written "imagistically," and centered on young male protagonists, Martin Howe and John Andrews. What makes the novels better than some of his self-conscious aesthetic pronouncements of these years is that his emotional energy permeates them, and commits him to writing powerfully about experiences and newly developed feelings. Even though he still felt somewhat trapped by what he called the "bell-glass" atmosphere of Harvard and its Boston society, his novels convince the reader that war is more than a rhetorical problem or a social one, that the lives of all men are valuable, and that Dos Passos's purpose as writer is to present enough of the bones of the experience that readers can then add on the flesh. In *One Man's Initiation*, for example, there is little attention to political events which preceded and surrounded the war. Dos Passos's interest, and focus, falls on a few soldiers faced with their first encounter with death—of both physical bodies and cultural ones. The experience of the novel is immediate and concrete.

What makes these two novels a crucial part of the artistic progression Dos Passos's writing career evinces is that the methods he uses in them are very similar to the methods he was then employing in his poems. Instead of choosing a dramatic structure of rising action-climax-falling action, Dos Passos sets one scene against another. Events distant in time become related thematically as they are presented in a non-linear montage. His reaction against a time-sequential, plot-oriented novel is clear in his statement that "happenings meant nothing in themselves anyway—and . . . I tried to give that impression—by the recurrence of words and phrases."

Like his poems, the prose of *One Man's Initiation* is governed by factual detail shown concretely and by a painter's reliance on color. Yellow crates and white hand-kerchiefs are shaded with the brown hues of the wharf as the book opens, and soon "the rosy yellow and drab purple" buildings of the New York skyline pass the ship. In the swatch of colors Dos Passos interjects the relatively stark dialogue of the young soldiers:

> "This your first time across?"
> "Yes . . . . Yours?"
> "Yes . . . . I never used to think that at nineteen I'd be crossing the Atlantic to go to war in France." The boy caught himself up suddenly and blushed. Then swallowing a lump in his throat he said, "It ought to be time to eat."
>
>> God help Kaiser Bill!
>> O-o-o-old Uncle Sam.
>> He's got the cavalry,
>> He's got the infantry,
>> He's got the artillery;
>> And then by God we'll all go to Germany!
>> God help Kaiser Bill!
>
> The iron covers are clamped on the smoking room windows, for no lights must show. So the air is dense with tobacco smoke and the reek of beer and champagne. In one corner they are playing poker with their coats off . . .
>
> *Dos Passos* Initiation *44–5*

The contrasting glimpses of bravado and fear take the story quickly from the early tone of comfortable pastiche to the stolid irony of most of the narrative. Throughout *One Man's Initiation*, or *First Encounter* as it was titled in England, Dos Passos sets the unrelieved horror of physical war against the propagandist version of that war, with snatches of popular songs serving as punctuation. These opposing views of war form the bases for the novel: scenes set in graphic montage to dupli-cate the effect the sights of war have on Martin Howe.

Even as the prospective soldiers drink and gamble to allay their fears, these fears surface in their conversations. Dos Passos shows fear in both the abstract and the specific, and in the latter, in a scene in which a soldier reports that death from the German's "new gas" means "five to seven days of slow choking," the fear results from home-front propagandists. Juxtaposed with this scene is the cloying dialogue between Howe and the patriotic girl (imaged through her unbelievably white teeth), who relishes telling stories about German atrocities.

The much shorter second chapter serves as an image for both the war and its scarifying effect on Martin Howe. In the midst of descriptions of the flowers for sale in the French market looms the damaged human face, used as a leitmotif throughout the book. In the midst of roses (for good luck) and daisies (for love), Howe sees the image that haunts him: "Between the pale-brown frightened eyes, where the nose should have been, was a triangular black patch that ended in some mechanical contrivance with shiny little black metal rods that took the place of the jaw" (Dos Passos *Initiation* 54).

The novel continues, making scenes expand into more and more physical horror: the reader is taken through the destruction of the abbey, the slow deaths of ambulance patients, and the depravity of the soldiers. Dos Passos's use of the physical imagery of mutilation begins with the triangular patch, then changes to "a depression, a hollow pool of blood lying where the middle of a man had been," and culminating in the memory of a German prisoner's being blown to bits by a grenade. This last image recurs as the cause of psychological torment to a supposedly hardened soldier and, in later descriptions, the author adds more and more graphic details.

One Man's Initiation—1917 is not exclusively about war. Martin Howe is also naïve about romance, about the important qualities of women, and about the role of religion in a person's life. Reminiscent of Eliot's J. Alfred Prufrock, Dos Passos's Martin Howe survives the war—but only in part. He watches his friends die; he sees the Frenchmen with whom he has talked blown to pieces; he finds no answers to questions of either war or peace. With a narrative trajectory that is all too predictable, the novel comes to its conclusion in mock crucifixion scenes, in the rantings of a deranged soldier calling for everybody's death, and in too many glimpses of "shapeless, sacked bodies of the dead."

Dos Passos's approach in *Three Soldiers* was meant to change the predictable nature of a book about war. This book is longer and more complex; the protagonist, John Andrews, a composer, is forcing himself to deny the importance of class, parentage, education. He assumes friendships with two lower class soldiers, Chris Chrisfield and Dan Fuselli. Forcing the reader's attention away from the military action abroad, Dos Passos created a psychological study of three very different young men. *Three Soldiers* is five times as long as *One Man's Initiation—1917*.

Its narrative, unfortunately, leads to a similar resolution of horror: John Andrews deserts, and is eventually arrested as a deserter. One of the other men kills not only the enemy but his superior officer. Despite a better control of color imagery and a broader context for the immensity of the happenings of war, Dos Passos's second novel has little freshness of either writing or content.

The author spoke to this quandary, later, as he reminisced about the choices beginning writers make.

The basic raw material is everything you've seen and heard and felt, it's your childhood and your education and serving in the army, and travelling in odd places, and finding yourself in odd situations. It is those rare moments of suffering and delight when a man's private sensations are amplified and illuminated by a flash of insight that gives him the certainty that what he is seeing and feeling is what millions of his fellowmen see and feel in the same situation, only heightened.

This sort of universal experience made concrete by the individual's shaping of it, is the raw material of all the imaginative arts. These flashes of insight when strong emotions key all the perceptions up to their highest point are the nuggets of pure gold.

Virginia archive

What use Dos Passos was eventually to make of his World War I experiences came as he approached writing his chronicle of his country. By the late 1920s, having earned the success that greeted his 1925 *Manhattan Transfer*, and several of his experimental plays, Dos Passos was more likely to see himself as Walt Whitman instead of Prufrock. When he wrote the first book of what would become his *U.S.A.* trilogy, a 1930 novel he titled *The 42nd Parallel*, he used poetic prose as one of the four kinds of narrative that comprised the book. Dos Passos never left poetry.

The poetic "Camera Eye" sections were often subjective, and sometimes even autobiographical—but always imaged as scenes. Dos Passos never relied on the "I" point of view. In each perfectly realized prose poem, the scene comes to life, and tells the reader why this particular scene is important. The Camera Eye sections begin with Dos Passos as small boy, remembering "The first time He[3] came He brought a melon and the sun was coming in through the tall lace windowcurtains and when we cut it the smell of melons filled the whole room" (Dos Passos *U.S.A.* 29–30). Some phrases appear as heard language—"Longago Beforetheworldsfair Before youwereborn"— several during later childhood when the protagonist worries that he has not been baptized, that other boys will make him fight ("the bloody sweet puky taste" of his injuries), that as a college man he may remain an inept, Prufrockian figure.

Usually paired with one of Dos Passos's inventive "Newsreels," montages of actual quotes from news media as well as the filmic newsreels, the Camera Eye sections grow less personal as the three novels progress. By the time Dos Passos comes to the war years in *1919*[4] he is placing more emphasis on the Newsreels, for their juxtaposition of parts allows more ironic impact. (It is also clear that Dos Passos wants to emphasize the economics of both going to war and waging war; he spends much of his space for "Biographies" on the political and economic leaders of the world.)

In one of the earliest of his Camera Eyes from *1919*, he recounts the life of the ambulance driver:

remembering the grey crooked fingers the thick drip of blood off the canvas the bubbling when the lungcases try to breathe the muddy scraps of flesh you put in the ambulance alive and haul out dead/ three of us sit in the dry cement fountain of the little garden with the pink walls in Recicourt.

Dos Passos U.S.A. *446*

The image is strengthened after much geographic description, when Dos Passos brings the reader back to those three men, "happy talking in low voices . . . about après la guerre that our fingers our blood our lungs our flesh under the dirty khaki feldgrau bleu horizon might go on sweeten grow until we fall from the tree ripe like the tooripe pears . . . ."

There is the irony of Dos Passos being concerned about the 11,000 "registered harlots" at the front, about the humor in the submarine crew's having to bring rosies to the surface to empty them, about the false valor of the men commanding the Red Cross units, or about the steady need for care of the terribly wounded man. But most often, the Camera Eye focus is on death. When the Armistice has been signed, Dos Passos walks in the French countryside and describes the impact of losing the war:

we're going to walk a long way get good wine full of Merovingian names millwheels glassgreen streams where the water gurgles out of old stone gargoyles Madeleine's red apples the smell of beech leaves we're going to drink wine the boy from Philadelphia's got beaucoup jack   wintery purple wine   the sun breaks out through the   clouds on the first day in the year
    in the first village
    we stop in our tracks
    to look at a waxwork
    the old man has shot the pretty peasant girl who looks
like Madeleine but younger she lies there shot in the left breast in the blood in the ruts of the road pretty and plump as a little quail
    The old man then took off one shoe and put the shotgun under his chin pulled the trigger with his toe and blew the top of his head off   we stand looking at the bare foot and the shoe and the foot in the shoe and the shot girl and the old man with a gunnysack over his head and the dirty bare toe he pulled the trigger with   Faut pas toucher until the commissaire comes process verbale
    on this first day
    of the year the sun
    is shining.

Dos Passos U.S.A. *574–5*

Master of the unexpected even in juxtaposition, Dos Passos creates remarkable effects as he stays within the simple language (often intermixed with French or German) of the military recruit, of the common person not only facing but submerged—and hopeless—in war. Using spaces within lines (reminiscent of the typographical practices his college friend cummings had practised) and very little punctuation, Dos Passos relied on the synergy between the reader's eye and his or her implied voice.

The Dos Passos manuscript collections show the plethora of cut-and-paste materials (actual print from newspapers set against the author's typed responses to newsreels and other media bulletins), and even as his readership dwindled throughout his later more conservative writing, he was hard at work to use the *real* in his presentations. When he died in 1970, outliving both Hemingway and Faulkner (and living long past F. Scott Fitzgerald, Edith Wharton, and Willa Cather), he was no longer hopeful of winning the Nobel Prize for Literature— or any other literary prize. Fiction based in fact had been overwhelmed by the curious non-factual way Hemingway and Fitzgerald used the truths of their surroundings; novelists seemed forced by that most imaginative writer of the century—William Faulkner—to admit that the writer's created world might be more convincing than reality.

Somewhat ironically, the best-known war novel early in the 1920s was Willa Cather's *One of Ours*. Despite negative reviews by both Edmund Wilson and Hemingway, Cather's story of Claude Wheeler, the remotely dissatisfied farm boy from Nebraska, was awarded the Pulitzer Prize for Fiction in 1922. Unlike Hemingway's early war novels, as well as Dos Passos's novels of World War I, in this book Cather allows Wheeler to die, making his heroic sacrifice for his men—a man remembered by all those who served with him. Heroism, unlikely though it seemed to be for a character like Wheeler, fed most readers' appetites.

Cather's novel seemed unusual for her; she admitted she had never planned to write a war novel. She began as a muckraking journalist and an editor at *McClure's* Magazine. She published poems and stories and then her first novel, *Alexander's Bridge*. In 1913 she made an even more successful debut as a Plains novelist: *O Pioneers* was much acclaimed. In 1915 *The Song of the Lark* privileged the career choices of the professional woman singer. In 1918 *My Antonia* appeared. Cather had seemingly not cared much about drawing male characters. Yet the first (long) half of *One of Ours* is Claude's story, set in his domestic circumstances. The middle of his family's sons, he is talented and bright, but he is rarely motivated. He goes through the paces of getting an education but once his father sees a way to increase

---

EXCERPT FROM WILLA CATHER'S *ONE OF OURS*, pp. 83–4

. . . his heart was growing a little heavier all the time. The Erlich boys had so many new interests he couldn't keep up with them; they had been going on, and he had been standing still . . . . The thing that hurt was the feeling of being out of it, of being lost in another kind of life in which ideas played but little part . . . . Coming here only made him more discontented with his lot.

the family fortune, and announces that Claude's college years are over, he accepts his father's decision: he drops out of college and runs the family farm (with only mediocre success).

In living a homey life with his mother and their black maid, Mahailey, Claude seems to be content. He reads to his mother at night, or she reads to him: he is truly replete with domesticity. What he misses acutely, however, is his involvement in the Ehrlich family's life. Taken into that home by a college friend, Claude read their interactions as stemming from their interesting intellectual lives. Aside from his mother, Claude on the farm felt that he belonged only to a people who "worked hard with their backs and got tired like the horses, and were too sleepy at night to think of anything to say" (Cather *Ours* 84).

Trying to transfer the Ehrlichs's contented home life into his own environs, Claude proposes to the unlikely Enid, who at first refuses to marry him. He diligently builds their house, board by board; she finally accepts his offer, but on their wedding night, she refuses to admit him to her sleeping compartment.

The environment that Claude creates at home is one of purposelessness.[5] If young American men should be noted for their ambition, their drive to achieve some version of the American dream, then Claude Wheeler is clearly a misfit. It is that sense of what Wilson calls "romanticization" that is the keystone for criticism of this novel. But in the second half of *One of Ours*, Cather includes more actual "war" than any of the war writing accomplished by either Hemingway or Dos Passos. On board ship, she creates seasickness and then the death-dealing influenza, signaled first by unusual nosebleeds. Nearly all the men Claude has come to know die, even the old doctor, Tannhauser, his death marked by "frightful sounds that came from his throat, sounds like violent vomiting, or the choking rattle of a man in strangulation" (Cather *Ours* 299).

Sent to a French training camp near Rouen, the young recruits are bombed; the result is twenty-six men buried and eleven in hospital. With the talented violinist Gerhardt as his roommate, Claude and he spend two weeks in the trenches, living in "No Man's Land," bathing in a sink hole which turns out to be the burial site for German corpses. Claude's friendship with Gerhardt makes him more confident, leads to his promotions in the field. Important to Company B, Claude—ironically turning twenty-five at that juncture—is asked to hold "the nastiest bit of line" for a day and a night. Snipers are rampant but Claude stands above his men in the trenches, directing their rifle fire: "He felt no weakness. He felt only one thing; that he commanded wonderful men."

Cather's description of Claude's death is psychologically accurate (and might have influenced Hemingway as he wrote about Henry's wounding in his 1929 novel): she writes that Claude

> felt the ground rise under him, and he was swept with a mountain of earth and rock down into the ravine. He never knew whether he lost consciousness or not. It seemed to him that he went on having continuous sensations. The first, was that of being blown to pieces; swelling to an enormous size under

intolerable pressure, and then bursting. Next he felt himself shrink and tingle, like a frost-bitten body thawing out." Later in the sequence, "he felt as if he were full of shell splinters.

Ours *298*

Cather then creates the harsh irony—had Claude lived, he would have quickly learned that he had, in effect, sent his best friend Gerhardt to his death from shelling. Claude does not live to know that. What the ending of *One of Ours* solidifies, as Claude's mother reads all his letters, is that her son had found happiness—a sense of purpose and perhaps an ennobling peace. The novel concludes in Mrs. Wheeler's words, "For him the call was clear, the cause was glorious" (*Ours* 458).

As both Jennifer Haytock and Sharon O'Brien have made clear, Claude's being characterized as purposeless is central to what Cather establishes. O'Brien makes the point that Claude is very much like his creator, and that Cather was herself influenced by the deaths of both her nephew, G. P. Cather, and her young violinist friend, David Hochstein, in battle in France (O'Brien 189). She read letters, interviewed returning veterans, tried to build an archive of materials about the American men who fought, even as she resisted writing a war novel.

In Haytock's assessment, *One of Ours* is both domestic novel and war novel, and from that combination stems inevitable tension. Men, even though they are isolated in battle, have difficulty adopting female roles, yet all people when they are alone in foreign countries and faced with possible death, try to create comfort. As she says, "the idea of home still maintains its appeal" (Haytock *At Home* xxv). Claude writes his mother regularly; she treasures his letters, and what they tell her about his growth to maturity. Readers who understand gender equivalence in the twenty-first century do not blink at O'Brien's comment that "Cather's war is a mother-son story in which women gain the power men relinquish" (O'Brien 193). They might, however, insist that the category of domestic fiction reaches here to make Cather's presentation of Claude as a soldier truly viable. He revels in having found himself, and he has found himself through the relationship of man with man, soldier with soldier. The crucible of possible death has bound this band of brothers more tightly than any civilian experiences, in any domestic setting.

American readers in the early 1920s were not intent on reading about the war that had finally ended. What they wanted were stories of individual civilian promise—leaving the damaged or dead bodies out of their imaginative consciousnesses. The immense economic successes in the postwar marketplace, increased during the 1920s because so much of European industry had been damaged, meant only prosperity—luxuries, homes, college educations—and the most significant of American novels were dealing with postwar, profitable United States life.

It is in this context that the most impressive young American fiction writer becomes Sinclair Lewis, with his break-out novel *Main Street* published in 1920. Vying for the first Pulitzer Prize in Fiction, that book was denied the accolade (which in 1921 went instead to Edith Wharton's retrospective *The Age of Innocence*, a novel that just as ironically as had *Main Street* exposed the flaws of being guided in all decisions by social propriety).[6] Looking back in time with Wharton's story of love subverted was less threatening than Lewis's accurate expose of small town America, admittedly prosperous in the post war climate. History provided a gloss of separation.

Main Street gave the readership of the world a sense of true irony. Beginning with the somewhat ambiguous characterization of Carol Kennicott, the novel was filled to overflowing with the pride of the confident, and prosperous, merchants of the Midwestern provincial town. Even though Lewis had serialized his earlier novels in the *Post*, he kept Main Street secret; in fact, he changed publishers to bring out this novel. He knew readers would find it "shocking and iconoclastic." As Miles Orvell points out in his 2012 *The Death and Life of Main Street*, Lewis's was the first book to ridicule and criticize that homey nest of small town America. In 1920 one half of America's population lived in villages of under 2500 people.

In most readers' views, the small American town—even one named "Gopher Prairie"—was the place to achieve the long-awaited American dream. When Dr. Will Kennicott saw the prosperity that surrounded him, he absorbed the pride of his friends as rightfully his: what was the *dream* but to get ahead, to change residences so that your living space showed your financial prosperity to the world. So entrenched was the identification between dream and household that no reader would question the characters' behavior in *Main Street*. Orvell points out that whereas most Americans did not go to college, they had all been reared on the conservative *McGuffey's Readers*. Carol moves to a place in which people lead "seriously purposeful lives," and the fact that those townspeople are also anti-immigrant, anti-Jewish, racist, and conservative does not lessen their self-satisfaction (Orvell 84, 92). As this critic pointed out later, small towns are white; cities are non-white. Or, less directly, "Perhaps it is enough to say that the small town has always been ruled by a powerful elite at pains to conceal the practices of exclusion through hearty proclamations of the principles of community." (Orvell 6, 131.)

It is Gordon Hutner who traces the idea of the "American dream" to the 1931 book by James Truslow Adams. His *The Epic of America* expresses the middle-class fantasy of individual fulfillment, of the efficacy of a social order that lets individuals come to fruition—and not just economically (Hutner 108). The concept moves forward and backward, and influences both conventional readings of United States culture and satiric readings: Edna Ferber's *So Big*, Marjorie K. Rawlings' *The Yearling*, Caroline Miller's *Lamb in His Bosom*, H. L. Davis's *Honey in the Horn* and fiction by Glenway Wescott are set against Lewis's *Main Street*. (Between 1920, when the latter novel appeared, and 1925, no other American novel matched its sales. Even more important than Lewis's 1922 novel, *Babbitt*, *Main Street* kept its readership.)

As Lewis handled Babbitt, his successful and prosperous title character of the 1922 novel, he drew more criticism than had any of the figures within *Main Street*. In the 1920 novel, Carol Kennicott does leave Will for a period, but she returns. She has learned enough about life in Gopher Prairie that she can find tranquil happiness with her spouse, his friends, and the inherently simple culture of their town. In *Babbitt*, both the title character and his close friend Paul are dissatisfied with their wives. Paul, in fact, tries to kill Zilla. The bullet strikes her in the shoulder, but she lives; he is sentenced to three years imprisonment. Partly as a response to seeing what action came from his and Paul's complaints, George Babbitt ends his flirtations with Ida Putiak, the manicure girl, and Tanis Judique, a more mature friend (both of questionable nationality), and returns to Myra, his supposedly objectionable wife. Her attack of appendicitis brings him thoroughly around, and George Babbitt becomes a more satisfied, complacent citizen. When his son Ted secretly marries his young girlfriend (Ted saying he was determined to do something he *wanted* in his life), George feels pride in the boy's action.

Even though the 1920s literary life seemed to revolve around Paris and New York, Sinclair Lewis drew strength and information from his childhood in Sauk Centre, Minnesota. He had gone to college at Oberlin and Yale; he had lived in Upton Sinclair's colony for progressive thinking. He had written several romantic, bad novels. Through his scrutiny of American readers and American beliefs, Lewis knew his treatment of United States ideals in *Main Street* would be controversial. But he understood irony, and he persisted. Hutner points out that the fiction of the later 1920s is

> most notable, not for its classics of American modernism or even the moralism that the Pulitzers glorify, but for the intensity of its efforts to represent a bourgeois America. Through stories devoted to arbitrating modern troubles, novel after novel chronicles the pressures facing the New Woman, the challenges of doing business in an immoral age, the trials endured in the suburbs, the frustrations of rearing children .... plots of these novels provide marked routes through everyday confusions.
>
> *Hutner 76*

Critics more recently have placed *Main Street* in what they term "the anti-village tradition," linking it back to Mark Twain's *The Man That Corrupted Hadleyburg* and pairing it with the "rotten onion" trope that governed Edgar Lee Masters's *Spoon River Anthology*. Sherwood Anderson's "grotesques" in his *Winesburg, Ohio* were also revealing, and comments by H. L. Mencken, Zona Gale, Floyd Dell, and Van Wyck Brooks supported the idea that there was such a movement. Carl Van Vechten called it "The Revolt from the Village" (Orvell 75).

It is Orvell who points out that the deification of the American small town had only just begun in 1920. He draws attention to the fetish Henry Ford showed as he created the Ford Museum and Greenfield Village, artificial structures where the children of many Ford workers (some, immigrants) were educated. He points to the creation of the village at Williamsburg, Virginia, and to the popularity of Norman Rockwell's illustrations. Orvell sees Garrison Keillor and his *A Prairie Home Companion* as a more modern reification of this impulse. "Main Street is the material embodiment of the dream. Moreoever, my tacit assumption is that there is an equivalence of sorts between Main Street and America, that Main Street, in its broadest significance, *is* America" (Orvell 7, 28, 45). With even more emphasis, Orvell states, "the idea of the small town lies at the heart of the American ethos, with a strong and continuing appeal for Americans" (Orvell ix).

Notes

1 During the 1920s, much drama was truly experimental, so such writers as John Howard Lawson, Edna St. Vincent Millay, Elmer Rice, Gertrude Stein, DuBose and Dorothy Heyward, Owen Davis, Paul Green, Thornton Wilder, and Dos Passos and cummings should be added to this listing.
2 Mark Spilka says that Hemingway remained nineteen—when these losses occurred, both unexpectedly—and that much of his personal life stemmed from what was this late adolescent loss. Hemingway was apparently fixed (in emotional age) "at about nineteen. That was the year of his war wound in Italy and of his hospital romance" (Spilka 258).
3 Born to Lucy Addison Sprigg Madison, then unmarried because her lover, John Roderigo Dos Passos, could not leave his invalid wife, the author was known as John Roderigo Madison until his parents could marry (in 1910). He then assumed the name of John Dos Passos. His childhood was spent largely abroad, traveling with his mother, with occasional visits from Dos Passos.
4 Praised by Jean Paul Sartre in an influential essay, *1919* led to Dos Passos's being positioned along with Hemingway and Faulkner as the triumvirate of American modernism, leaders in new trends in international literature.
5 In Cather's 1923 novel, *A Lost Lady*, she draws an opposing set of characters: here the stable heart of a family is the older man, caring for his young and beautiful—and unconventional—wife. Flipping gender, so to speak, Cather tells Marion's story through the adoring voice of the young boy who lived nearby. Praised by F. Scott Fitzgerald as the best novel of the year, his creation of Nick Carraway as the narrative voice for the Gatsby story may borrow something from Cather's work here.
6 Sinclair Lewis did win a Pulitzer Prize for Fiction in 1926 but more impressively, he was awarded the Nobel Prize for Literature in 1930. (It would be another twenty years before either Faulkner or Hemingway received the latter.) After *Main Street* came *Babbitt* in 1922, *Arrowsmith* in 1925, *Mantrap* in 1926, *Elmer Gantry* in 1927, *The Man Who Knew Coolidge* in 1928 and *Dodsworth* in 1929.

Suggested further reading

Stanley Cooperman. *World War I and the American Novel*. Johns Hopkins UP, 1967.
Paul Fussell. *The Great War and Modern Memory*. Oxford UP, 1975.
Frederick J. Hoffman. *The Modern Novel in America, 1900–1950*. Henry Regnery, 1951.
Hugh Kenner. *A Homemade World: The American Modernist Writers*. Knopf, 1975.

5

FITZGERALD, FAULKNER, AND WOLFE AS AMERICAN ROMANTICS

The tendency to create worlds of the widest possibility is inherent in writers and artists. Such practice burgeoned early in the twentieth century: it was not only postwar aesthetics that privileged the imaginative. Led by previously unheard of originality of painting and sculpture world wide, writers, too, bought into such boundlessness. Realism and naturalism paled. Texts that could speak for greater personal freedom for the individual (i.e. the American dream), for the acknowledged rise of the middle class, for the struggle to free the psyche from restrictions set in place by the powerful classes—these works came to illustrate the promise of America. Joined with works that celebrated the natural, and spoke to the appeal of the remote, the variety possible in postwar writing came to fruition as more and more publishing houses were formed—Alfred A. Knopf was established in 1915; Boni & Liveright in 1917; Harcourt, Brace in 1919; and Viking in 1925, among others. It was a heady time to begin a literary career.

To a certain extent, all writers at work after World War I have positive aims in mind: to support the existing (and victorious) social, political, and economic beliefs the population evinced. The United States believed in democracy, of government by and for its people, and in religious freedoms. Americans believed in a government of the unified common mind, expressed through the mechanism of the vote. Most postwar writing, especially in non-fiction and fiction, was to support such beliefs. Writers then as now work from the desire to inform and to persuade, to arouse feeling and influence readers' behavior. At base, writers believe that language—used effectively—can both create and change behavior.

The postwar milieu in America gave rise to fear as well as hope. In reaction to the surge of less-than-desirable immigration that swept through the Statue of Liberty's arc, existing Americans found themselves suspicious of such cultures as the Irish, the Italian, and the German (people who were frequently Catholic—and therefore, using some twisted logic, "un-American"). Urged on by temperance workers, particularly the Women's Christian Temperance Union of countless and diverse Protestant churches, in 1919 the United States Congress passed the Eighteenth Amendment, which prohibited the sale of liquor. That Amendment went into effect in mid-January, 1920. The Volstead Act accompanied it, criminalizing a great deal of individual behavior that had never before been considered immoral—"all activities related to manufacturing, selling, and transporting alcoholic beverages." People breaking these laws could be imprisoned; at the very least, they could be fined. "In fact, in 1929 the Volstead Act was supplemented by the Jones Act, which increased the maximum penalty for Prohibition violators to five years in prison and $10,000—even for first offenders—and made any liquor violation a felony" (Drowne 8).

Historian Kathleen Drowne points to the incessant law-breaking during the 1920s and until 1933, when the Eighteenth Amendment was repealed, as inimical to basic respectful attitudes toward law and government control: not only was effective law enforcement impossible in many areas of the United States, but even some police and federal troops had little sympathy for the strictures of Prohibition. In order to subvert the Eighteenth Amendment, new establishments were created—drug stores which sold illegal products, speakeasies, nightclubs, good time flats, blind pigs, roadhouses—and the musical world was filled with songs about alcohol-fueled conflicts ("popular Tin Pan Alley, jazz, blues, and hillbilly songs"), augmented by the tremendous increase in phonographs and radios sold for personal use. As Drowne concludes, "Prohibition politicized what had previously been essentially apolitical events." She points particularly to what she terms "prohibition culture, widespread and transgressive behaviors that became popular during the 1920s, such as women drinking, petting, smoking cigarettes, and dressing more alluringly" (Drowne 4, 8).

American restrictions against drinking alcohol led quickly to an exodus of the young, the artistic, and the rebellious for Europe; it was not only the favorable exchange rate that lured postwar men, women, and couples to leave the States. Anger at a government that assumed legislating morals was one of its rights might have been seldom expressed, but the irony that people had fought for their freedoms, losing lives and health in World War I, only to be censured for one of the behaviors that going to war had led them to develop—drinking, drinking, drinking alcohol, drinking wine, drinking beer—seemed a true misuse of power. Even as the Methodist church insisted that its children sign sobriety pledges, many young Methodists were flocking to France and Italy. It goes without saying that legislating morality was one means of stifling the power of "foreign" beliefs, and of supporting the "Americanism" that the largely white Protestant heterosexual population upheld. At issue were religious, racial, and sexual practices, not to mention the very definition of "normal." While Sinclair Lewis met these issues head on, the writers who focused on wartime chronicles were, whether intentionally or not, avoiding some of the most vexed cultural issues for United States readers.[1]

Another feeder for the malaise that Prohibition had in some part occasioned was the increasing pressure on young men of the middle and upper classes to go to college. College behavior, at least as Dorothy Parker and F. Scott Fitzgerald drew it, was a kind of romance in itself—separating characters from families, from towns, from churches—and readers read hungrily to learn the mores of this new kind of adventure (one approved by the progressive tenets of Americans). As the spokesperson for characters' college experiences, F. Scott Fitzgerald drew on all his memories of his years at Princeton: creating the Jazz Age and the flamboyant sleek-haired and short-skirted flapper, he used scenes and dialogue that were less romanticized than some readers thought.

One of the myths about modernist American writers is that they did not go to college. While Hemingway circulated that belief, to his own personal advantage, John Dos Passos had graduated from Harvard, as had e. e. cummings, John Reed, Edwin Arlington Robinson, Wallace Stevens, Gertrude Stein, Alain Locke (who was chosen to be one of the first Rhodes scholars there), and others; Willa Cather graduated from The University of Nebraska; Ezra Pound took an M.A. degree in Romance Languages from The University of Pennsylvania, where Marianne Moore, H.D. (briefly), and William Carlos Williams became a part of Pound's aesthetic group. Williams was completing his medical degree there.

W. E. B. Du Bois, Carl Van Vechten, T. S. Eliot, and Thornton Wilder—among others—did graduate degrees at Harvard. Zora Neale Hurston studied at Columbia University with Franz Boas, and was later rewarded with a Guggenheim fellowship. After graduating from The University of North Carolina, Thomas Wolfe did graduate study at Harvard. Gertrude Stein studied medicine at John Hopkins.[2]

F. Scott Fitzgerald, along with Edmund Wilson and John Peale Bishop, went to Princeton, but Fitzgerald often dropped out during spring semesters for reasons of health (and busyness as he wrote scripts for spring musicals). He did not graduate; rather he left school to join the military, and he subsequently pretended that what was a very uneven academic record was lost to his memory.

It is William Faulkner, who spent parts of intermittent terms at The University of Mississippi after he returned from the Canadian air corps, who completed the "uneducated" myth that Hemingway originated. In many ways like Hemingway, Faulkner read his way through a wide-ranging literary curriculum, concentrating his energies on drama, poetry, and fiction of the contemporary period throughout the world. The capacity to read and digest immense quantities of writing—which both Faulkner and Hemingway evinced—and make superb use of their highly subjective and inductive learning, marked each writer's accomplishment as he worked his rapacious reading into his own inimitable style.

Fitzgerald and the 1920s

When Fitzgerald broke onto the American literary scene in 1920, he was only twenty-four and had published a very few short stories. Both his novel, *This Side of Paradise*, and his first collection of stories, *Flappers and Philosophers*, fed the appetites of readers who were curious about college life (and young Americans' behavior). With the send-off of these two books, Fitzgerald became a spokesperson

EXCERPT FROM EZRA POUND ON "INVENTORS AND MASTERS"

When you start searching for "pure elements" in literature you will find that literature has been created by the following classes of persons:

1   Inventors. Men who found a new process, or whose extant work gives us the first known example of a process.
2   The masters. Men who combined a number of such processes, and who used them as well as or better than the inventors.
3   The diluters. Men who came after the first two kinds of writer, and couldn't do the job quite as well . . . .

for the young. Interviewed wherever he went, he was suffused with the sense of fame. He knew he could make it as a writer; he became expert at mining the full range of the hedonistic behavior associated with the Jazz Age. Married to his chic younger wife, Zelda Sayre, Fitzgerald wrote with an eye to describing the lives of couples: never moralistic, the author instead created a romantic context to elevate the foibles of early 1920s life in both the small Southern towns he had learned about from Zelda and the urban contexts he already knew.

Never confident of his ability or his personhood, Fitzgerald needed to carve out a career that would compensate for the failures he saw as dominating his early life: his father's business failures, his mother's defeated social hopes, his life in St. Paul, Minnesota, and his continuing unhappy boyhood at boarding school. He was also undecided about both his Irish heritage and his Catholicism. After leaving Princeton in 1917, without graduating, he spent two years in the Army and then worked in New York, learning advertising. During these years he wrote several drafts of *This Side of Paradise,* and on the basis of Max Perkins' accepting the manuscript for Scribner's, Zelda Sayre (whom he had met while he was stationed in Alabama) agreed to marry him.

Their honeymoon weeks in New York created the image of the public Fitzgeralds: they became the epitome of the glamorous if somewhat unreal people who frequented the city in the Jazz Age. Scott and Zelda appeared to be living the American dream of beauty, imagination, and wealth.

Fitzgerald's second novel, *The Beautiful and Damned,* was published in 1922. *Tales of the Jazz Age,* another collection of stories, also appeared then and *The Vegetable,* an unsuccessful play, in 1923. During these years, Fitzgerald also wrote many stories for high-paying magazines. By the end of his career he had published 178 such stories, including some written with or by Zelda. So long as Scott's name appeared as author, the stories commanded fees of up to $4,000 each. Yet, as though uncontrolled, the Fitzgeralds ran through this income so quickly that they were often broke.

Fitzgerald's 1925 novel, *The Great Gatsby*—a smaller financial success than his earlier fiction but a greater critical one—is a testimony both to Fitzgerald's seriousness about his writing and to his increased understanding of the directions that modern fiction was taking. The craft of the novel—its remarkable economy and its disciplined attention to details that acquire symbolic significance—marks it as a remarkable advance. In many ways, Fitzgerald's themes went back to his beginning in *This Side of Paradise*, with its concern for "a new generation grown up to find all Gods dead, all wars fought, all faiths in men shaken." But there were important differences in technique. Like Joseph Conrad in his Marlow stories and Cather in *A Lost Lady*, Fitzgerald here uses Nick Carraway as the narrative consciousness for Gatsby's story and thereby gives the reader contrasting perspectives that call both Gatsby's and Nick's motivations into question. The complex texture and structure of this short novel about the tragic consequences of America's naïve optimism make it evocative beyond its length.

Somewhat defeated by the relatively moderate praise that greeted *The Great Gatsby*, Fitzgerald retreated. It would be nine years before he published his fourth novel, *Tender Is the Night*. Debilitated by his drinking and his constant debt, Fitzgerald had difficulty facing his personal feelings of social inferiority. He was, after all, Midwestern, Irish, and Catholic and he would never be mistaken for someone who was an integral part of Ivy League culture. As his classmate Edmund Wilson wrote, Fitzgerald "has an instinct for graceful and vivid prose that some of his more pretentious fellows might envy." (Gertrude Stein, too, recognized the lithe surety of Fitzgerald as wordsmith—his was a skill that could be encouraged but it could not be taught.) In Wilson's analysis, Fitzgerald brings to his writing a sensibility that is "not Anglo-Saxon. For, like the Irish, Fitzgerald is romantic . . . . He casts himself in the role of playboy, yet at the playboy he incessantly mocks. He is vain, a little malicious, of quick intelligence and wit, and has an Irish gift for turning language into something iridescent and surprising" (Wilson *Axel's Castle* 32–3).

Often referred to as a romantic, Fitzgerald developed the tactic of creating a sense of non-reality—or of combining the real and the persuasively unreal. Even though the story of James Gatz, a man who has made himself into "the great Gatsby," is far from romantic, Fitzgerald embeds romantic moments within the narrative. The first sight Nick has of Daisy and Jordan, for instance, is not only other worldly; it is evanescent.

Lawrence Buell, in his 2014 study, *The Dream of the Great American Novel*, describes one set of conventions that people have used to cast *The Great Gatsby* in that niche—of a romantic treatment of a traditional American dream. Buell states, "The long-embedded assumption of the United States as a project in the making, forever grasping after—and fighting about—the elusive promise of freedom, equal rights, equal respect for all" (Buell 463). In a work that capitalizes on what Buell calls "enshrinement by reinvention," *Gatsby* offers readers any number of strong characters. Glossed by Kathleen Drowne's reading of the way Prohibition and its resulting crime undergirds plot in Fitzgerald's novel, other recent commentators have brought to the work interesting discussions of class. John F. Lavelle, for example,

---

EXCERPT FROM *THE GREAT GATSBY*

We walked through a high hallway into a bright rosy-colored space, fragilely bound into the house by French windows at either end. The windows were ajar and gleaming white against the fresh grass outside that seemed to grow a little way into the house. A breeze blew through the room, blew curtains in at one end and out the other like pale flags, twisting them up toward the frosted wedding-cake of the ceiling, and then rippled over the wine-colored rug, making a shadow on it as wind does on the sea.

The only completely stationary object in the room was an enormous couch on which two young women were buoyed up as through upon an anchored balloon. They were both in white, and their dresses were rippling and fluttering as if they had just been blown back in after a short flight around the house. I must have stood for a few moments listening to the whip and snap of the curtains and the groan of a picture on the wall. Then there was a boom as Tom Buchanan shut the rear windows and the caught wind died out about the room, and the curtains and the rugs and the two young women ballooned slowly to the floor . . . .

---

comments on what he calls "social fields." In *Gatsby*, according to this critic, such fields are "many, intricate, and blur into one another. Nick associates with Tom and Daisy within their field through performativity and emulation spurred only by his ideology of privilege." Because of their birth and family position, he (and Jordan) are accepted as subordinates.

This top level of society is, however, a "group under siege" (Lavelle 234). American fiction has never been about the very wealthy; it more often takes as its province the underdog, if not the underclass. Its focus highlights the middle class. In *The Great Gatsby*, there are many variations of the middle class.

> Nick is a member, separated by the same discourses as those separating East and West Egg. George Wilson's wife, Myrtle, after meeting Tom on the train, has pretensions of moving into a higher class than her husband might provide by acquiring from Tom the economic ability to assume the signs of higher classes. Myrtle's acquaintances at the apartment Tom has rented for their liaisons are mostly of the middle class, yet of a different middle class than Nick. The group, including Myrtle, is oblivious of the fact that money . . . will not gain them access to Nick's middle class . . . . The characters in Tom and Myrtle's apartment speak of what they *do*, rather than who they *are* . . . . They are upstarts, as is Myrtle, and, . . . misinterpret not only the signs of class but also the correct way of producing the signs of class, a sign in itself.
>
> *Lavelle 232–3*

Myrtle sees the dog as one of these elevating signs: she does not understand the bases, or the functions, of class.

Lavelle sees Fitzgerald's novel as a way of exposing the fallacies of class superiority. Once Gatsby is dead—even before his death, Nick learns that neither Daisy nor Tom is in any way morally superior. In Nick's efforts to give Gatsby a respectable funeral, he aligns himself with the striving that motivated Gatsby's life: Nick wants to be as honest as Gatsby has been. Gatsby becomes the fresh and idealistic America/American (despite his life of crime), an image for the views of the Dutch sailors. Like Wilson and his father, Jay Gatsby believes in an equalitarian America—a person can, through effort, succeed. Through the events of *The Great Gatsby*, Fitzgerald shows the ineffective rationale that "privileged" beliefs—those held by not only Tom and Daisy but also by Jordan and Nick—provide for modern Americans.

Fitzgerald's *Gatsby* was the instructive American novel, through which readers could judge their own morality and empathy. He could call into question some of the verities that Sinclair Lewis was drawing as fact in his *Main Street* and *Babbitt*, and know—or at least hope—that his readers would appreciate his skepticism. In Lavelle's terms, one could say that the social fields of *Main Street* and *Babbitt* are much narrower than the panoply of those fields within *Gatsby*.

In this regard, Richard Gray notes that Fitzgerald's use of Nick as narrator enables him to "maintain a balance [between] the idealist, the romantic who believed in perfectability and the pragmatist, the realist convinced that life is nasty, brutish, and short." The book's "alternating rhythm of action and meditation" provided openings for all kinds of readers. But what remains after the experience of reading *The Great Gatsby* is the sense that

> Gatsby believed in an ideal of Edenic innocence and perfection . . . . So did America. Gatsby tried to make the future an imitation of some mythic past. So did America. Gatsby tried to inform his life into an ideal, that strangely mixed the mystic and the material. So did America. Gatsby's dream is, in effect, the American dream.
>
> *Gray 198–9*

No critic denies that it was the contextual trappings of Gatsby's life that first attracted readers. As Frederick Lewis Allen explained about the early 1920s in the United States, "the revolution in manners and morals were all 100 percent American. They were prohibition, the automobile, the confession and sex magazines, and the movies" (Allen 90). What Gatsby's parties provided readers was echoed by Hollywood films (it is no accident that Fitzgerald enjoyed writing for the movies)—celebrity culture, even if it was not labeled as such then, gave readers a way out of mundane and sometimes restricting lives. The automobile began the process of sexualizing male-female relationships, foreshadowing the kinds of freedoms the pill would provide decades later, and added to the behaviors of thousands of American women, for whom experience provided safeguards of all kinds. (Zelda herself epitomized that adventurous American girl, though she defined herself as a

New Woman and a belle rather than as a flapper.) Much of the heart of *The Great Gatsby* is imaged in Daisy—both her retrospective scene of trying to delay marrying Tom and crying over Gatsby's letter as it falls into wet shreds in her bath, and her euphoric statements ("Do you always watch for the longest day of the year and then miss it? I always watch for the longest day in the year and then miss it" [Fitzgerald *Gatsby* 12]).

Readers do not question that Gatsby is motivated by his pure, idealized love for this woman. By a stroke of genius, Fitzgerald saw that the American dream belonged, in its most intense form, not to the respectable, the educated, and the sensitive Nick Carraway, but rather to a fugitive, an outsider, a man born without any pedigree but with a great capacity for hope. In Gatsby, Fitzgerald shut down the naturalists' theories even as he used some of their methods and thus created a new version of the outrageous lowborn, even criminal, American "hero." Gatsby may well be descended from that earlier lowborn, Huck Finn. But Fitzgerald's creation is a new protagonist of great force who brings America's established social codes into direct confrontation with conflicting codes of human behavior, belief systems, and class.

By 1937 Fitzgerald was so ill from the effects of his alcoholism—and his sorrowful realization that his beloved Zelda would not ever fully recover from the breakdowns that had plagued her life for the entire decade—that writing had become almost impossible for him. When he died in December 1940 at the age of forty-four, after several heart attacks, he was struggling to complete *The Last Tycoon*. The seriousness of his vision in both *Tender Is the Night* (1934), the complex narrative of a psychiatrist and the woman he both loves and fears, and *The Last Tycoon*, a story about Hollywood life, demonstrated again how far Fitzgerald had moved from his early aim of, simply, making good money by writing about his culture. The gravity of his personal predicament comes through even more directly, however, in "The Crack-Up," a three-part essay that appeared in *Esquire* in 1936. As if Gatsby has returned to speak for his own lost promise, Fitzgerald's voice here is less modern than it is nostalgic.

Critic Timothy Galow summarizes the decline of Fitzgerald's writing, and life, during the 1930s, [Fitzgerald]

> was repeatedly connected with the distant glamour of the 1920s and did not produce enough work, or grab enough headlines, to significantly modify the public's opinion of him. In such a context, Fitzgerald's scattered meditations on his past persona and the difficulties of producing quality writing only worked to reinforce the sense that the author's best writing was behind him. By 1936, even those critics and writers who knew that Fitzgerald possessed a keen literary mind had a hard time seeing the "Crack-Up" essays as anything more than an embarrassing admission of failure or a desperate grab for attention.
>
> *Galow 164*

To add to this assessment, one might connect these last unexpected essays to what Fitzgerald had achieved—perhaps unknowingly—in *The Great Gatsby*: for the writer who lived to write, and to love, the loss of both his passions left little but the ache of loss, along with the sobering recognition that, in Gatsby's words, "'Can't repeat the past?'....'Why of course you can!'" In the romance of F. Scott Fitzgerald's life and work, only a few moments of greatness lit the darkness of his last decade.

Faulkner and Wolfe: the world of the South

If readers in the 1920s were fascinated by the exotic, the American South might have been seen as one compelling source of interest. Yet, aside from H. L. Mencken's 1917 essay "The Sahara of the Bozart," the literary world paid that quarter of the United States little attention. Given the influence of Mencken—in not only his essays and books but his reviews and columns, it may be that this seminal essay put the kibosh on serious considerations of Southern writing. Mencken closes this essay by noting,

> it is impossible for intelligence to flourish in such an atmosphere. Free inquiry is blocked by the idiotic certainties of ignorant men. The arts, save in the lower reaches of the gospel hymn, the phonograph and the Chautauqua harangue, are all held in suspicion. The tone of public opinion is set by an upstart class but lately emerged from industrial slavery into commercial enterprise—the class of "hustling" business men, of "live wires," of "drive" managers . . . in brief, of third-rate southerners inoculated with all the worst traits of the Yankee sharper.

As the paragraph continues, Mencken mourns what he calls "the old romanticism" and "an old tradition of chivalry." If F. Scott Fitzgerald was trying to overcome his pedigree of being Irish, Catholic, and Midwestern, William Falkner (later changed to the spelling of *Faulkner*) was faced with his outright lack of any college experience, or connections, and his all too obvious Southernness.

Relegated to a territory of old conventions, of racism, of stigmatizations of inferiority that losing the Civil War conveyed, the South had been so torn through Reconstruction that industrial prosperity had—for the most part—fled north. The paucity of good roads and air conditioning meant that few people who knew such modern comforts chose to abandon them: and those that were attracted by the climate and the beauty of the Southern natural world harbored irrational fears of such exclusively Southern elements as angry African Americans or, more logically, the Ku Klux Klan (made vivid through D. W. Griffith's 1915 film, *The Birth of a Nation*, based on Thomas Dixon's 1905 *The Clansman*). For those would-be writers born to Southern families and living in small Southern towns, when they wrote about their environs, readers felt some sense of cliché. In critic Joseph Allen Boone's words, in the twentieth century "the defeated and divided state of the South becomes a microcosm for the post-World War I Eliotic wasteland itself" (Boone 302).

Susan V. Donaldson has recently written, adding to C. Vann Woodward's classic 1960 *The Burden of Southern History*, that all writing about the South must begin with the Civil War and the South's resounding defeat (Donaldson 266). It is Donaldson who points out that Faulkner could have been supported by the

Vanderbilt Fugitive-Agrarian group (Donald Davidson, Robert Penn Warren, Cleanth Brooks, and Allen Tate), white Southern men who developed a powerful academic influence through both their poetry journal (*The Fugitive*, published in the early 1920s) and their 1930 Agrarian manifesto, "I'll Take My Stand." Given Faulkner's lack of academic connections, the Vanderbilt cadre might have brought his fiction to the literary world—as it had supported Eudora Welty's writing and their own powerful poetry and fiction. But Faulkner's tendency to move away from the romantic, nostalgic Southern world—exemplified in his characterizations of Quentin Compson in his *The Sound and the Fury*—lost their respect.[3] In this critic's summary, Faulkner's novels seemed intent on repudiating what the Fugitives stood for. In *Sanctuary, As I Lay Dying, Light in August, Absalom, Absalom!, Pylon, The Hamlet,* and *Go Down, Moses,* the writer "began to address issues of race, racialization, segregation, and eventually slavery on a level that almost immediately set him apart from Agrarian politics" (Donaldson 275).

David Minter, too, notes this possible connection—describing the fact that

> In villages, where the South still lived in 1929, they had observed people who lived in slow time and acquired a sense of sequence and shared know-ledge. But they had also seen history batter people with failures and defeats, leaving them with the sense of being entangled in many stories whose beginnings and endings were hazy.
>
> *Minter 256*[4]

Born in Jefferson, Mississippi, in 1897, Faulkner was unquestionably a son of the South. The oldest of four children, all boys, he very naturally seemed obsessed with his region—he asked for stories about histories, especially those that included his ancestors; he probed people's memories for details about each happening. All writers start with their early years in their imaginative reservoir—their recollections and experiences from childhood—because it provides the detailed and accurate fabric of their memory. Faulkner was no exception to this pattern, although he later spent some months in New Orleans, New York, and Paris, plundering those cities and the friendships he made for non-Mississippi information. And his brief experience in the Canadian military gave him more fodder for his own sometimes implausible recollections of "experience."

Wherever he was, Faulkner was more of a listener than he was a story teller. When Sherwood Anderson portrayed his young southern friend in his short story, this was the characterization he chose to use. And when Faulkner described Anderson's influence on him, he then told the story of Anderson's advice:

> to be a writer, one has first got to be what he is, what he was born . . . . You have to be somewhere to start from: then you begin to learn. You're a country boy; all you know is that little patch up there in Mississippi where you started from. But that's all right too. It's America too.
>
> *Faulkner Essays 8*

There was much that Faulkner loved about the South. He recalled having told people that the South was "the only really authentic region in the United States, because a deep indestructible bond still exists between man and his environment" (Faulkner *Lion* 72). Whether he hunted in that natural world that surrounded him, or paused to appreciate its flowering spring trees, Faulkner was deeply aware of that world—whether it ran wild or was cultivated; whether it existed on his own land or in his mother's carefully tended garden.

Economically, he had little choice but to remain in Mississippi. Both because of his lack of education and his temperament, Faulkner had few employment credentials. Because of the interest of his friend Phil Stone, practicing law and willing to spend his money to buy the newest books of interest,[5] Faulkner read voraciously, and then part of his reading led him to explore his own ancestry more deeply. He immersed himself in the tales of Civil War bravery (as well as World War I stories), of the lives of Southern land owners, of his grandfather the somewhat famous novelist. He also knew the stories of African American Caroline Barr and her family, juxtaposed with the white Southern tales his mother told him. This continuing stream of story may be one of the reasons that he visited his mother nearly every afternoon that he lived at Rowan Oak (see Sensibar, Blotner, Gray, R.).

When Faulkner lost his Estelle after she married a successful businessman, his real-world inabilities became clear and the self-glamorization (of himself as returning war hero and poet) more visible. He was clear-sighted about himself: a failed post office worker, a not very enthusiastic house painter, a man dependent on his family for financial support—no wonder the historical narratives of his family glowed in comparison. Being small, being somewhat effeminate in an age that valued prize-fighting and "masculine" interests, "Billy" was unusually emotionally dependent on his family's support, especially his mother's. One of the motivations for his learning to fly—witness both his volunteering for the Canadian air corps and his private flying, a pastime to which he indoctrinated his beloved youngest brother, John—was to achieve that macho quality that nature had withheld.

Before people recognized the study of anthropology or the social sciences, Faulkner was compiling an archive of Southern stories. Obviously, the Southern tendency to aggrandize the past, particularly the Civil War past, came easily to him. This tendency to romanticize history began with early eighteenth century existence and ended before World War I—it made him cognizant of social and religious customs, and he drew from both literary and narrative information as he developed his own sense of the leisurely, aesthetically pleasing Mississippi (that was, clearly, no longer in existence). As Faulkner traced the frightening mortality of war in his first novel, *Soldiers' Pay*, and the aesthetic community made real in his second, *Mosquitoes*, he embellished both with seemingly digressive passages that reflect his carefully-acquired knowledge about the South.

William Faulkner spent nearly fifteen years of his life writing poems. His persistence in learning a largely romantic style of poetics is illustrated by the fact that in all those years he published only one poem. But he was composing books of his poems, treating their juxtaposition into texts as if they were narratives, searching through his sometimes ornate description and use of language for *story*.

Very seldom during these years did Faulkner write in free verse; his conception of good poetry was formal, marked by imagery that might sometimes rhyme—but more often, not.

> Soft hands of skies
>
> Delicately swung the narrow moon above him
> And shivered the tops of trees . . . .

Often, descriptions of the natural world carry entire Faulkner poems. Many of these appear in Carvel Collins' edition of Faulkner's early poems. In that same edition, Collins quotes Faulkner's query in the midst of his rejection of the world view (and the form, or lack of it) of both Eliot's *The Waste Land* and Pound's *Mauberley*:

> Is there nowhere among us a Keats in embryo, someone who will tune his lute to the beauty of the world? Life is not different from what it was when Shelley drove like a swallow southward from the unbearable English winter . . . . Here is the same air, the same sunlight in which Shelley dreamed of golden men and women immortal in a silver world . . . . Is not there among us someone who can write something beautiful and passionate and sad instead of saddening?
>
> *in Collins 118*

As Faulkner's poems themselves progressed, his interest in characterization became more evident: poetry is often a difficult vehicle for that mode. Robert Browning had chosen one tactic in his dramatic monologues; Edwin Arlington Robinson, a less ambitious other. Faulkner's own poems showed that he knew the work of each writer, but that he was still searching for a poetic form that would allow him to create complex figures. At times he equated characters with the natural world, as in "A Poplar,"

> Why do you shiver there
> Between the white river and the road?
> You are not cold,
> With the sun light dreaming about you;
> And yet you lift your pliant supplicating arms as though
> To draw clouds from the sky to hide your slenderness.
>
> You are a young girl
> Trembling in the throes of ecstatic modesty,
> A white objective girl
> Whose clothing has been forcibly taken away from her.
>
> *in Collins 60*

Faulkner's sense of the Orient in this opening suggests his familiarity with Pound, and the poem then builds through image after image in the best Imagist manner.

After such work as this in the early 1920s, Faulkner continued to rely on imagery as he created narratives from separable poem sequences. In Poem III of *A Green Bough*, for example, he equated the woman he loves with music:

> The cave is ribbed with music; threads of sound
> Gleam on the whirring wings of bars of gold
> Loop from the grassroots to the roots of trees
> Thrust into sunlight, where the song of birds
> Spins silver threads to gleam from bough to bough.
> Grass in meadows cools his fancy's feet:
> Dew is on the grass, and birds in hedges
> Weave the sunlight with sharp streaks of flight,
> Bees break apple bloom, and peach and clover
> Sing in the southern air where aimless clouds
> Go up the sky-hill, cropping it like sheep,
> And startled pigeons, like a wind beginning,
> Fill the air with sucking silver sound.
>
> *18–19*

Between Faulkner's publication of his 1924 *The Marble Faun* collection and the 1933 *A Green Bough*, he expressed much of his consistent view about Imagist poetry (calling it "a tide of aesthetic sterility," which he illustrated by mentioning "Mr. Vachel Lindsay with his tin pan and iron spoon . . . Mr. Carl Sandburg with his sentimental Chicago propaganda") ("Turns and Movies" 1921). Perhaps his real answer for the trendiness of the most modern of American poetry was the sheer excellence he managed to create in the sequenced poems of *A Green Bough*. Throughout that collection, Faulkner attained what is a more pervasive rhythm for him; his longer-lined poems allow space for characterization. Rather than a two or three-line image, Faulkner in many of these poems uses an entire stanza to build a single effect.

Biographer Judith Sensibar makes a strong case for Faulkner's having learned the essentials of writing good prose from his collecting poems into meaningful sequences. One might also mention as part of his progression the series of fifteen sketches he published in the New Orleans *Times-Picayune* (from January to September of 1925). Varied topics handled in germane ways, Faulkner's sketches about characters both exotic and common are reminiscent of early prose by both Hemingway and Dos Passos. In every case, the writers knew that what they had learned from writing poetry would be relevant.

By 1925, Dos Passos had completed not only *One Man's Initiation-1917*, *Three Soldiers*, *Streets of Night*, and his poem collection *A Pushcart at the Curb* but also *Manhattan Transfer*. Hemingway had published single poems and stories, the lower-case *in our time* and the Liveright *In Our Time*, and was working on the novel that would become *The Sun Also Rises*. Sinclair Lewis had shared the prestige of popular novels with F. Scott Fitzgerald—Lewis's *Main Street* and *Babbitt* not only being best sellers, but films—and Fitzgerald's *This Side of Paradise* and *The Beautiful and Damned*, best sellers, with *The Great Gatsby* marking a diminishment of that writer's attraction. The long-lasting Sherwood Anderson had increased his popularity, following the 1919 publication of *Winesburg, Ohio* with *The Triumph of the Egg, Many Marriages*, and *Dark Laughter*. Book sales show the popularity of such women writers as Edith Wharton (*The Age of Innocence* in 1920, *The Glimpses of the Moon* in 1922, *A Son at the Front* in 1923, *Old New York* in 1924, and *A Mother's Recompense* in 1925), Anzia Yezierska (*Hungry Hearts* in 1920 and *Bread Givers* in 1925), Evelyn Scott's *The Narrow House* in 1921, Elinor Wylie's *Jennifer Lorn* in 1923, Edith Summers Kelley's *Weeds* in 1923, Ellen Glasgow's *One Man in His Time* in 1922 and *Barren Ground* in 1925, and Cather's *A Lost Lady* and *The Professor's House* in 1923 and 1925 respectively, following *One of Ours* in 1922.

In the midst of this flurry of book publication, William Faulkner had only his self-published poem collection, *The Marble Faun*, to show. Energies are at work, however, and it is in 1926 that Boni & Liveright (Anderson's publisher) brings out Faulkner's first novel, *Soldiers' Pay*. In 1927 they also publish *Mosquitoes*. Sales, however, are scant, and Faulkner seemed to be less involved in writing about the war wounded and New Orleans' artistic communities than he might be. With *Sartoris*, his first Southern novel and the first in which Faulkner appeared to have listened to Anderson's advice, he changed publishers. In 1929 Harcourt, Brace brings out *Sartoris*. Faulkner then moved to Cape & Smith for the publication of both *The Sound and the Fury* in 1929 and *As I Lay Dying* in 1930. It was a frantic effort—to create fiction that used every word, every sign, in the service of Faulkner's distinctively accurate characterizations—and he hardly had time to notice what else was happening in the literary world, either internationally or within the United States.

Throughout his early sketches and novels (with stories to come later, reversing the pattern that had been effective for both Fitzgerald and Hemingway), Faulkner seemed driven to create interesting women figures. The center of *Soldiers' Pay*, for instance, becomes Margaret Powers, who shepherds home the tragically wounded Lieutenant Mahon. "Impersonal, self-contained," Powers breaks all conventions for a woman (one who has lost her own love to battle) existing in postwar civilization. Even though her key quality is empathy, Faulkner describes her as someone Aubrey Beardsley would have "sickened for," a striking woman whose beauty attracts everyone but whose chief quality is strength. Powers' conversation with Joe Gilligan about the irrelevance of a woman's reputation foreshadows the attitudes of other women Faulkner created—Addie Bundren, Caddie Compson, Lena Grove, Eula Snopes, Jenny Du Pre and many others.

> "They'll think you are one of them French what-do-you-call-'ems the Loot brought back with him. Your good name won't be worth nothing after these folks get through with it."

"My good name is your trouble, not mine, Joe."

"My trouble? How you mean?"

"Men are the ones who worry about our good names, because they gave them to us. But we have other things to bother about, ourselves. What you mean by a good name is like a dress that's too flimsy to wear comfortably."

Faulkner Pay 104–5

Margaret Powers's attitudes suggest those of other Faulkner protagonists. Addie Bundren's scathing monologue about the ineffectuality of words is here prefigured in Powers's rebuff of Januarius Jones: "Let me give you some advice . . . the next time you try to seduce anyone, don't do it with talk, with words. Women know more about words than men ever will. And they know how little they can ever possibly mean" (Faulkner *Pay* 250). Faulkner's women are people who act: they sell mules, dig up graves, care for the disabled, and marry wounded soldiers—and they know that their personal willingness to act is superior to the rhetoric of men. As Margaret Powers explains to Gilligan, "I just happened to be the first woman you ever knew doing something you thought only a man would do. You had nice fixed ideas about women and I upset them" (Faulkner *Pay* 161).

If there is any pattern in Faulkner's characterizations of women, it is that women are never to be stereotyped. Faulkner's women are both unexpected and unpredictable. Jason Compson intends to malign them when he claims that he will never understand them, but Faulkner's presentations show his own personal incredulity—at women's bravery, humor, realism, unselfishness, and love. As he says about Southern women in *The Unvanquished*, each one is "incorrigibly individual."

One of the best-drawn women characters in Faulkner's early fiction remains Caddy Compson, the sister who is never given a voice. The three sections of *The Sound and the Fury* that preface the conclusion are given over to the vacant voicelessness of the non-speaking Benjy, then to Quentin's disoriented yet effusive expressions, and finally to Jason's terse action-oriented solutions. Throughout these separate sections runs the voice (always heard second-hand) and the actions (always purposeful) of the problematic sister, Candace. For her, nagged by a suspicious and unfeeling mother, life is a set battle. As a child, Caddy provides the only love Benjy is ever to know; as an adolescent, she understands Quentin's anguish better than he does himself; as an adult, she is motivated only by her love for her daughter—named *Quentin* for her older brother—and she consequently becomes a pawn in Jason's manipulations. Like a younger and less confident Margaret Powers, Caddy is the victim of a social morality that considers the state of a woman's hymen the only important index to her value. Charity, love *per se* is worthless; and the Compson family completes its final somersault to damnation because it condemns its one caring child.

The real tragedy of Caddy's life is not so much her isolation and the bleakness of her existence, Faulkner's fiction suggests; it is rather than she has had so little effect on anyone. Quentin and Mr. Compson are dead; Jason lives largely to torment her and her child; Mrs. Compson muddles the girl Quentin's life just as she had Caddy's; Benjy can only wail—no one has learned to love, or to cope, from her example.

Reading *The Sound and the Fury*, keyed as it is to the dangers of Shakespeare's *Macbeth*, the self-aggrandisement of Jason Compson becomes the horrifying center of the novel. Faulkner's intricate arrangement of both chronological time and Biblical (shaping all important events around the Good Friday-Easter weekend of 1928, making readers flashback to all four of the children's earlier years and then, in Part II, to the day of Quentin's suicide his freshman year at Harvard, June 2, 1910) has both bewildered and intrigued readers for the past eighty years. Reading *The Sound and the Fury* evokes Henri Bergson's meditations about time and its value (or lack of value), and allows readers to understand Virginia Woolf's concept that lives are centered around what she called "moments of being," images of acts that shape all parts of people's lives.

This most intricate of Faulkner's modern fictions spoke to his personal relinquishment—he was sure no publisher would bring out this difficult work; he was sure no library would buy it; he was sure it would find no readers. Having given up, he then wrote everything he thought necessary to tell the Compson story. The structural juxtapositions, the flamboyant creations of individual characters, the resonating scenes of dialogue, above all, the relentless descriptions of pain—Faulkner's novel worked, as he had intended, as a testament to his unique understanding of human misalliances. As he wrote in an unpublished essay,

> One day I seemed to shut a door between me and all publishers' addresses and book lists. I said to myself, Now I can write. Now I can make myself a vase like that which the old Roman kept at his bedside and wore the rim slowly away with kissing it. So I, who had never had a sister and was fated to lose my daughter in infancy, set out to make myself a beautiful and tragic little girl.
>
> Virginia archive

To study the hand-written manuscript of *The Sound and the Fury* at the University of Virginia Alderman Library is to note how perfectly the book had flowed from Faulkner's hand. What he added once the novel is begun is more description of the way the men playing golf appear to Benjy's limited view. "Plot" rather than tone or import is what needed to be expanded.

To read Faulkner's *The Sound and the Fury* as another exemplary modernist text is to lean more heavily on the author's actual prose. With Hemingway, readers could view a dialogue scene as a pro forma "image" and could then drain out all kinds of meaning from the interchange. But with Faulkner's writing, the *manner* in which the author contextualized those dialogue scenes was, in many cases, as significant as what the scenes themselves conveyed. For example, Part III of *The Sound and the Fury* ("Jason's section") begins abruptly with that character's voicing of his misanthropic behavior:

> Once a bitch always a bitch, what I say. I says you're lucky if her playing out of school is all that worries you. I says she ought to be down there in that

kitchen right now, instead of up there in her room, gobbing paint on her face and waiting for six niggers that cant even stand up out of a chair unless they've got a pan full of bread and meat to balance them, to fix breakfast for her . . . .

Faulkner Fury *180*

As Jason rants about Caddy's daughter, Quentin, transferring all his anger at his sister onto his niece, Faulkner's skill in replicating "redneck" insults—to both women and African Americans—images that character's violent demeanor. In studied and effective contrast, Part II of the novel, which presents Quentin's last day alive, opens,

---

EXCERPT FROM WILLIAM FAULKNER'S *THE SOUND AND THE FURY* (MANUSCRIPT)

Through the fence, between the curling flower spaces, I could see them hitting.
 Then they came on toward where the flag was and I went along the fence. I passed where T. P. was leaning against the flower [tree?]. Then they stopped hitting where the flag was and Ike [they] went to the table and hit again and went in. I went along the fence and T. P. came away from the flower tree.
 "Here, Caddy," one of them said.
 The boy came to him and then he hit again and went along the fence . . . .

EXCERPT FROM WILLIAM FAULKNER'S *THE SOUND AND THE FURY* (PRINT VERSION)

Through the fence, between the curling flower spaces, I could see them hitting.
 They were coming toward where the flag was and I went along the fence. Luster was hunting in the grass by the flower tree. They took the flag out, and they were hitting. Then they put the flag back and they went to the table, and he hit and the other hit. Then they went on, and I went along the fence. Luster came away from the flower tree and we went along the fence and they stopped and we stopped and I looked through the fence while Luster was hunting in the grass.
 "Here, caddie." He hit. They went away across the pasture. I held to the fence and watched them going away.
 "Listen at you, now." Luster said. "Aint you something, thirty-three years old, going on that way. After I done went all the way to town to buy you that cake. Hush up that moaning. Aint you going to help me find that quarter so I can go to the show tonight."

When the shadow of the sash appeared on the curtains it was between seven and eight oclock and then I was in time again, hearing the watch. It was Grandfather's and when Father gave it to me he said I give you the mausoleum of all hope and desire, it's rather excruciatingly apt that you will use it to gain the reducto absurdum of all human experience which can fit your individual needs no better than it fitted his or his father's. I give it to you not that you may remember time, but that you might forget it now and then for a moment and not spend all your breath trying to conquer it. Because no battle is ever won he said . . . .

Faulkner Fury 76

Solipsistic as Quentin's memories of the language of his learned father (a man now drowning in his alcoholism) may be, the sonority of great words, great ideas, has effectively stunted his own personal growth. Just as Quentin cannot read the numerals on the watch, neither can he understand what literal words, here, mean. Although he stays alive until he has been at Harvard nearly the full year, respecting the financial sacrifices his father has made to send him north, Quentin is a man without a firm place in any country—and it takes Faulkner until the end of his second "Quentin" novel, *Absalom, Absalom!* in 1936, to make clear the boy's love-hate relationship with the South. (Quentin there replies to his Canadian Harvard roommate Shreve, when he asks him why he hates the South, "'I dont hate it,' Quentin said, quickly, at once, immediately; 'I dont hate it,' he said. *I dont hate it* he thought, panting in the cold air, the iron New England dark: *I dont. I dont! I dont hate it! I dont hate it!*'" (Faulkner *Absalom* 303).

One of the painfully dominant themes that had come to occupy Faulkner's writing by the time of *Absalom, Absalom!* was the tendency of nearly all Southerners to denigrate other people on the bases of either gender or race. Dilsey Gibson's role within *The Sound and the Fury* signaled Faulkner's view, that the African Americans employed by Southern whites held families together: "They endured," as the author emphasized in his late-added glossary to that novel. After he had written a different kind of novel in *As I Lay Dying*, capturing what he consistently saw as Southern humor in Anse Bundren's always inappropriate behavior, he returned to questions of race, or the impossibility of either discovering—or under-standing—a character's racial make-up. In *Light in August*, the character Joe Christmas was never shown to be either African American or Mexican—but all promise for his life was ruined because of the dark shade of his skin. Faulkner in this novel emphasizes the ignorance of the Southern townspeople as they hunt and kill Christmas: more importantly, he places the "story" of inherent and vicious racism within a larger context.

The philosophical Faulkner appears as early as 1932, and continues—largely through the more abstract contextualizations of the characaters' action. Reversing the sense that "meaning" could accrue from scattered and separable images, in most of his 1930s novels Faulkner gave readers passages that were not only memorable, but quotable.

EXCERPT FROM WILLIAM FAULKNER'S *LIGHT IN AUGUST*

Memory believes before knowing remembers. Believes longer than recollects, longer than knowing even wonders. Knows remembers believes a corridor in a big long garbled cold echoing building of dark red brick sootbleakened by more chimneys than its own, set in a grassless cinderstrewnpacked compound surrounded by smoking factory purlieus and enclosed by a ten foot *steel-and-wire* fence like a penitentiary or a zoo, where in random erratic surges, with sparrowlike childtrebling, orphans in identical and uniform blue denim in and out of remembering but in knowing constant as the bleak walls, the bleak windows where in rain soot from the yearly adjacenting chimneys streaked like black tears.

In the quiet and empty corridor, during the quiet hour of early afternoon, he was like a shadow, small even for five years, sober and quiet as a shadow. Another in the corridor could not have said just when and where he vanished, into what door, what room. But there was no one else in the corridor at this hour. He knew that. He had been doing this for almost a year, ever since the day when he discovered by accident the toothpaste which the dietitian used . . . .

Never timorous about his convictions, Faulkner wrote and wrote and wrote about racism unbridled: his passion was, first, to show meaningful family relations in practice, saving lives of promising children, helping to right the wrongs of the post-Civil War South; and second, to show the poisons that the culture's splenetic racism spewed into all kinds of families, all kinds of belief systems. It is probably no accident that Faulkner arranged his studied composition of those black lives and white in his 1942 novel, *Go Down, Moses*: misleadingly termed a collection of stories, the book was always a forceful novel, and its publication came soon after the death of Caroline Barr. Beloved by Faulkner, held to totemic significance because of her devoted love for the four Faulkner boys, Caroline Barr was the essential piece in Faulkner's transformation of the "African American" Lucas Beauchamp into a "white" ancestor, set against the renunciatory Ike McCaslin but capable of living his own male life without approval from white Southern culture.

Paired with Faulkner's 1948 novel, *Intruder in the Dust* (a continuation of sorts of the Lucas Beauchamp narrative), *Go Down, Moses* was the clearest description of the contradictory racism that bifurcated the South. After Faulkner's death, both these novels grew in importance. Critics began to see anticipations of Faulkner's critique of patterns of uneasy black-white lineage (for example, among Judith, Clytie, and Miss Rosa in *Absalom, Absalom!*) And they began to stop quibbling about what a story like "Pantaloon in Black" was doing in *Go Down, Moses* at all: the story of Rider's bereavement after his young wife's death is the closest Faulkner ever comes in any of this fiction to sharing pain. In this provocative section, the author's psyche—like Rider's—walks a narrow line between sanity and madness, trapped in life by the very strength that has provided its former balance. Here Rider becomes the surrogate for the author himself, bereft of both Caroline Barr and his brother John.

It was in 1947 that Ernest Hemingway wrote to Faulkner—acknowledging that he owned all Faulkner's novels, and attempting to give him the highest praise. Hemingway begins with his reservations about the fiction of John Dos Passos, but the heart of the letter deals with Faulkner:

> "Dos I always liked and respected and thought was a second rate writer on account of no ear. Second rate boxer has no left hand, same as ear to writer, and so gets his brains knocked out and this happens to Dos with every book . . . ." "You are a better writer than Fielding . . . and you should know it and keep on writing. You have things written that have come back to me better than any of them . . . . You should always write your best against dead writers that we know what stature (not stature: evocative power) that they have and beat them one by one . . . . Beat Turgenieff—which we both did soundly . . . . You and I can both beat Flaubert who is our most respected, honored master . . . ."
>
> *Hemingway* Letters *623–4*

Hemingway's clear effusion was unexpected (and may have been prompted, too, by his realization that Fitzgerald was now long dead), but both Hemingway and Faulkner had regularly spoken about the accomplishments of one another. It is in Faulkner's infamous "list" of America's great writers that he places Hemingway fifth, after himself. The list runs, privileging Thomas Wolfe as number one, creating a "splendid magnificent book" as he tried to "put the whole history of the human heart on the head of a pin." The second writer on Faulkner's list was Erskine Caldwell (perhaps for his sense of the humor of Southern living); the third was John Dos Passos, and the fourth was Faulkner himself (Faulkner *Lion* 81).

Not surprisingly, Thomas Wolfe's *Look Homeward, Angel*, published by Scribner's in 1929 (so that critics paired it with Faulkner's *The Sound and the Fury*) in itself gave Wolfe a permanent place among America's modernist writers. Judging from his modest notes and postcards to his mother—during the two years he was writing the book in longhand, the year it was then being typed by one of his former students, and the months that Max Perkins was seeing it through the production process, Wolfe did not understand that his novel might change his life. (Living in Asheville, North Carolina, Wolfe felt that he had generations of living to do outside the South before he could become a professional writer.) He had graduated from the University of North Carolina in 1920 and had gone immediately to Harvard, where he completed a two-year M.A. in drama. He then taught composition at New York University—living frugally so that he could travel in Europe (and sometimes taking semesters off in order to continue his writing while he lived—more cheaply—abroad.)

His ambition was always modest. Even though David Seed, like David Minter, equates the scope of Wolfe's fiction with the country of America (Seed 198), Thomas Wolfe remained imaginatively a permanent resident of Asheville, North Carolina. It was as if his sense of story had burrowed in behind the mountains—or, more accurately, as if all that mattered about any person's story was to be found in that single, stunning location, as well as the relationships among the people who lived there.

Wolfe's modesty showed in his many letters to his mother. On September 11, 1926, he wrote her from London, describing "I have two rooms in Chelsea, a quiet part of the city, where I have been hard at work on a book. I am alone—know few people, and therefore have to work" (Wolfe *Letters* 131). Wolfe's book then was unnamed; the fusion between his longer letters to his mother—in which he wrote about children's positions in families, for example—meant that his fiction suffused his letter writing. In November of 1926 he wrote, "I suppose in every family there's always a stranger, always an outsider. In our family Ben was the stranger until his death—I suppose I'm the other one" (Wolfe *Letters* 136). In another passage he noted, "Strangers we are born alone into a strange world. We live in it, as Ben did, alone and strange, and we die without ever knowing anyone" (Wolfe *Letters* 145). In the same fall, Wolfe told his mother that the book would be dedicated to her, "the best and truest friend I have ever had—the one person who has given love, comfort, and understanding to my lonely and disordered life" (Wolfe *Letters* 132).

Wolfe's letters home showed that he was ever conscious of being a Southerner. He wrote his mother that "The Southerner on the whole is a better fellow than the Yank. He is, God knows, just as ignorant, he has the same superstitions, but he is quieter, kinder, slower, and less offensive" (Wolfe *Letters* 143).

Yet even as Wolfe knew he was true to his Southernness, he also knew he wanted to write modern fiction. He had already learned that Modernism never did anything the easy way. In order to be a significant "new" writer, Wolfe understood the caveats of the modern—Brancusi's sculptures, Picasso's paintings, Stravinsky's music, and he had read widely in Joyce, Pound, Yeats, O'Neill, Dos Passos, Millay, Stein, Anderson, Hemingway and Faulkner. He knew what *avant garde* meant, and he spent time repeatedly in Europe absorbing the currents of the new to be found there.

Despite Maxwell Perkins's repeated admonitions that Wolfe needed to condense his prose, *Look Homeward, Angel* was a roiling (yet gorgeous) fabric of language. Instead of Wolfe's using classic juxtaposition, as Faulkner and Hemingway often did, this author poured what might be called "digressions" into his texts. Juxtaposition was in itself psychologically protective, keeping any reflection of autobiography out of readers' assessments. Yet Wolfe was not self-protective; he went wholeheartedly into his story—often, his story was his family's story—and taunted the reader with the necessity of unravelling the language. One meaningful section—because it describes the mother Eliza's bargaining with a teacher over the cost of Eugene Gant's education—shows this almost frantic amalgamation of information.

He told her the tuition was one hundred dollars a year. She pursed her lips lingeringly before she answered.

"Hm–m!" she began with a bantering smile, as she looked at Eugene. "That's a whole lot of money. You know," she continued with her tremulous smile, "as the darkey says, we're pore-folks."

Eugene squirmed.

"Well what about it, boy?" said Eliza banteringly. "Do you think you're worth that much money?" . . . .

[Eliza tells Mr. Leonard that she once taught school. He replies with interest.]

"Yes," said Eliza, "I remember my father—it was long before you were born, boy," she said to Eugene, "for I hadn't laid eyes on your papa—as the feller says, you were nothing but a dish-rag hanging out in heaven— I'd have laughed at any one who suggested marriage then—Well, I tell you what [she shook her head with a sad pursed deprecating mouth], we were mighty poor at the time, I can tell you.—I was thinking about it the other day—many's the time we didn't have food in the house for the next meal.—Well, as I was saying, your grandfather [addressing Eugene] came home one night and said—Look here, what about it?— Who do you suppose I saw to-day?—I remember him just as plain as if I saw him standing here—I had a feeling—[addressing Leonard with a doubtful smile] I don't know what you'd call it but it's pretty strange when you come to think about it, isn't it?—I had just finished helping Aunt Jane set the table—she had come all the way from Yancey County to visit your grandmother—when all of a sudden it flashed over me—mind you [to Leonard] I never looked out the window or anything but I knew just as well as I knew anything that he was coming—mercy I cried—here comes—why what on earth are you talking about, Eliza? said your grandma—I remember she went to the door and looked out down the path—there's no one there—He's acoming, I said—wait and see—Who? Said your grandmother—Why, father, I said—he's carrying something on his shoulder . . . ."

Wolfe Look *174–5*

Wolfe too was cognizant of the difficulty of reading modernist texts, but he made impressionistic use of diacritical marks, especially the dash, as he created a scene of the often coy Eliza making her narrative do double and triple duties. This is Eugene Gant's proud mother, who knows that he is "worth" the cost of this education. But Eliza is also the proud former schoolteacher, weighing what Mr. Leonard really had to offer.

The romance of *Look Homeward, Angel* occurs in both the author's view of the Gant family's chronicle (that, somehow and at least for some of the children, life will be promising) and in the language Wolfe chooses to employ in the story's telling. As a preface to Eugene Gant's great love for the older woman Laura, for example, he creates the mountain dark:

> The wasting helve of the moon rode into heaven over the bulk of the hills. There was a smell of wet grass and lilac, and the vast brooding symphony of the million-noted little night things, rising and falling in a constant ululation, and inhabiting the heart with steady unconscious certitude. The pallid light drowned out the stars, it lay like silence on the earth, it dripped through the leafy web of the young maples, printing the earth with swarming moths of elvish light.
>
> *Wolfe* Look *362*

The love affair between Eugene and Laura is one of the important sub-themes of the novel, and in the passion they know for each other, Wolfe's description becomes more focused, more pointed toward the heartbreak that will come. (After Laura leaves town, to return to her family in Richmond—ostensibly for a summer reunion—her "goodbye" letter admits that she has been engaged to a businessman there for over a year, and that they will marry during the coming week.)[6]

Within the family narratives and the love narratives, Wolfe interjects passages that describe what Eugene Gant has come to realize—that he will be a writer.

> As the war developed, and the literature of war-enchantment began to appear, Margaret Leonard gave him book after book to read. They were the books of the young men—the young men who fought to blot out the evil of the world with their blood. In her trembling voice she read to him Rupert Brooke's sonnet—"If I should die, think only this of me"—and she put a copy of Donald Hankey's *A Student in Arms* into his hand, saying: "Read this, boy. It will stir you as you've never been stirred before. Those boys have seen the vision!"
>
> He read it. He read many others. He saw the vision. He became a member of this legion of chivalry—young Galahad-Eugene—a spearhead of righteousness. He had gone a-Grailing. He compared dozens of personal memoirs, into which quietly, humorously, with fine-tempered English restraint, he poured the full measure of his pure crusading heart. Sometimes, he came through to the piping times of peace minus an arm, a leg, or an eye, diminished but ennobled; sometimes his last radiant words were penned on the eve of the attack that took his life. With glistening eyes, he read his own epilogue, enjoyed his post-mortem glory, as his last words were recorded and explained by his editor. Then, witness of his own martyrdom, he dropped two smoking tears upon his young slain body.
>
> *Wolfe* Look *291*

Comic in its self-absorption, this paean to Eugene Gant's ambition is just one of the passages a reader remembers. Each section of *Look Homeward, Angel* works from its structural, emotional origin into a suitably staged denouement. Wolfe's prose gives his readers the leap into a scene, the lush description of surroundings, the sometimes pinched dialogue between characters—Thomas Wolfe made the modern American novel his own, and in doing so, he made it particularly southern.

Notes

1 Hemingway had had some taste of a readership pushed to outrage when his 1926 *The Sun Also Rises* was lambasted because of the heavy drinking, and the seemingly indiscriminate sex, of that book's characters. No such objections greeted his 1929 *A Farewell to Arms*, though the sex between Catherine and Frederic was never sanctified through marriage.
2 Many of the immigrants that Americans feared, such as Abraham Cahan, were well-educated in European and Russian schools; their language abilities were honed into clarity through not only learning but discussion.
3 Ironically, it was the French academic community, led by existentialists under the wing of Jean Paul Sartre, that saw Faulkner's greatness, and won for him the most important international literary accolade, the Nobel Prize in Literature in 1949.
4 Minter goes on to say that "more and more Southerners were beginning to buy into the dream of becoming rich and powerful enough to impose their wills on their environment. Having lost hold on an older sense of living in a world made for them . . . Erskine Caldwell's 1933 *God's Little Acre*" reflected these attitudes (Minter 256).
5 In Phil Stone's book orders during 1922, for example, are Cather's *My Antonia*, Edna Ferber's *The Girls*, James Joyce's *A Portrait of the Artist as a Young Man*, H.D.'s *Hymen*, Zona Gale's *Miss Lulu Bett*, Aldous Huxley's *Crome Yellow*, H. L. Mencken's *The American Language*, D. H. Lawrence's *Aaron's Rod*, Percy Lubbock's *The Craft of Fiction*, John Parris's *Kimono*, H. A. Shands's *White and Black* , and other fiction by Joseph Hergesheimer, Louis Hemon, Gerald Gould, Maxwell Bodenheim, Waldo Frank, Henry Adams, and others (Faulkner's Library).
6 An almost asexual description, Wolfe writes about Laura through Eugene's eyes: "When he held her hand, he felt as if he had already seduced her. She lifted her lovely face to him, pert and ugly as a boy's; it was inhabited by a true and steadfast decency . . . . All the young beauty in the world dwelt for him in that face that had kept wonder, that had kept innocence, that had lived in such immortal blindness to the terror and foulness of the world. He came to her, like a creature who had travelled its life through dark space, for a moment of peace and conviction on some lonely planet, where now he stood, in the vast enchanted plain of moonlight . . ." (Wolfe *Look* 363).

Suggested further reading

Gordon Hutner. *What America Read: Taste, Class, and the Novel, 1920–1960.* U of North Carolina P, 2009.
Kevin Jackson. *Constellation of Genius: 1922: Modernism Year One.* Farrar, Straus and Giroux, 2013.
Alfred Kazin. *On Native Grounds.* Harcourt, Brace, 1942.
John T. Matthews, ed. *A Companion to the Modern American Novel 1900–1950.* Wiley-Blackwell, 2009.

6

THE HARLEM RENAISSANCE AND AFTER

Separating out the modernist writings of African Americans may have at one time been a useful demarcation but emphasis throughout the twenty-first century (and even during the later twentieth century) has been on seeing *all* ethnic writers as part of the full stream of *American* literature. The division of "Harlem Renaissance" is even more misleading because not all writers of color lived in New York (and many who did were not located in Harlem).

Today's critic must also question the fact that this so-called "Harlem Renaissance" is said to begin in 1925, when Alain Locke edited and published his far-reaching collection *The New Negro: An Interpretation*. Locke, a professor of philosophy at Howard University, was well-placed; he included James Weldon Johnson, Arthur Schomburg, J. A. Rogers, Albert C. Barnes, Langston Hughes, Countee Cullen, and Claude McKay, and shaped his book as a kind of answer to W. E. B. Du Bois's cry for the "Talented Tenth" of African Americans to lead an artistic charge. As Cheryl A. Wall summarized, Locke's call for "a revised racial identity" took an offensive position, not a defensive (Wall *Women* 1–2). In the process, African American artists and musicians explored all the dimensions of vernacular cultures, and thereby "yielded new genres of poetry and music" (ibid.)

Locke specified that "the new Negro" should not be buried under faddish concepts of sociology or politics, but neither should he or she be confined to images that had existed through history (the "old" Negro concepts of servility or rebellion). What would characterize the new Negro would be the spirit of discovery, of pride, of the search for origins—many of them African—that would lend a different complexity to art and literature and music. The situation in the mid-1920s was different; it was, according to Locke, "prophetic."[1]

One of the reasons circumstances for blacks had changed so radically was that Negroes had come to Harlem as residents early in the twentieth century (more than 87,000 blacks moved there during the 1920s and by the end of that decade,

EXCERPT FROM ALAIN LOCKE'S "THE NEW NEGRO"

The tide of Negro migration, northward and city-ward, is not to be fully explained as a blind flood started by the demands of war industry coupled with the shutting off of foreign migration, or by the pressure of poor crops coupled with increased social terrorism in certain sections of the South and Southwest. Neither labor demand, the bollweevil nor the Ku Klux Klan is a basic factor, however contributory any or all of them may have been. The wash and rush of this human tide on the beach line of the northern city centers is to be explained primarily in terms of a new vision of opportunity, of social and economic freedom, of a spirit to seize, even in the face of an extortionate and heavy toll, a chance for the improvement of conditions. With each successive wave of it, the movement of the Negro becomes more and more a mass movement toward the larger and the more democratic change—in the Negro's case a deliberate flight not only from countryside to city, but from medieval America to modern.

they numbered over 200,000).[2] For the first time in American history, blacks of upper, middle, and lower classes had created a largely African American urban area. In Harlem, the Negro was no longer the minority. Fitzgerald's naming this decade "The Jazz Age" underscored the centrality of black music and its importance to cultures both here and abroad. As Carl Van Vechten pointed out, jazz and other black music has "an inexorable rhythm"; it combines passion with pleasure. And, further, "Nearly all the dancing now to be seen in our musical shows is of Negro origin [Cake-Walk, the Bunny Hug, the Turkey Trot, the Charleston, the Black Bottom, and the Lindy Hop]" (Van Vechten *Dance* 38–9).

The American (and French) fascination with jazz stemmed partly from its improvisational nature, its spontaneity, its finding form in random patterns, its sensuality, and its premise that cooperation and good musicianship could lead to art. This antirational approach signaled deeper underlying convictions that emotion was as important as intellect and that an empathetic audience would respond. The immense success of black American dancer and comic Josephine Baker, particularly in Paris, spoke to the great attraction of the improvisational and the sensual.

In the world of writing, free forms in poetry and less traditional structures in fiction, as illustrated in the work of both Jean Toomer and Langston Hughes—whose poetry collections *The Weary Blues* and *Fine Clothes to the Jew* were key publications of 1926 and 1927, paralleled the improvisational forms of African American music, and the use of both dialect (the real, the emotionally true) and folk idioms changed literary language. The rationale for the shape of many of Langston Hughes's poems was often the dialect that dominated their language (a mother talks to a son, the voice laments its black heritage); speech patterns created meaningful line breaks.

EXCERPT FROM LANGSTON HUGHES'S "THE NEGRO ARTIST AND THE RACIAL MOUNTAIN"

. . . The road for the serious black artist . . . who would produce a racial art is most certainly rocky and the mountain is high. Until recently he received almost no encouragement of his work from either white or colored people. The fine novels of Chesnutt go out of print with neither race noticing their passing. The quaint charm and humor of Dunbar's dialect verse brought to him, in his day, largely the same kind of encouragement one would give a sideshow freak (A colored man writing poetry! How odd!) or a clown (How amusing!).

The present vogue in things Negro, although it may do as much harm as good for the budding colored artist, has at least done this: it has brought him forcibly to the attention of his own people among whom for so long, unless the other race had noticed him beforehand, he was a prophet with little honor . . . . I know a young colored writer, a manual worker by day, who had been writing well for the colored magazines for some years, but it was not until he recently broke into the white publications and his first book was accepted by a prominent New York publisher that the "best" Negroes in his city took the trouble to discover that he lived there . . . .

For critic Jonathan W. Gray, a more significant book than Locke's *The New Negro* was James Weldon Johnson's 1922 *The Book of American Negro Poetry*, because it provided an earlier, and a wider, showcase for African American achievement. Although Johnson, too, avoided including much work by Marcus Garvey's black nationalist followers, his collection, according to Gray, is "the first modern anthology of African American literature" (Gray 236). It also placed a premium on poetry instead of fiction, a form that came easily to black writers who had been reared in the African American churches. (Few histories of this period today mention the highly influential poets Gwendolyn Bennett, Anne Spencer, Countee Cullen, Georgia Douglas Johnson, Claude McKay, Arna Bontemps, and Sterling Brown.) With Johnson's collection appearing in 1922, followed the next year by Jean Toomer's *Cane*, readers such as Gertrude Stein and Ernest Hemingway in Paris were perhaps more impressed than New Yorkers themselves with the versatility of black writing.

Toomer's *Cane* appealed particularly to Stein because in one slim book this previously unknown author packed not only a variety of poems—some formal, more idiomatic—as well as the same wide-reaching variety of short story. Following the tendency of most modern writers to be less self-conscious about distinctions among genres, Toomer here combined long stories with others compacted into prose poems, as well as both poetry and a drama. In the unified segments of *Cane*, Toomer evinced a great deal of knowledge about both American and European modernism.

As Thadious Davis has recently pointed out, none of the 1920s African American writers considered themselves professionals. Even as they "enjoyed a wider access to more varied publishing outlets both within and outside the black community, as well as in small private and large commercial ventures,"[3] they earned their living in other ways.

> Countee Cullen, for example, was a schoolteacher, as were Bontemps and Jessie Fauset. McKay and Wallace Thurman did manage to work as editors, but Rudolph Fisher was a medical doctor, Georgia Douglas Johnson a government worker, and Nella Larsen a librarian. Others, such as Hughes and Hurston, were primarily students who earned a living by performing a variety of short-term jobs.
>
> *Davis* Southscapes *141*

Perhaps the most extensive clarification of the rationale for separating literature written by African Americans from the work of white Americans exists in James Smethurst's 2011 *The African American Roots of Modernism*. As his title suggests, some critics have reversed the origins of American modernism—drawing from writing that already based its forms on speech rhythms, on privileging the common, and on aiming to be read by all participants interested in both written and spoken language. It was the work of African Americans, Smethurst contends, that influenced early Modernism in America. He begins his discussion of U.S. modernism by describing late nineteenth century

> bohemias, characterized by racially and ethnically distinct, though significantly overlapping, communities. Whether one is speaking of "black bohemia," the largely white bohemia in such communities as New York's Greenwich Village and Chicago's Towertown, or the avant garde artistic subcultures of immigrant communities, such as the circles of Yiddish- and Russian-speaking Jewish artists and intellectuals who frequented the cafes of New York's Lower East Side.
>
> *Smethurst 123 and see Boone 205ff.*

Within these communities, the roots of European politics, such as socialism, were dominant, so the aesthetic principles of a somewhat more elite British cultures merged with bohemian radicalism. To view the new *vers libre* poetry, for example, as being the product of Ezra Pound and T. S. Eliot, omitted the work of socially conservative African American poets William Stanley Braithwaite and Fenton Johnson, and their less conservative friend Paul Laurence Dunbar.

Smethurst discusses writing by both African Americans and mainstream writers to show amalgamation where race alone might suggest prejudice, but he attends primarily in his last chapter to the geography of the United States. Here he considers what he calls "the larger anxiety about divisions within the United

---

**EXCERPT FROM WILLIAM CARLOS WILLIAMS'S
SELECTED LETTERS (TO HORACE GREGORY, JULY 22,
1939, ABOUT GREGORY'S PREFACE FOR WILLIAMS'S
IN THE AMERICAN GRAIN)**

Let me begin by telling you something of how I came to write the book. Of mixed ancestry, I felt from earliest childhood that America was the only home I could ever possibly call my own. I felt that it was expressly founded for me, personally, and that it must be my first business in life to possess it; that only by making it my own from the beginning to my own day, in detail, should I ever have a basis for knowing where I stood . . . .

States." What was agreeable in the north may not have been acceptable in the south. "The articulation about race by white modernists was strongly connected to journeys along the North–South axis largely introduced by black writers and to the early African American migration narrative" (Smethurst 192).

Using as illustration William Carlos Williams, whose Puerto Rican mother was descended from Jewish, and perhaps black, lineage, Smethurst incorporates many of Williams's descriptions of African American characters within his poems. Williams's interest in African American music, as well as literature and the plastic arts, meant that he was constantly reinforcing what he felt as racial difference. (Smethurst comments that some present-day critics refer to Williams as "Afro-Latino")(Smethurst 194).

Illustrating the fragility of racial classification (as well as suggesting that categories of gender and sexual preference may be similarly fluid), Smethurst prompts readers to consider a range of books usually associated with Harlem writers. He mentions Jessie Fauset's *Plum Bun*, Nella Larsen's *Quicksand*, Rudolph Fisher's *The Walls of Jericho*, Wallace Thurman's *Infants of the Spring*, Claude McKay's *Home to Harlem* and *Banjo*, as well as Toomer's *Cane*, pointing out that "interracial presence" seems to be necessary for characterization. He continues, "These bohemias also seem to require . . . transgressive interracial and often queer, if not gay, sexual pairings." Gay networks during the 1920s were important ways for publishers to discover interesting and competent African American writers, as in the cases in which Carl Van Vechten brought new writers of color into Alfred A. Knopf's ken[4] (Smethurst 201).

In illustration, one might notice the frontispage for Fisher's first novel, *The Walls of Jericho*, (published by Knopf in 1928), a page designed to promote the Knopf series called "The Negro in Unusual Fiction." The designed page contained five books, each title on the first line followed by the author's name on the second:

Nigger Heaven
by Carl Van Vechten

The Autobiography of an Ex-Colored Man
by James Weldon Johnson[5]

The Fire in the Flint
by Walter F. White

Flight
by Walter F. White

Latterday Symphony
by Romer Wilson

In Fisher's novel, his appendage "An Introduction to Contemporary Harlemese" ("Expurgated and Abridged") appeared at the conclusion of the book; in Van Vechten's *Nigger Heaven*, similarly, he titled his appendage a "Glossary" of the unusual Negro words and phrases employed in this novel. Pretending that cultural difference was a matter of language rather than custom, both Van Vechten and Fisher showed their competence in translation without relinquishing their right to use an African American vocabulary.

Van Vechten's book makes itself a kind of a literary companion by including favorite works that the character Mary Love, a librarian, admires—Louis Bromfield, Jean Cocteau, Aldous Huxley, Somerset Maugham, and Elinor Wylie. Mary owns signed editions by Charles Chesnutt (*The Conjure Woman*), James Weldon Johnson (*Fifty Years*), Claude McKay (Harlem Shadows), Jessie Fauset (*There is Confusion*), Walter White (*The Fire in the Flint*), W. E. B. Du Bois (*The Souls of Black Folk*), and Jean Toomer (*Cane*). The narrator also makes references to now-classic modernist texts such as Gertrude Stein's "Melanctha" as well as works by Sherwood Anderson, Anatole France, Jean Toomer, Langston Hughes, James Branch Cabell, and Norman Douglas. (Van Vechten makes clear that all the blues lyrics used within the novel were written specifically for the book by his friend, Langston Hughes.)

Just as Mary has created her own very literate world, proving herself an authority in works written by both black writers and white, American and European, Van Vechten has chosen to write his own version of African American lives in New York during the 1920s. Greeted by a divisive firestorm of controversy, *Nigger Heaven*[6] featured issues of black characters passing, or thinking about passing; deliberating on questions of class—usually determined by whether or not they had gone to college, and by whether they had there surrounded themselves with white people as well as—or instead of—black; and by the machinations of finding drugs and alcohol during the height of Prohibition. For example, the naïve character Byron Kasson, who has graduated from the very white culture of the University of Pennsylvania and therefore seems to be adrift in New York, cannot appreciate Mary's love for him. He finally destroys everything that might be possible for him through his various addictions (including the sexual). In his apparently murdering the man he thinks is his competition for the professional prostitute that he prefers to Mary, he faces death in an American prison. And Van Vechten's implication is that Mary Love will remain, ironically, unloved.

In Emily Bernard's assessment, Van Vechten's 1926 novel was an expansion on Du Bois's conviction that African American novels should be about "uplift." She saw it as Van Vechten's

> declaration of his right to write about black Harlem life just as he pleased. For black writers, the novel was their way of declaring the same, and they gloried in the scandal that Van Vechten had created—although Van Vechten himself was distressed by it—because the book afforded them an opportunity to distance themselves from conservatives who thought that black stories should be written only by black people.
>
> *Bernard 8*

That Mary Love was a New York librarian may have been a nod of approval for Van Vechten's friendship with Nella Larsen. In 1928 Alfred Knopf published Larsen's first novel, *Quicksand*, and followed that book in 1929 with her second, *Passing*. A well-educated mulatto, Larsen was born in 1893 in Chicago to a Danish mother and a black West Indian father. When her mother married a white man after the early death of her father, Larsen married physicist Elmer Imes, a professor at Fisk University; eventually she traveled to Demark in search of her roots, attending classes there at the University of Copenhagen. Then she studied nursing at Lincoln Hospital Training School in New York, graduating in 1915 and taking the position of superintendent of nurses at Tuskegee Institute. She then returned to New York but in 1921 began work in the children's division of the New York Public Library—where she also took up writing.

For all the solemnity of the title of her first novel, *Quicksand* was a fairly routine *roman a clef* about a displaced, racially mixed, heterosexual woman. Helga Crane searches for romance in many places, but her natural sexuality troubles her—and she ends pregnant, married to a highly unsuitable mate. A definite feminist novel, Larsen's book shows clearly that, for women, sexuality leads to pregnancy and pregnancy—in many cases—to weary overwork and the possibility of death. Larsen's *Quicksand* rewrote Gertrude Stein's "The Gentle Lena" with even greater intensity.

It is also a novel about class, and embroiders the differences between the lives of Southern blacks and the urban African American elite. Larsen's sophistication about conditions throughout the world, especially for characters whose non-white skins call attention to them, mirrored one of the traits Van Vechten had long developed: when she writes about the privilege Helga Crane refuses while she lives in Denmark, her attitudes become a hook for readers already wary of the choices Helga might make. Marrying the man of God in his small poverty-stricken Southern town turns out as the dramatic irony Larsen intended. Helga's personal slavery to the bigot Mr. Green turns her into a nonentity: after her fourth pregnancy and her life in poverty with her children and the distasteful self-righteous husband, Larsen writes "She knew only that, in the hideous agony that for interminable hours—no, centuries—she had borne, the luster of religion had vanished; that revulsion had come upon her; that she hated this man" (Larsen *Quicksand* 129). Determined to leave Mr. Green and their children, Helga is then stymied by her realization that she is once again pregnant.

Larsen's treatment of this combined *bildungsroman* and quest novel works well. She presents the suspicion of people of several cultures as they watch the beautiful, educated protagonist. Cultural reaction is that there is something *wrong* with this woman; why does no one desire her? Moving far beyond African American issues, Larsen writes a testimony to difference, that the woman seeking self-betterment and learning does not fit most gendered stereotypes.

With her second novel, *Passing*, as with Jessie Fauset's *Plum Bun*, feminist issues might seem to be submerged beneath the world's attention to skin color. Larsen uses as epigraph for this novel Langston Hughes's lines,

My old man died in a fine big house.
My ma died in a shack.
I wonder where I'm gonna die,
Being neither white nor black?

Fauset, similarly, draws her title from the nursery rhyme, "To Market, to Market/ To buy a Plum Bun," emphasizing women's lack of choices. In the context of her novel, the light-skinned woman's temptation to *pass* takes on sinister overtones.

These discussions of skin color and the options—or lack of options—dark skin provides, are reinforced by the empathetic fiction of Wallace Thurman, when his novel *The Blacker the Berry*...appears from Macaulay Publishing in 1929. Presenting Emma Lou Morgan who has three years of college at University of Southern California, Thurman stresses that with skin as dark as hers, Emma Lou has little chance of finding either employment or love in New York. Sure of her own potential, reliant on skin lightening potions, Emma Lou has just broken up with John, the first New Yorker to make love to her. Thurman points out that Emma Lou tends to move geographically whenever she is unhappy: here she has once more "fled into an unknown town to escape the haunting chimera of intra-racial color prejudice" (Thurman *Blacker* 38).

Relentless in his description of her bad luck, her occasional wins and more frequent losses, Thurman writes a novel that keeps readers' attention. Emma Lou, because she works as a maid for white actresses (and would not consider working for black women), is often surrounded by whites. Her inability to move back into African American circles makes her as displaced as was Byron Kasson in Van Vechten's novel. A snob, Emma Lou walks through Harlem looking for employment agencies that are suitable for her patronage:

> ... she was looking for a job. Sour smells assailed her nostrils
> once more. Rasping voices. Pleading voices. Tired voices.
> Domineering voices.
>
> *Thurman* Blacker *45*

Reading *The Amsterdam News* and counting "a half a dozen empty gin bottles bearing a pre-prohibition Gordon label," Emma Lou almost succumbs to caring for a worthless lover's disabled baby. But she escapes that trap, and readies herself to leave. Thurman's giving Emma Lou the ability to resist motherhood is a positive marker, even in an urban culture so dominated by illicit alcohol, illicit drugs, and illicit sex that little reasoning ability remains.

Toomer's *Cane*, a collage of poetry, fiction, and drama

Critic Cary Wintz called Jean Toomer

> by far the most talented and promising black writer to surface in the early
> 1920s ... whose experimental novel *Cane* created a sensation among black
> writers. The book had a tremendous impact on the young black artists who
> read it. Hughes, Cullen, Hurston, Rudolph Fisher, and Wallace Thurman ...
> were deeply affected by it. Countee Cullen praised *Cane* as a "real race
> contribution, a classic portrayal of things as they are".
>
> *Wintz 75*

Revered by not only African American writers, *Cane* prompted Waldo Frank and his Greenwich Village friends to probe American writing for what Frank called "buried cultures." In Frank's case, the less visible culture would be Native American and in Toomer's, *southern* African American. For Frank, Toomer's *Cane* related to Sherwood Anderson's *Winesburg, Ohio*, with the same kind of accurate emphasis on characters who were themselves comparatively inarticulate (Wintz 79).

As evocative of the South as cotton was, the imagery of sugar cane portrayed beauty and richness wound through with deep poverty, as well as the mistreatment of African American workers and the hopelessness of the worn-away soil. Toomer was fully aware that this far-reaching image could fuse his fragments of black life— whether that life was lived in Washington, DC, his home,[7] or in Georgia, where he went briefly to join administrators at Sparta Agricultural and Industrial Institute. It also is a homonym for the Biblical Cain, whose name suggests the destruction of brotherhood and introduces the concept of familial violence.

Never didactic, Toomer's *Cane* explores the sexual lives of African Americans, and much of its narrative is expressed from a male perspective—although many of its characters are female. In the five stories about women ("Karintha," "Becky," "Carma," "Esther," "Fern"), Toomer forces the reader to see that these prose-poems are women-centered, specific to each character in their careful formalism.

Besides being fascinating in themselves, Toomer's portraits of women characters show his aim to integrate his philosophy (more Eastern than Western) with his aesthetics. He viewed the elements of water, fire, wind, and sun as primary and necessary, for life and for sacrifice. Besides the literal name "Carma" (karma) appearing in the listing of women characters, Toomer's descriptions of each figure stress one or another of these natural qualities. "Karintha" suggests the wind: "Karintha, at twelve, was a wild flash that told the other folks just what it was to live. At sunset, when there was no wind . . . her sudden darting past you was a bit of vivid color, like a black bird that flashes in light . . . . Karintha's running was a whir" (Toomer *Cane* 1). "Fern" suggests water: "Face flowed into her eyes. Flowed in soft cream foam and plaintive ripples . . . the curves of her profile, like mobile rivers . . . . Like her face, the whole countryside seemed to flow into her eyes" (Toomer *Cane* 14–15). In his poetic language, Toomer includes many references to Eastern culture, to the state of people's souls, to the harmony that would lift people beyond sexuality or dissension to a nirvana that might be attainable. ("Kabnis," the play that ends the book, attends to those very large themes.)

In negative contrast, "Becky" is written in cryptic, blunt prose with harsh assonance; it tells a story that is without mercy, just as the community has shown no mercy toward the woman they were convinced could not be redeemed. More centrally, "Carma," with its synthesis of Eastern and African cultures, introduces a strong thematics for *Cane*. It also describes an important stage in the development of essential black womanhood. Karintha is a passively sexual object; Carma is much more aggressive. "Carma, in overalls, and strong as any man, stands behind the old brown mule, driving the wagon home . . . . She, riding it easy," the narrative begins. Assuming power from her own self-knowledge, Carma does what she pleases, and that pleasing includes making love with men she finds attractive. She accepts the results of her acts and does what she can to protect herself from social disapproval. Her trickery in the canebrake, making her angry husband think she had killed herself, leads to his killing an innocent man—and ending up in prison. But Carma is untouched by his outcome, and her narrative is appropriately open-ended (Toomer *Cane* 10).

Although Carma is too fascinated by her own pleasure to have reached nirvana, she is at a different stage than are Fern, Esther, or Becky. Women such as Muriel in "Box Seat" and Bona in "Bona and Paul" share some of Carma's qualities—realistic and aggressive, they do not see themselves through the eyes of the men who view them. They exist on their own terms.

Throughout *Cane*, Toomer works with the image of woman as primitive force, as a rooted center for life, in several of the middle-section stories. In "Box Seat," for example, in the midst of the tormented Dan Moore's aberrant behavior, Toomer embeds the surreal image of a black woman who knows herself and her place in the world:

[Dan] shrivels close beside a portly Negress whose huge rolls of flesh meet about the bones of seat-arms. A soil-soaked fragrance comes from her.

Through the cement floor her strong roots sink down. They spread under the asphalt streets. Dreaming, the streets roll over on their bellies, and suck their glossy health from them. Her strong roots sink down and spread under the river and disappear in blood-lines that waver south. Her roots shoot down. Dan's hands follow them. Roots throb. Dan's heart beats violently. He places his palms upon the earth to cool them. Earth throbs. Dan's heart beats violently. He sees all the people in the house rush to the walls to listen to the rumble. A new-world Christ is coming up. Dan comes up. He is startled. The eyes of the woman don't belong to her. They look at him unpleasantly.

Toomer Cane *62*

In the midst of images of sterility at the theater, the black woman's powerful, searching roots are a vivid contrast. To counter the sense of her life as bountiful, open to all who ask, Toomer creates the hostile second stage of Dan's recognition. After he has plundered her, following those roots in a kind of surreal rape image, the woman's eyes change; she does not welcome his using her. Similar imagery connects the less violent "Fern" with the narrator, and he remarks to himself, "When one is on the soil of one's ancestors, most anything can come to one" (*Cane* 17).

The dichotomy between the naturalness of black life in Georgia—primitive though it may be—and the skewed sophistication of the Washington, D.C., existence provides steady contrast as *Cane* unfolds. Smethurst sees that Toomer's inclusion within *Cane* of many journeys "to and from the folk motivated by desire, anxiety, alienation and brutal racial violence . . . mirrored his extremely complicated relationship with the usual divisions of racial identity in the United States. Structurally [too] it represented his lifelong search for a physical, mental and spiritual wholeness" (Smethurst 202).

In order for "Kabnis" to provide closure as well as continuity for *Cane*, readers needed to be comfortable with the metaphoric images—Father John, the meditative stonelike old man who lives in the basement, may allude to the Kaaba, the black stone which is the most sacred Moslem object, housed as it is in the center of the Great Mosque of Mecca. Kabnis cajoles Father John (calling him "You old black fakir") and Carrie Kate has learned moral values by caring for Father John's needs. The male characters of the play represent different stages of will, desire, and knowledge. Halsey may suggest Arjuna, the wheelwright of the *Bhagavad-Gita*, instructing Kabnis in the life patterns he finds meaningful. Kabnis's self-definition as "orator" does not stand completely intact: he also admits to a feminized self, to the capacity to empathize with others, and to his ongoing search for a meaningful soul. By the end of Toomer's play, Kabnis has accepted his role as laborer, man, black man, southern black man. Though he fights his education at the hands of all his compatriots—resisting Halsey's practical injunctions, Lewis's expanding definitions of purpose, and Carrie Kate's religious insistence, Kabnis at least survives his *Walpurgisnacht*, admitting that his lust has been only cold ash, a temporary solution to his many problems. Going into the cellar for his orgy, coupling there with a Kore/Cora figure, and then returning to a higher stratum, suggests the Demeter–Persephone myth, with the power of procreation and fertility resting finally with the matriarch.

Experimental as Toomer's writing is, "Kabnis" yet continues the themes that are at last obliquely expressed in the short fiction, poems, and prose poems of *Cane*: that people must find a source of personal and emotional sustenance and lead their lives as they plan them, choice after choice; that the optimum stage is that of a realistic nirvana, without dissension, conflict, or vain striving for material objects; yet that people must not live their lives away in sleep, passively accepting whatever force assaults them. The women in *Cane* awaken and come to their own sense of themselves and stop being only sexual objects, and at the close of "Kabnis," the title character literally wakes from sleep and ascends the stairs to resume his work. A few years later, Toomer had become a serious follower of Gurdjieff and through his teachings, the metaphor of awakening—of claiming one's own consciousness—was always positive: sleep suggests a trance state that results from negative self-awareness. This theme appeared clearly throughout *Cane* in 1923. The book may have been Toomer's first work, but it was in many ways to serve, as did Wallace Stevens's *Harmonium*, as a touchstone (or a mandala) for all the author's other writing.

Women and men writing. . .

Sara Blair describes the way Harlem came to work. She notes in a recent essay that "Like the Village, Harlem in its 1920s heyday boasted a spectacular salon life. Pacesetter A'Lelia Walker—nicknamed the Great Black Empress, she had inherited a substantial fortune from her mother, who sold hair straightening products to striving African Americans—sponsored high society gatherings with impressive guestlists. Dancing on the parquet floors. Visiting her top-floor library. She had verses from Langston Hughes's 'Weary Blues' displayed on a wall." Jessie Fauset's salon, in contrast, was "decidedly soberer." Regular attendees were W. E. B. Du Bois, Alain Locke, and labor activist A. Philip Randolph. The group sometimes conversed in French.

Blair points to the serious disagreement between the camps: "If culture czar Du Bois—progressive, elitist, and high bourgeoise—would espouse an aesthetics of didacticism, by which the 'Talented Tenth' (the leaders of the race) rises and pulls all that are worthy of saving up to their vintage ground," "younger writers like Langston Hughes and Zora Neale Hurston would vigorously oppose his ideology of uplift with an investment in the black vernacular and in such 'low' forms as folktales, lying contests, and the blues" (Blair 169). When she was in New York, Zora Neale Hurston also held a weekly soiree, on Sunday nights (Mitchell and Davis 131). According to the memoirs of Dorothy West, Hurston "has millions of marvelous anecdotes." More entertaining than most literary get-togethers, Hurston let her evenings wander where they would, and her own storytelling skills were often substantially featured.

Of all the figures of the Harlem Renaissance, Langston Hughes was omnipresent. Working in poetry (and illustrated poems as well), in essays that appeared in newspapers as columns, and then in 1929, in the novel, Hughes had quite easily become the voice of African American writing in the United States. When he began *Not Without Laughter*, the novel that was to appear from Knopf in 1930, he had just replicated Toomer's immersion in Southern life: Hughes had traveled South with Zora Neale Hurston as she undertook anthropological investigations. So Hughes' understanding of Southern racism, and of Southern African American life, had a more sophisticated underpinning, that of anthropological study.[8]

Beginning in Kansas with a storm reminiscent of that in *The Wizard of Oz*, Hughes' novel recounted the daily lives of western black families. The title suggested a blues philosophy, a way to meet the hardships of life and survive them; the protagonist was a young Langston Hughes. (Hughes himself was Midwestern, and part of the power of the fiction comes from his vivid description of this non-urban life.) During his work on this novel, he was supported by Mrs. Charlotte Mason, the benefactor of many African American writers and artists; unfortunately, her support ended after the novel appeared, and Hughes then experienced a deep depression. He returned to his life work of writing poetry, and also became interested in drama. [9]

During the late 1920s and 1930s, Arna Bontemps—already known as a poet who had won the *Crisis* poetry prize—wrote a variety of fiction, from his wrenching short story "A Summer Tragedy," about the suicide of a black sharecropper couple as they faced illness and poverty in old age, to the novels *God Sends Sunday* in 1931 and *Black Thunder* in 1936. The latter book represented a new direction in African American fiction, that of historical romance. Bontemps records that he had found a large collection of slave narratives in the Fisk University Library and, intrigued by the will to freedom which each narrator conveyed—especially moving during the depths of America's Depression—Bontemps chose a narrative about Gabriel's insurrection to use as frame for his imaginative retelling of the story. Told by Bontemps's fictional Gabriel, the story of the June 1800 Virginia uprising is an effective if impressionistic novel, which makes good use of rapidly shifting points of view. Bontemps wrote a vivid account of the slave rebellion that—were it not for unusual torrential rains—might have succeeded. In subject matter, *Black Thunder* was an historical romance, but in form it was as modern as most other novels of the Harlem Renaissance.

Critic Robert Stepto makes an essential point in his 1979 discussion of Afro-American literature when he notes that black writers are often criticized for their use of established forms (i.e. the sonnet in poetry, for example). Yet even if critics respect the conviction that accompanies their choices of subjects, they may fault black writers for the lack of innovation. Stepto states that many African American writers may use conventional forms but then add inversions (or subversions) to those forms, so that the work reflects a variant pattern: "Of special interest is the play or counterpoint within a given author's writings between 'received' forms (the sonnet at one aesthetic extreme, the ballad at the other) and 'indigenous' forms (blues, folk sermon, etc.)" (Stepto 796–7). From Paul Laurence Dunbar and James Weldon Johnson to Langston Hughes and Zora Neale Hurston through Margaret

Walker, Gwendolyn Brooks, Richard Wright, and Ralph Ellison, struggles over this use of counterpoint have marked black writing.

No African American writer's *oeuvre* so clearly illustrates this practice of writing in a traditional form only to vary from the expected as that of Zora Neale Hurston. Trained as a folklorist under Franz Boas, Hurston spent much of the late 1920s and early 1930s researching black culture—both abroad and in the small all-black Florida town of Eatonville where she was born. She wrote a number of effective short stories during these years, and some plays, but her first novel, *Jonah's Gourd Vine*, was not published until 1934. In 1935 came her first collection of folk lore, *Mules and Men*, followed in 1937 by her novel *Their Eyes Were Watching God*. Much more than Janie's story to her friend Pheoby Watson, Hurston's second novel adapted its simple frame of retrospective telling to incorporate a number of folktales from African and African American culture. By so doing, Hurston created a mythic, heavily symbolic story that stretched past its visible structure.

Beginning at the end of Janie's three marriages, with her return to Eatonville after her third husband's death, Hurston's protagonist shares the story of her life with her childhood friend. Through Pheoby, Janie's story will reach the rest of the community: "Ah don't mean to bother wid tellin' 'em nothin', Pheoby. 'Tain't worth de trouble. You can tell 'em what Ah say if you wants to. Dat's just de same as me 'cause mah tongue is in mah friend's mouf" (*Eyes* 17). This connection with the town is important because Janie, at this time in her life, is moving toward community relationships rather than the marriages that shaped her early history. By serving to bring her back into community, Janie's narrative is a kind of confession, although her motive is pride and accomplishment, not guilt or shame.

Hurston's *method* of narration—relying on an apparently artless recreation of idiomatic speech—forces the reader to accept the voice and language of the black woman storyteller. There is a deliberate emphasis on Janie's telling her story in a "womanly" way—emotional, impulsive, fragmented, intimate—and to a woman. Hurston's approach allows Janie's story to be truly woman identified and widens the distance between the comparatively conventional narratives of Nella Larsen and Jessie Fauset, which were published with the approval of the powerful male writers of the Harlem Renaissance. Hurston did not want for a minute to be confused with that "Talented Tenth" that was supposedly responsible for the excellence of current black art, and her insistence on using as protagonist a poor southern black girl, educated primarily by her grandmother (a former slave), stemmed from that stubborn insistence that the true life of African American culture was in its realism—*real* characters, *real* situations, *real* antipathies. For Janie, marriage and its reliance on the control of a black man was the only way out of the poverty she had been born into.

Hurston's changes in point of view and tense fit no prescribed formula. They suggest that readers are at the mercy of a whimsical speaker who makes such changes whenever she wants, yet the truth is that Janie's narrative is immediate and compelling. Hurston's flexible point of view is achieved partly by maintaining the idiom throughout, even when Joe Starks, Janie's second husband, takes over the

---

EXCERPT FROM ZORA NEALE HURSTON'S "SWEAT"

"Mah Gawd!" he chattered, "ef Ah could on'y strack uh light!"

The rattling ceased for a moment as he stood paralyzed. He waited. It seemed that the snake waited also.

"Oh, fuh de light! Ah thought he'd be too sick"—Sykes was muttering to himself when the whirr began again, closer, right underfoot this time. Long before this, Sykes' ability to think had been flattened down to primitive instinct and he leaped—onto the bed.

Outside Delia heard a cry that might have come from a maddened chimpanzee, a stricken gorilla. All the terror, all the horror, all the rage that man possibly could express, without a recognizable human sound . . . .

---

story. (Joe's incompatibility with Janie comes partly from his usurping her power as a human being. He does not allow her to participate in any community activities, to speak in public, or to have opinions. If language reveals, and perhaps creates, personality, Janie is bereft. It is therefore ironically suitable that Joe "speaks" this section of Janie's story.) As Hurston moves to the use of restricted third person, Janie realizes her lack of freedom and when she comes into her own storytelling near the end of the novel, that "voice" signals her possession of her self. As incisive as her killing Tea Cake to save her own life is her assuming control of her own story.

Hurston's language is significant because it tells Janie's story but also because, in it, the power of the "folk" comes to life. Not only does much of the action during the community scenes in Eatonville and in the Everglades revolve around telling stories, amusing one's friends, and creating myths and legends, but a great concern with orality had fueled black writers' arguments throughout the twentieth century. *Oral*, not written, speech had been the mainstay of the African American culture. The argument in the twentieth century was whether to abandon that orality in its written form or to duplicate narratives by white writers. Camps were bitterly divided, and anthologies were composed of black works that either testified to the importance of writing in black dialect or of using a language that could have been written by whites as well as blacks. Hurston, by conveying so much of both characterization and plot through black idiomatic language, casts her allegiance in the ongoing argument with Toomer, Hughes, and Sterling Brown rather than with Du Bois. When Janie says to Pheoby, then, "Ah been a delegate to de big 'ssociation of life. Yessuh! De Grand Lodge, de big convention of livin' is just where Ah been dis year and a half y'all ain't seen me," she is making a clear political and aesthetic statement (Hurston *Eyes* 18).

In addition to phrasing, contractions, and dropped consonants, Hurston relies on maxims from actual speech. "Unless you see de fur, a mink skin ain't no different from a coon hide . . . . We been kissin'-friends for twenty years . . . livin' in de white folks backyard." She relies heavily on metaphor, as in using the blossoming pear tree to image Janie's budding sexuality as a teenager (and throughout the novel). One of the oldest symbols for lust and sexuality in Western literature, the pear tree suggests Hurston's ability to draw from different bodies of knowledge to enrich Janie's story. More ethnic identified is the series of stories about Matt Bonner's yellow mule, representative of the many animal tales from African lore (and a character as well in *Mule Bone*, the play Hurston and Langston Hughes wrote together, [10] as the mule of Matthew Brazzle, who still buys side meat by the slice to prove his cheapness.)

After the yellow mule's death, scenes with the waiting buzzards are further illustration of the efficacy of the animal folktale, and the reader learns a great deal about Joe Starks from listening to the words of the Parson, the ruler buzzard. *Their Eyes Were Watching God* also includes a root doctor, a hurricane (drawn from the quantity of black hurricane lore, like tales of floods and apocalypse, intensified after the 1928 hurricane), the rabid dog as devil, and a number of more overtly mythic elements. Yet as Hurston weaves these materials into the text, readers assimilate them easily because Janie's story remains dominant.

Many elements of Janie's story are humorous. Through intentionally comic language and events, Hurston draws her reader into and along what might have been a relentlessly somber account of the woman's search for maturity and freedom. As Hurston has created the character of Janie, her protagonist succeeds, and her novel is truly comic. She has learned about life through her three marriages but rather than being a dependent woman, Janie is able to exist alone. She comes to know herself and what she can accomplish, and she is able to grow tall and straight (hence, the comparisons with trees or treelike shapes). As Pheoby says at the end of Janie's narrative, "Lawd! . . . Ah done growed ten feet higher from jus' listenin' tuh you, Janie. Ah ain't satisfied wid mahself no mo'. Ah means tuh make Sam take me fishin' wid him after this. Nobody better not criticize yuh in mah hearin'" (Hurston *Eyes* 284).

At the close of her story, Janie has become a traditional hero. Taking on herself the double role of protector and initiate, Pheoby serves to prove that Janie Woods (a veritable bevy of trees) has come to fruition, has found her horizon, and has achieved contentment. In the course of her journey, Janie has found the silver fleece of W. E. B. Du Bois's cotton field, the spacious vision so different from the limited inward-turning view of Toomer's *Cane* and the horizon image of Frederick Douglass's narrative. More than simply Janie's story, *Their Eyes Were Watching God* is a literary *tour de force*, but the reader's recognition of that fact does not detract from the book's effect. It instead allows it a central place in American modernism.

Notes

1 Material in *The New Negro* was originally published in a special issue of Locke's *Survey Graphic* (Volume 6, March 1925); in that collection Locke published two essays, "Harlem" and "Enter the New Negro."

2 Rafia Zafar notes that such population growth resulted from

push and pull vectors . . . the Niagara movement, which led to the formation of the NAACP; Marcus Garvey's electrifying call to build once more a black kingdom in Africa, and the common people's embrace of his UNIA movement; the return of African American veterans who demanded freedom at home . . . flocks of rural folk fleeing agricultural serfdom, the boll weevil, and drought; the horrors of lynch mobs and Klan activity; the encoding of separate but equal in the Supreme Court's *Plessy v. Ferguson* decision; the attractions of 'the North' itself, believed to be less racist than the South, and with greater educational and job opportunities, whatever their limitations.

Zafar 287–8

3 Davis lists *The Messenger, Crisis,* and *Opportunity,* the official organs of the Brotherhood of Sleeping Car Porters, the NAACP, and the Urban League; "in *Fire!!!* and *Harlem,* short-lived independent magazines; and in *Survey Graphic,* the *Atlantic Monthly,* and *Forum*" (Davis *Southscapes* 141).

4 Less sexually defined, Eric Walrond's move into elite New York circles is described by his biographer James Davis:

within four years, he would be dining downtown with Alfred and Blanche Knopf, James Weldon Johnson, Carl Van Vechten, Zora Neale Hurston, Countee Cullen, Langston Hughes, Alain Locke, and other literati. He would take them to A'Lelia Walker's parties, heir to the fortune of the first African American millionaire, and dance the Charleston until the early morning in the gin-soaked cabarets of Prohibition-era Harlem.

Davis 43

5 This important book was originally published anonymously in 1912; it was Van Vechten who brought it to Knopf and suggested that it be attributed to its author (Bernard 6). Bernard points out that many of Van Vechten's black friends saw "no racial divide between themselves and Van Vechten."

6 Early in the novel, Van Vechten explains through the character of young Ruby that Harlem is truly "Nigger Heaven." The freedoms available to African Americans there are dazzling as well as bewildering. It is Ruby's repetition of the word that, supposedly, legitimates it, echoing Van Vechten's longer statement that sometimes "nigger" is a term of endearment, even though "its employment by a white person is fiercely resented" (Van Vechten *Nigger* 15, 26).

7 Jean Toomer was born Nathan Pinchback Toomer in 1894; after his parents had divorced, the boy moved back to Washington with his mother and lived with his grandparents (P.B.S. Pinchback had been lieutenant governor of Louisiana during Reconstruction). He was raised by those grandparents after his mother's early death. Appearing to be white, Toomer attended college in several states, never graduating but amassing a wealth of knowledge in philosophy and aesthetics.

8 Spending two years in the writing of *Not Without Laughter,* Hughes was hurt by the critique of W. E. B. Du Bois, who preferred that African American novelists wrote *romances* rather than novels. Du Bois could not stomach the 1920s emphasis on the sexual. His own novels, *The Quest of the Silver Fleece* in 1911 and *Dark Princess* in 1928, were pastiches of realism and naturalism, with the good, simple African American characters being rewarded for their moral choices with happiness.

9 In Eugene Redmond's assessment, whereas he sees James Weldon Johnson as the first "groundbreaking poet of the blues," Langston Hughes came to carry that banner, beginning with Hughes' blues poem written from a woman's perspective, "Young Gal's Blues," published in 1927 (Smethurst 144).

10 As Mitchell and Davis describe the 1931 controversy over the joint authorship of this play, Hurston reportedly claimed that *Mule Bone* was hers. When Wallace Thurman was

hired to revise the play, he refused the work, since he could see where the argument was heading. According to these authors, "Hurston could be two-faced . . . frequently playing people off against each other as she did with Langston Hughes and Alain Locke, Langston Hughes and Mrs. Mason, and Langston Hughes and Carl Van Vechten" (131–2, 136).

Suggested further reading

Houston A. Baker, Jr. *Modernism and the Harlem Renaissance*. U of Chicago P, 1987.
Bernard W. Bell. *The Afro-American Novel and Its Tradition*. U of Massachusetts P, 1987.
George Hutchinson. *The Harlem Renaissance in Black and White*. Harvard UP, 1995.
James Smethurst. *The African American Roots of Modernism*. U of North Carolina P, 2011.

7

RECONSTRUCTING THE 1930s

The American thirties still resonate with a pervasive message of loss. Whether using the end of the 1920s as a standpoint position—including the visible "crash" occurring in late October, or seeing the flamboyant prosperity of the twenties as the apex of American financial ingenuity, readers find a definite change in United States writing that begins in 1930. The contrast between 1920s high Modernism and the 1930s, an age that demanded anything except *self-involved* art, was striking, and gave some observers reason to think that Modernism might be over.

Even in literature that seemed motivated largely to express the radical political sentiments of the 1930s, however, many stylistic techniques stemmed from the earlier modernist period. Writers saw no conflict between continuing to use methods they felt were effective, even if their themes had changed. John Dos Passos, for example, crafted *The 42nd Parallel*, published in 1930, to show his characters' daily lives: the way a person earns a living, maintains romance, friendship, and political alliances, and describes contemporary value systems at work, as well as newspaper and screen ("Newsreel") headlines, popular song lyrics, and colorful descriptions of home interiors, clothing, customs. This first book of what was to become his trilogy *U.S.A.* used more modernist techniques than any other thirties novel except some of William Faulkner's, yet it was considered a *proletarian* novel.[1]

In her recent book, *The Middle Class in the Great Depression*, critic Jennifer Haytock lists some visible social changes resulting from this decade's economic unease, if not deprivation: "lower marriage rates . . ., a drop in childbirth, increased incidences of marital desertion, and a reduction in divorce rates because few couples could afford to end unhappy marriages" (Haytock 3). As she concludes, problems previously impacting the poor were now affecting middle-class families.

A bevy of economic theorists contend that even when 25% of the working population had lost their jobs, 75% of Americans saw little change: they were, however, affected by fears of personal loss, and the once-strong undergirding of a belief system that was founded on the promise of the American dream began to stagger. As critic Amy Kaplan pointed out in *The Social Construction of American Realism*, "realism serves as a strategy for imagining and managing the threats of social change" (Kaplan 10).[2] The fear was often interior: would people's beliefs in the promise of America hold up? It was true that the teeming immigrant population was still seen as a threat; yet, cultural beliefs still privileged the accessibility of work. Americans, both newly-arrived and long resident, believed that their country would provide work opportunities. They saw, however, that they might have to struggle to obtain the privilege of working. As Haytock creates her definition of 1930s literature, she notes,

> Literature of the Great Depression engages the American Dream possibly more and more directly than literature of any other decade. It was one thing for a middle-class, native-born American to envision an immigrant face on poverty; it was quite another to see one's neighbor having to give up his house.
>
> *Haytock 4*

Gordon Hutner states more directly that so-called "proletarian" literature did not dominate the decade. At its highest peak, according to this critic, these texts "occupied only a small part of literary discussion." Rather, readers commented on the "decline of modernist satire and the rise of regionalism, historical fiction, and the family saga, all of which combined, apparently, to replace '20s debunking with a new kind of earnestness and a new desire for explanation" (Hutner 155).

Haytock terms these serious literary approaches to region and family matters, "the rise of 'middlebrow fiction.'" Drawing from the work of Lawrence W. Levine (particularly in his *Highbrow/Lowbrow: The Emergence of Cultural Hierarchy in America*), Haytock credits the financial and emotional uncertainties of the 1930s with making readers appreciate narratives about the "reality" of contemporary lives. Just as Levine considers the influences of a new wave of immigrants, settling into work experiences that might have been given to non-immigrant Americans, Haytock notes both the "specialization and professionalism" that resulted from economic uncertainties—as well as "an expanding middle class" (Haytock 5).

Haytock's 2013 study canvasses what she terms "middle-class" novels so that readers understand the contributions made by such critically overlooked writers as Margaret Ayer Barnes, Fannie Hurst, Edna Ferber, Mary Roberts Rinehart, Dawn Powell, Josephine Lawrence and others. Her efforts are significant, but as Hutner points out, the novels that last into later decades appear to be those that "assail" the middle class. (For example, why does Sinclair Lewis's *Babbitt* remain a classic of the middle life, even as Josephine Lawrence's *If I Have Four Apples* slips into obscurity?) Hutner, accordingly, asks, "Why do the books that fall out of favor inevitably treat the middle class, while revenge narratives *against* the middle class manage to survive?" (Hutner 63).

Recently, British critic Peter Conn has provided a similar injunction against claiming too much importance for the proletarian novel: "to see the thirties exclusively as 'the red decade' is to reduce a complex palette to a monotone." Conn continues that no reader today should view the United States in the 1930s as dominated by

> Left aesthetics and politics. In fact, the United States in the 1930s was—as it has always been, and despite the pressures of the Depression—a place of enormous ideological and imaginative complexity, and the uses to which writers put the past can assist in recovering the heterogeneity of intellectual life in the decade.
>
> *Conn 6*

Conn's view wars with opinions expressed in a recent essay by Barbara Foley, when she defines proletarian fiction as "inseparable from its historical context," which she specifies as

> the political and economic crisis of the Depression; the emergence of Soviet socialism and its far-flung challenge to capitalism; the growth of the American Communist Party (CPUSA), which exercised widespread influence upon writers, first through the John Reed Clubs and subsequently through the League of American Writers and its larger American Writers Congress gatherings.
>
> *Foley Matthews 353*

Foley stresses as well the politics of the proletarian novels' influence: geared to chart people's everyday lives, the novel focused particularly on "the lives of working-class people from an anti-capitalist perspective, one that was intended to arouse militant . . . class consciousness" (Foley Matthews 355). She divides these works into five thematic categories. The first is the "strike novel," beginning with the Gastonia, North Carolina mill strikes, moving to Steinbeck's *In Dubious Battle* as well as *The Grapes of Wrath*, and merging in Myra Page's *Gathering Storm* with more overt Russian wooing.

The second is the political novel that centers on race and racism. Fielding Burke's *A Stone Came Rolling* is paired here with William Attaway's *Blood on the Forge* and other historical novels. Foley here inserts Richard Wright's *Uncle Tom's Children* because its stories deal with blatant racism.

The third category is "Bottom Dogs," the name drawn from Edward Dahlberg's expose of the poverty that created the homeless and the hobo: Nelson Algren's *Somebody in Boots*, Tom Kromer's *Waiting for Nothing*, Louis Coleman's *Lumber*, James T. Farrell's *Studs Lonigan* trilogy, the 1920s novels of B. Traven and—extending into the 1940s—Richard Wright's *Native Son* and *Lawd Today!* Foley makes the point that these are works about *non*-class conscious workers. David Minter attributes the effectiveness of what he calls "the authority of the tough-guy, bottom-dog male writers" to the subjects explored in the novels—"Coal miners, steelworkers, bricklayers . . . each of them is the story of a witness who has seen up close the wounded, damaged lives they represent" (Minter 230–1).[3]

Foley's fourth category depends upon books that feature the development of class-consciousness (and often, of Red beliefs). Jack Conroy's *The Disinherited*, Agnes Smedley's *Daughter of Earth*, Isidor Schneider's *From the Kingdom of Necessity*,

Myra Page's *Moscow Yankee*, Albert Maltz's *The Underground Stream*—in these novels, even if they have been well-reviewed, their tendency to proselytize is obvious.

Foley's fifth category is reserved for the majority of these novels—books about the everyday working classes and their lives. Meridel Le Sueur and Tillie Olsen's writings here join Conroy's 1935 novel *A World to Win*, Thomas Bell's *All Brides Are Beautiful*, Josephine Herbst's *Rope of Gold* trilogy, Michael Gold's *Jews Without Money*, William Carlos Williams' Stetcher trilogy, beginning with *White Mule*, and Dos Passos's *U.S.A.* (Foley Matthews 358–9).[4]

The best description of the literary production of the 1930s remains Alan Wald's critical trilogy, represented here by his books published in 2002 (*Exiles from a Future Time*) and 2007 (*Trinity of Passion: The Literary Left and the Antifascist Crusade*). In his discussions, Wald honors the key earlier books about the radical American novel (Daniel Aaron's *Writers on the Left* and Walter Rideout's *The Radical Novel in the United States, 1900–1954*), but extends his broadly-based commentary to reach a plethora of texts that have long been forgotten. Considering the novels recently brought back into print by Wald's series at University of Illinois Press,[5] Foley's judgment that perhaps only 100 novels fit her descriptors of proletarianism might be questioned.

Janet Galligani Casey assesses the decade (in her introduction to her essay collection, *The Novel and the American Left*), and sees the importance of what she terms "the documentary book, including Erskine Caldwell's and Margaret Bourke-White's *You Have Seen Their Faces* (1937) and James Agee's and Walker Evans's *Let Us Now Praise Famous Men* (1941)."[6] She places the significance of photographs in line with the deep-rooted American belief in linear progress: motion is good, stasis is frustrating. She describes this as "the dichotomy between aimlessness and direction, fixity and loco-motion" and connects the 1930s industrial vocabulary to the nineteenth century working–class culture that identified progress with such terms as "*speed-up, work stop-page, walkout*, and *strike*," strategies in a socioeconomic war (Casey x).

Casey's consideration of the novel *per se* leads her to what she calls

> an intriguing moment in the history of the American novel. Despite asser-tions that the novel has been less efficacious in addressing working-class culture and concerns than such genres as autobiography or reportage, the art of fiction in this period was at the forefront of left-intellectual inquiry in that numerous socially conscious novels were indeed written and the role(s) and theory of fiction were widely debated. Moreover, one novel—Steinbeck's *The Grapes of Wrath*—was arguably the century's most influential arbiter of Depression iconography and broadly leftist sentiment. The contentions, on one hand, that politics and aesthetics are not profitably mixed and, on the other hand, that all art is essentially political, have worked to minimize the specific achievements of a large group of Depression-era novels that can be construed as leftist in a rich variety of ways, and whose serious investigation has been even further, if unintentionally, constrained by the perceived necessity of pooling texts that share the same foundational forms of leftist.

> *Casey xi–xii*

This critic admits that on first glance, the political novel of the 1930s appears to be written by white, male authors, but she lists a number of non-male and non-white mainstream writers as integral to her investigation: Margery Latimer, Tess Slesinger, Meridel Le Sueur, Tillie Olsen, Pietro Di Donato, Arna Bontemps, Waters E. Turpin, Countee Cullen, Myra Page, Caroline Slade, Edith Summers Kelley, Claude McKay, Richard Wright, Clara Weatherwax, and others. It remains for Marcus Klein to recover specifics about the range of 1930s fiction and non-fiction. As he notes in *Foreigners,* "these [writers] were ghetto blacks, midwestern 'bohunks,' Lower East Side Jews, or the rural poor of the South." He lists a number of titles as he suggests that "true Americans became the subjects of literature," pointing as he does to "the Americanness of non-Americans." His list includes Wright's *Native Son,* Anderson's *Puzzled America* and *Hometown,* Dreiser's *Tragic America,* Louise Armstrong's *We Too Are the People,* Erskine Caldwell's *Say! Is This the U.S.A.?* and *Some American People,* Paul S. Taylor's *An American Exodus,* Nathan Asch's *The Road: In Search of America,* Eleanor Roosevelt's *This Is America,* Benjamin Appel's *The People Talk,* James Agee's *Let Us Now Praise Famous Men,* Walker Evans's *American Photographs,* Louis Adamic's *My America,* Joseph Freeman's *An American Testament,* the WPA's *These Are Our Lives,* and the Federal Writers' Project's *American Stuff* [7] (Klein 37).

Some of the most effective writing about the conditions of the poor occurred in theater productions. As throughout the world, dramatists viewed performance as a primary tool for change, so Clifford Odets[8]—writing both *Waiting for Lefty* and *Awake and Sing* in 1935—knew audiences would respond to his evocation of pain. Called a one act play, "Waiting for Lefty" is five separate scenes, each one set in the midst of people in need, each group of actors waiting for the character—Lefty—who does not appear. In the reassuring words of Joe in the first scene, saying that he does not know Lefty's whereabouts:

> . . . he didn't take no run-out powder. That Wop's got more guts than a slaughter house. Maybe a traffic jam got him, but he'll be here. But don't let this red stuff scare you. Unless fighting for a living scares you. We gotta make up our minds. My wife made up my mind last week, if you want the truth. It's plain as the nose on Sol Feinberg's face we need a strike.

Complete with racial slurs, Joe's allegiance is reassuring. Later in his speech, he quotes "the wife" who reminds him "eighty cents ain't money—don't buy beans almost" (Odets *Lefty* L D, 1710).

Odets' second scene is of a middle-class home after the furniture has been repossessed; the third, of a laboratory employee refusing to be dishonest; the next, of a girl going out to a dance with a man her mother disapproves of ("I gotta right to have something out of life. I don't smoke, I don't drink. So if Sid wants to take me to a dance, I'll go." Immediately the reader translates smoking and drinking into costs, and then the dialogue segues to the reason Sid is so objectionable: "It's that he ain't got nothing." He's a taxi driver and as her brother reminds her, "Today they're makin' five and six dollars a week. Maybe you wanta raise a family on that") (Odets *Lefty* L D, 1717).

The next episode introduces Tom Clayton, a labor organizer who was active in the Philadelphia taxi cab drivers strike; one of the hecklers in the audience knows he is really "Tom Clancy, from the old Clancys, way back" and that he infiltrates union meetings in order to disband them. He is a company spy. Sabotage from within is one of the problems labor and its members face. In the last scene, a senior Jewish doctor is being blackmailed by his hospital so that a relative of a board member can join the staff: his ethnicity means he will never work again if he protests.

When Odets returns the action to the union meeting, with the call that its members become "Stormbirds of the working-class. Workers of the World .... Our Bones and Blood," as they plan to strike, it is then that Lefty's body is found, "behind the car barns with a bullet in his head" (Odets *Lefty* L D, 1726).

Produced countless times in small theaters and large, (for a nominal production charge), Odets' first play prepared audiences for the longer family drama. In *Awake and Sing* the three-generation lower class Jewish family faces the trauma of questioning whether they can stay in their small Bronx apartment despite prejudice. At root, however, the dilemma is a financial one, and the way the status-conscious mother, Bessie Berger, forces her husband and son to make money shreds the fabric of family. The money Uncle Morty leaves his nephew may save the Bergers' status but the loss of his uncle drives Ralph into Marxism. Originally titled *I Got the Blues*, the play was directed by Harold Clurman, running for over 200 performances at the Belasco Theatre in New York.

To mount any play, production costs were prohibitive—especially given the paucity of funding for what would be seen as "subversive," even "Red" dramas. Listing Broadway plays, even off-Broadway plays, shows that most drama available was still conservative, politic only in its non-labor subject matter: in 1929 Elmer Rice won the Pulitzer Prize for Drama with *Street Scene*—despite John Howard Lawson's *The International* (scenes based on music and carnival acts) and John Dos Passos's *Airways, Inc.* about capitalistic maneuvering.[9] Edna St. Vincent Millay's *The Princess Marries the Page* was done in 1932. In 1934 Lillian Hellman's *The Children's Hour* introduced unusually demanding subject matter even as T. S. Eliot's verse drama *The Rock* drew on religious sonority. 1935 saw the production of Eliot's morality play, *Murder in the Cathedral*, as well as e. e. cummings' ballet *Tom*. This play, followed in 1939 by Eliot's *The Family Reunion*, made its author, now a British citizen, famous world-wide (and probably led to his receiving the Nobel Prize for Literature in 1948). Any observer could see how differently Odets' 1935 plays, particularly *Waiting for Lefty*, would affect audiences in that same year: in 1936 Lillian Hellman wrote her strike play, *Days To Come*, at least partly out of Odets' force.

American playwright and novelist Thornton Wilder won the Pulitzer Prize for Drama in 1938, with his return-to-nostalgia production, *Our Town*. Wilder had an earlier Pulitzer for his 1927 *The Bridge of San Luis Rey*, and his motivation was to return the literary world to normalcy. Miles Orvell linked Wilder's 1938 play to the writing of both Sherwood Anderson's *Home Town* and Archibald MacLeish's 1938 *Land of the Free*, a book which made extensive use of the Farm Security Administration (FSA) photos. Orvell saw these works as a way of comforting United States citizens because there was little comfort economically, no matter what individual circumstances were. He called *Our Town* "an exemplar of the period . . . a meditation on that favorite construction of thirties culture, the common man . . . . it echoed as well the period's fascination with facts, which pervaded the visual, literary, and dramatic arts of the time." Orvell goes on to point out that "Wilder steers clear of any literal realism, not only in staging but also in characterization" (Orvell 118). His reading of *Our Town* is commensurate with his contention that the small town in all types of U.S. literature became "an icon of American democracy," triggering people's nostalgia for the "GOOD—American dream—years" (Orvell 102).[10]

Observers of the 1930s also realize that signs of (attempted) economic and philosophical change were in evidence long before the crash in October, 1929: the international furor over the executions of Nicola Sacco and Bartolomeo Vanzetti in 1927 involved such writers as Edna St. Vincent Millay, Edmund Wilson, Mike Gold, Genevieve Taggard, John Dos Passos, and others. Postwar America had seen a number of repressive, antiliberal events—the Espionage Act of 1917, the Sedition Act of 1918, the beginning of Prohibition with the passage of the 18th Amendment (prohibiting the making, selling, or transportation of alcohol in the United States), *Schenck v. United States* and *Abrams v. United States* in 1919, increased membership in the Ku Klux Klan as well as the groups' more visible and aggressive acts, the passing of the 19th Amendment in 1920 giving women the vote. In 1921 Congress set a limit of 357,000 new immigrants per year, and the Supreme Court ruled that labor unions could be prosecuted for restraining interstate trade.

Not all measures were legal ones. Workers felt the pinch as most wages in industrial sectors were cut. Then came the Scopes trial in 1925 and the frightening labor strikes, especially the Gastonia, North Carolina, cotton mill strike in 1929 (covered by international media because of the murder of Ella May Wiggins, the woman who led the strikers). As attitudes throughout America became more and more restrictive, whether in fear of Communism or in support of national isolationism, the country dedicated itself to legislating people's morals. These policies seemed to be approved by whatever power influenced prosperity, perhaps because the United States economy was burgeoning. Much of the country interpreted financial prosperity as a sign that its political and social beliefs were correct.

By the time of the 1930s, the energy of isolationism stemmed from the fear of losing work, and its resultant prosperity—and eventually, financial standing. Klein states that the literature of the thirties was to show "the direct experience of the lowly" (Klein 130). Most readers did not want to learn about that class of people, and avoided exposure to the texts that described those people and their chosen work; they preferred reading and learning about what Michael Denning calls "ethnically unmarked middle-class American people" (Denning 153). It is Denning who points out that ethnic figures in literature, music, and entertainment often changed their names to erase whatever taint ethnic roots might convey: Man Ray changed his name from Emmanuel Radnitzky; Nelson Algren modified his given name, Nelson Ahlgren Abraham; Artie Shaw had been Arthur Arshawsky; Steve Nelson changed his name from Stjepan Mesaros; Mike Gold changed his name from Itzok Granich; V. F. Calverton changed his from George Goetz; Dorothy Parker had been Dorothy Rothschild; Edwin Rolfe had been born Solomon Fishman; Elmer Rice had originally been Elmer Reizenstein; Nathanael West had been christened Nathan Weinstein (Denning 153).

Denning makes a wider assumption that is relevant when he states that

> the popular arts of the age of the CIO, like most of the successful forms and genres of United States mass culture, had developed out of "lowbrow" working-class culture and were sanitized, Americanized, and whitened to attract a "respectable" middle-class audience . . . . Thus, on the surface, the mass culture of the 1930s and 1940s seems to be a "classless" and "American" culture, with white covers of black music and Jewish and Italian stars with Anglicized stage names.[11]
>
> *Denning 153*

In the often-vaunted melting pot of American democracy, issues of class had remained submerged under a patina of polite society: if the character Simon Rosedale (from Edith Wharton's *The House of Mirth*) was invited to a party, no one mentioned his Jewish roots. Or at least no other character commented on his Jewishness. It goes without saying that every culture has its cadre of the poor, but the United States was accustomed to only so many poor people; in earlier times, churches and other kindly institutions could help alleviate unfortunate peoples' distress. That level of comfort changed dramatically after 1929.

EXCERPT FROM ALICE DUNBAR-NELSON'S "THE PROLETARIAT SPEAKS"

I love beautiful things:
Great trees, bending green winged branches to a velvet lawn,
Fountains sparkling in white marble basins,
Cool fragrance of lilacs and roses and honeysuckle. . .

And so I work
In a dusty office, whose grimed windows
Look out in an alley of unbelievable squalor,
Where mangy cats, in their degradation, spurn
Swarming bits of meat and bread;
Where odors, vile and breath taking, rise in fetid waves
Filling my nostrils, scorching my humid, bitter cheeks. . .

Poverty during the depression

Described in the mildest possible of terms, United States residents—immigrant as well as native—were crushed by not only their own existing poverty, but by the ongoing threat of increasing financial difficulties. As Frederick Lewis Allen wrote in his landmark study, *Only Yesterday*, published just at the start of the decade of the 1930s, "Investors who had dreamed of retiring to live on their fortunes now found themselves back once more at the very beginning of the long road to riches. Day by day the newspapers printed the grim reports of suicides."

Ironic as the financial condition was (since Herbert Hoover was known as a genius of a businessman, and a friend of Wall Street),

> Coolidge-Hoover Prosperity was not yet dead, but it was dying. Under the impact of the shock of panic, a multitude of ills which hitherto had passed unnoticed or had been offset by stock-market optimism began to beset the body economic . . . . Nor was that all. Prosperity is more than an economic condition; it is a state of mind. The Big Bull Market had been more than the climax of a business cycle; it had been the climax of a cycle in American mass thinking and mass emotion. There was hardly a man or woman in the country whose attitude toward life had not been affected by it in some degree and was not now affected by the sudden and brutal shattering of hope.
>
> *Allen 256*

From the Prologue to the first issue of *New Masses* came this indictment:

> The Thirties began with the cold hell of hunger, the unparalleled assault of starvation: The hunger. The wrecked home. The family on the city pavement. The grandmother in her rocking chair, dry-eyed, on the sidewalk. In rain. Hopelessness. The crying child. The staring, anguished mother. The shamed, bitter father. The cold Hooverville. Waste, refuse: humankind on the dump. I repeat: the hunger. Milk dumped into rivers, obscene . . . . Oranges burned, wheat burned . . . to keep the prices up.
>
> *New Masses I 1926*

Sherwood Anderson wrote in his introduction to his 1935 *Puzzled America*, "There are, everywhere in America, these people now out of work. There are women and children hungry and others without enough clothes" (Anderson *Puzzled* ix).

One of the most moving accounts of physical hunger occurred in Richard Wright's *Black Boy*, the protagonist (Wright) looking back on the deliberate enervation of continuous hunger:

> Hunger stole upon me so slowly that at first I was not aware of what hunger really meant. Hunger had always been more or less at my elbow when I played, but now I began to wake up at night to find hunger standing at my bedside, staring at me gauntly. The hunger I had known before this had been

no grim, hostile stranger; it had been a normal hunger that made me beg constantly for bread, and when I ate a crust or two I was satisfied. But this new hunger baffled me, scared me, made me angry and insistant. Whenever I begged for food now my mother would pour me a cup of tea which would still the clamor in my stomach for a moment or two, but a little later I would feel hunger nudging my ribs, twisting my empty guts until they ached. I would grow dizzy and my vision would dim . . . . I could not understand why some people had enough food and others did not.

Wright Black *14–15, 19*

Critic Halford E. Luccock assesses the writing of the 1930s through the lens of the authors' creation of hungry characters, noting that throughout books written in the 1920s, almost nothing was said about eating—or about being able, or unable, to eat (Luccock 34). In contrast, writing from the 1930s showed that plots could be determined by the hunger of protagonists and antagonists. Such novels as Jack Conroy's *The Disinherited* and Tom Kromer's *Waiting for Nothing* have little story to tell except the appeasement of characters' hunger. In their co-written nonfiction work, *They Seek a City* (alternately titled *Anyplace But Here*), Jack Conroy and Arna Bontemps use the image of six adolescent boys—three black, three white—riding the rails north from the South to reach Detroit, where they hope to get work in the auto plants. Here in a "hobo jungle," the luminous image of community is a meal:

All had been foraging for food and were now pooling their combined catch for a "mulligan": a ham bone, a can of tomatoes for which one had been compelled to yield a dime, some scraps of bacon, green corn from a near-by field.

They Seek *249*

More centrally, in Josephine Johnson's 1934 novel *Now in November*, which won the Pulitzer Prize for Fiction in 1935, the voice of the middle daughter Marget Haldemarne recounts that hunger and the efforts their father takes to avoid it. The Midwestern family moves from farm to farm, hoping for success yet realizing that they were once again moving toward "some awful and hopeless hour." The book begins with the family's simple birthday celebration for the father, an afternoon which ends with the accidental, ominous death of their beloved dog. Marget's voice leads readers through ten years of their hard life on the always marginal farm, but sequence is less important than essence. Here she describes the man who stays so distant from them all:

Father couldn't see the masterpiece of a maggot or be satisfied with the shadow of a leaf, in which ways we were older than he was, but young in being so blind we could not see the heaviness of his responsibility or know the probe of that fear which made him want security at the expense of our happiness.—I think sometimes that he would have been a milder, more patient man had there been some sons instead of nothing but girls' talk all the time and women-voices. Life's lonely enough and isolated enough without the thick wall of kind to make it go even darker. Later we did not talk so much, but in the first year we were like a bunch of guineas, cackling and squawking at all hours. It irritated him to have us picking and pecking at lives of other people, and telling the things we'd hear. 'Shut up;' he'd shout.—'Shut up and keep out of others' business!' And at times we had hated him for it . . . . We never seemed able to make much over. All that we saved above what it cost to live—and live by mouth and mind only, with nothing new but the seasons or thoughts we had—all went into the mortgage-debt. It would have taken so little to make us happy. A little more rest, a little more money—it was the nearness that tormented. The nearness to life the way we wanted it

Johnson 36–7

At the end of several of these hard but unremarkable years, after a summer of drought in which the mother of the family has been badly burned and eventually dies, following the sister who drifts into madness and kills herself, Marget remains the stable center, trying to care for her sibling and the father who is now so broken he can barely function. She pronounces the epitaph that marked so many lives during the American thirties:

I do not see in our lives any great ebb and flow or rhythm of earth. There is nothing majestic in our living. The earth turns in great movements, but we jerk about on its surface like gnats, our days absorbed and overwhelmed by a mass of little things—that confusion which is our living and which prevents us from being really alive. We grow tired . . . .

Johnson 226

When Nelson Algren published *Somebody in Boots* in 1935, his first novel bore more of the marks of what readers think of as being a "collective novel," a work that is inclusive of the people caught in the depressed times and the places, so often urban. Here is Cass McKay, living in Chicago at the time of the second World's Fair, "A Century of Progress," observing

that night ten thousand kids in Tenement Town were sleeping when it rained. When it rains in Tenement Town sewers back up into basement flats. All over the World's Fair City, World's Fair spring or World's Fair summer, ten thousand kids slept in homes damp as kennels. Ten thousand kids didn't have enough to eat in that welter of diseased slum-streets. Sick kids sold papers, sniped tinfoil out of gutters, shot crap in hallways . . . . The Polock kids chased the Dagoes and the Dagoes chased the Jews. The Wops slunk behind fences on either side of the Loomis Street alleys and slung milk bottles over at each other's heads. They're half sick from birth—Black kids, Wop kids, Swede kids, Hunkey, Litvak and Chinese kids—the skinny tough dirty knockabout kids that had to knock down a fence to get into the World's Fair playground . . . . The highschool kids from '31 and '32 and '33 and '34 are still waiting for work, any kind of work. They booze while waiting. Their old men booze too . . . .

Algren 236

Juxtaposed with this kind of panoramic, didactic (and realistic ethnic) detail comes Algren's portrait of Cass, his protagonist—here, successfully back in his rented room after his first crime, robbing a cab driver and then taking a bus back home,

So weak with shock was he that twice on the staircase he had to sit down to rest. He sat with his head in his hands, and he whimpered. He rolled his head between his hands and pounded his temples with his fists to quiet the wild throbbing there. When he walked into the room Norah rolled off the bed and switched on the light. She took one look at him, and went for the whiskey. His shirt was drenched with sweat, and his face was so pale that its freckles stood out like moles. His socks were as wet as though he'd been wading. She sat up with him until he ceased to tremble, and by then it was too late to go to bed. Before that morning had passed, they moved. Just walked out and didn't come back . . . . He had gotten 41 dollars, and the sum lasted them 3 weeks.

Algren 194

Cass and Norah become the Bonnie and Clyde of Algren's novel, but they are never easy with their lives of crime. (From a realistic novel like Algren's, the move to the increasingly popular mystery and detective novel is slight: violence underlays both modes of writing, and in both, someone evolves into heroism.)

For all his education (Algren had graduated from the University of Illinois School of Journalism, but he had had trouble earning a living since 1931—and had ended up in Texas, where he learned to exist in the hobo life), he had no reputation as a writer. One of the more famous writers from this period, Jack Conroy, had no formal education, but he wrote about his life in a coal mining town of northern Missouri as one of nine children, most of whom joined the men to work in the Monkey Nest mine. Two of Conroy's brothers, like his father, died there. When in 1933 he published his first novel, *The Disinherited*, critics seemed to admire his lack of education. As critic Andrzej Gasiorek explained,

Among those who were sympathetic to the plight of the working classes— even if they didn't go so far as to espouse evolutionary politics—the difficulty of entering into working-class experience or of engaging with that predicament became as much a subject of their writing as any attempt to represent that experience.

Gasiorek 195

The authenticity of Conroy's fiction and non-fiction (including the series of children's books about American heroes that he co-wrote with Arna Bontemps) was unmistakable. Eventually, Conroy became the editor of a new little magazine, *Anvil*, and it was in that journal that Algren, then living in an abandoned gas station in Alpine, Texas, published a chapter of *Somebody in Boots*. In that same issue, Richard Wright, a Chicago postal employee, published his first poems. *Anvil* also published Erskine Caldwell, Langston Hughes, Meridel Le Sueur, and others. Conroy believed ardently that new and previously unknown writers would speak the language of the necessarily new thinking in the mid-1930s.

When in 1935 Conroy published a much more literary novel, *A World to Win*, a three-part narrative with Socialist/Communist leanings as the title suggests, critics then objected to the author's lack of authenticity. There are plenty of "authentic" moments in the book, but it tries to romanticize the reader's view of poverty, in the plot of young would-be writers and their circles, as well as the more descriptive narrative of Leo, the man who labors hard for his living. Here is a passage from the last segment of the book in which Leo, his very pregnant wife Anna, their five children and Leo's infirm father are in Utah weeding beet fields for the Mormon Bishop. The others working the seventeen-hour days are Mexicans.

> About four o'clock Leo had slackened his pace and had begun to worry about the time. He had been watching a Mexican woman from the next field leaving her work frequently and walking to the bank of a large irrigating canal near which he had eaten his own lunch. He supposed she was going to relieve herself . . . then he heard the Mexican woman scream. Turning, he saw her, a bright shawl fluttering from her shoulders like a banner, a bundle in her arms, running toward the men in the field, shouting words Leo could not make out. She stumbled and fell, but instead of raising herself, just laid in the middle of the beets and threshed about, howling. Occasionally, she talked rapidly . . . . When the blankets were thrown off and the "face of a dark Mexican baby about three months old" exposed, Leo and the others saw that 'The blankets were alive with large red ants, and the child's face was puffed and swollen until it resembled an overripe strawberry. Both eyes were swollen shut and a small round hole was the only indication of what had once been the mouth.
>
> *Conroy* World *290*

The racism of the Mormon family—who disregarded the Mexican family's need for child care even as they professed concern about Anna's pregnancy (Anna being a white woman)—is hardly subtle. Bishop Taylor drives the baby to town, but the infant dies before they reach a doctor. He then buries it as he is later to bury Anna after *his* son crashes a car with Anna in it. *A World to Win* charts a number of social problems as it tells the story of a laboring man who learns to live outside the law in order to survive. The only clear hero in the novel is Fatfolks, the black Communist who picks up the bombs thrown into the protesting strikers and hurls those bombs back into the police ranks—until a policeman shoots him in the back.

Another of the typical 1930s novels that aimed to speak for those mid-thirties voices was Albert Halper's *The Chute*. Based on the impersonality of piece work, the drudgery of repetitive tasks performed under incredible time pressures, the arduous labor this novel describes when Paul Sussman, marked by his Jewish name and appearance, is forced to take a job as runner for a mail-order house, earning twelve dollars a week, creates the substance of the long novel. His heart set on a career in architecture, Paul finds the frantic work not only demeaning but frightening, and the central chute into which all picked-up orders go becomes the metaphor for the whirling waste of his young life. "The packages were disappearing into a big black cavity, a hole which was centered in what appeared to be an upright black boiler standing upon its end" (Halper 16).

Fascinated by the urgency his peers devote to meeting their quotas, Paul learns how easily a foot slips and a life is lost to the hungry maw of the chute. Mesmerized by the chute, Paul approached it timidly, "just to look down its yawning mouth. He stood silently in awe, looking at a torrent of rushing goods" (Halper 39). The author also sets up a dichotomy between the blur of the young men's work at the mail-order business and the joy Paul experiences in his chosen isolation, doing his drawing as an apprentice. In Halper's descriptive choices, he changes the simplified remedy for lifting the poverty of the Depression—that a person finds work—to the heart-rending consequences of having to adjust to work that neither satisfies nor provides.

Difficult as it is to imagine the intensity of prejudice against Jewish people during the 1930s, Michael Gold's *Jews Without Money* traces the way anti-semiticism corrupted opportunities for both work and education. In David Minter's description, this autobiographical novel "stacks one brutal experience on top of another and then concludes with a formulaic celebration of the great revolution that will

---

EXCERPT FROM MICHAEL GOLD'S JEWS WITHOUT MONEY

On the East Side people buy their groceries a pinch at a time; three cents' worth of sugar, five cents' worth of butter, everything in penny fractions. The good Jewish black bread that smells of harvest time, is sliced into a dozen parts and sold for pennies. But that winter even pennies were scarce . . . .

Life froze. The sun vanished from the deathly gray sky. The streets reeked with snow and slush. There were hundreds of evictions. I walked down a street between dripping tenement walls. The rotten slush ate through my shoes. The wind beat on my face. I saw a stack of furniture before a tenement: tables, chairs, a washtub packed with crockery and bedclothes, a broom, a dresser, a lamp . . . .

Winter. Building a snow fort one morning, we boys dug out a litter of frozen kittens and their mother. The little ones were still blind. They had been born into it, but had never seen our world.

Other dogs and cats were frozen. Men and women, too, were found dead in hallways and on docks . . . .

finally set all the East Sides of the world free from poverty, exploitation, and misery" (Minter 229). Serving as editor of *New Masses*, Gold encouraged writers he found bluntly disparaging of the status quo (in this regard, he disliked Henry Roth's *Call It Sleep*, sensing that its effect relied on sentimentalism and shared sympathies). Rather, he admired Edward Dahlberg, Richard Wright, Arna Bontemps, Jack Conroy, Thomas Bell, Robert Cantwell, and others.[12]

In Werner Sollors' critique of the development of ethnic writing, he places Gold's *Jews Without Money* in the category of a work that challenged stereotypes—equating Jewish culture with moneyed success had been a trope that dominated American modernism, so here Gold worked against such an assumption. His characters were fighting the same relentless poverty that non-Jewish families faced. In other respects, Gold's novel charts the indignities of living in poverty in urban America: "the lack of privacy in overcrowded, filthy, and infested tenements, badly paying jobs and unemployment, gangsters, crime, and violence, and pimps, prostitution, and syphilis." It surrounds people in these circumstances, however, with the modern—the newsreels to be seen in the movie theaters, the child run over by a horse car, the elevated trains jammed with people intent on a Sunday outing. It includes a number of familiar ethnic themes: "greenhorns and Americanization, inter-ethnic encounters, name changes, the problem of ethnic slurs, the protective immigrant mother, the father's love for the Yiddish theater." Above all, Gold speaks for the individualization of his characters, noting that he knew few "racial types. My father, for instance, was like a certain kind of Irishman more than the stenciled stage Jew" (Sollors 391, 456).

For a text grounded in simple hunger, Meridel Le Sueur's *Women on the Breadlines* brings home both the physical condition of the deprived and the moral imbroglio of women faced with providing food for their families, as well as for themselves. Hunger becomes a double burden for women characters. As Le Sueur describes these who wait for work in an employment bureau, the specter of hunger dominates their consciousness: "We sit here every day, waiting for a job. There are no jobs. Most of us have had no breakfast. Some have had scant rations for over a year." She is not above editorializing, since her newspaper readers are, probably, less hungry: after all, they are able to buy a newspaper. "Hunger makes a human being lapse into a state of lethargy, especially city hunger . . . the timid crawl the streets, hunger like a beak of a terrible bird at the vitals" (Le Sueur 137).

Whether in her columns or, later, in her fiction such as *The Girl* and the journalism collected into books, Le Sueur includes food-related details. There is the nameless woman with no income who eats only a cracker a day, making no trouble, hoping not to be evicted from the room she can no longer afford. There is a seemingly harsh exchange between a young woman, out of work for eight months, who demands a job from the YMCA supervisor who reprimands her for her unshined shoes—cruel and unreachable because she knows that the girl is starving: "facing each other in a rage both helpless, helpless." There is the teacher who tries to get work from the welfare agency because she has no money at all, but because she still wears a suit and is a professional, she is turned away. So disoriented from her constant hunger that she cannot tell a convincing story about how she has been living, she does realize, finally, that she will never receive help, and after that recognition, she walks to a nearby bridge and jumps to her death. As Le Sueur had written elsewhere, "Not one of them [the out-of-work-women] but looks forward to starvation for the coming winter . . . . Not one of these women but knows that despite years of labor there is only starvation, humiliation in front of them." By choosing an ironic title, "Women on the Breadlines," for her collected columns, Le Sueur makes the searing point that even the hungriest of women were seldom included in food handouts or shelter programs sponsored by charities or governments. The hunger that beset these women was exponentially worse because they could not be cared for through the simple social medium of the breadline (Le Sueur 141).

The tragedy is unending. One of this author's most poignant stories is of

Mrs. Gray, sitting across from me, . . . a living spokesman for the futility of labor. She is a warning. Her hands are scarred with labor. Her body is a great puckered scar. She has given birth to six children, buried three, supported them all alive and dead, bearing them, burying them, feeding them. Bred in hunger they have been spare, susceptible to disease. For seven years she tried to save her boy's arm from amputation, diseased from tuberculosis of the bone. It is almost too suffocating to think of that long close horror of years of child-bearing, child-feeding, rearing, with the bare suffering of providing a meal and shelter.

As Le Sueur hammers home her journalistic details, the reader learns that Mrs. Gray is now fifty, unable to do any kind of work except washing streetcars, at which she labors

night and day, from midnight to dawn and offices in the early evening, scrub for fourteen and fifteen hours a day, sleep only five hours or so, do this their whole lives, and never earn one day of security, having always before them the pit of the future. The endless labor, the bending back, the water-soaked hands, earning never more than a week's wages, never having in their hands more life than that.

Le Sueur 147

Louis Adamic's nonfiction *My America, 1928–1938*, uses a statistical approach as he describes the ravages of the Depression. In reporting that there were 82 breadlines in New York City in January of 1931, serving approximately 85,000 meals a day, he chooses to give his reader the actual items the men waiting for that food received. For breakfast, oatmeal and coffee or rolls and coffee; for the other meals, "bread, soup, coffee; stew and bread; cheese or meat sandwiches and coffee; beans, bread, and coffee." Adamic itemizes to counter the anger of middle-class readers who—often insulated from such poverty—were critical of all relief efforts (Adamic 294).

By 1936, when James Rorty published his reportage as a book titled *Where Life Is Better: An Unsentimental American Journey*, the metaphor of hunger has become a given. What victims of the Depression have in common, according to this reading, is eternal optimism.[13] (In 1935, 22 million Americans were on relief, but Rorty summarizes the tone of United States poverty as "hopeful.") Reporting these attitudes with an undisguised cynicism, Rorty claimed that most Americans thought they could recover, that they and their families could both survive and—eventually-prosper. In Rorty's view, such *hope* was only *fantasy*. In his words, "I encountered nothing in 15,000 miles of travel that disgusted and appalled me so much as this American addiction to makebelieve. Apparently, not even empty bellies can cure it" (Rorty 13).

It goes without saying that the outrage of covering lives in the Depression gave rise to entirely new forms of writing. Just as Meridel Le Seuer used newspaper journalism to craft fiction, so Ruth McKenney created an entire city in her 1939 *Industrial Valley*. On the order of John Dos Passos's creating a pastiche of event through juxtaposed kinds of writing, McKenney composes her scenario of life in Akron, Ohio, through dated entries. For example, "Parade/January 2, 1932" is followed immediately by "Lethe/January 3, 1932," an account of seeing Greta Garbo "suffer all, even death, for love in a film called *Mata Hari*." (McKenney points out that tickets to the film cost forty cents.) That entry is followed by the catch-all category "News Items/January 4, 1932" and there the mayor announces that "after Wednesday all racketeers and bootleggers in town would be arrested." In sequence, William O'Neill, President of the General Tire and Rubber Company, urged an audience to "Come out of the gloom of the Depression and bask in the sunlight for a change." He reminded his listeners that Akron had long ago been officially dubbed the "City of Opportunity." The irony intensifies as McKenney reports on a meeting of Akron pastors, in which they joined in a campaign against "Depression gossip." They will support "a special anti-gossip Sunday in Akron churches." This group of entries ends with the January 15, 1932, report of the suicide of Gilbert Edgar, a bank vice-president. That item closed, "Mr. Edgar was Akron's first banker suicide."

The most dramatically different form of writing occurred in James Agee's 1941 *Let Us Now Praise Famous Men*, his evocative prose poem about share croppers in Alabama. Illustrated with Walker Evans' photographs of the three central families in Agee's text, the Gudgers, the Ricketts, and the Woods, the book combined the fascination of photo-documentary with the relentless reportage that Agee developed to tell this painful story. Begun in 1936 as an assignment for *Fortune* magazine, Agee's project started that summer as he and Evans traveled to Alabama to live with the nearly destitute white sharecroppers. In this work, Agee as writer leaves the role of observer and becomes participant. One of the most touching scenes in the book is the few hours when he has the Gudger house to himself so that he can scrutinize it: "They are gone. No one is at home, in all this house, in all this land. It is a long while before their return. I shall move as they would trust me not to, and as I could not, were they here" (Agee 119).

Highly sexual, Agee's language as he observes the poverty of the households—caught effectively in a survey of the contents of a drawer—insists on both literal and archetypal meaning. He moves from his guilt at being such an intense observer—"I am being made witness to matters no human being may see. There is a cold beating at my solar plexus" (Agee 120)—to memories of himself as a boy in "hot early puberty," alone in a house then that also allowed him sexual, as well as emotional, privacy. When Agee as writer emphasizes his own role in this supposedly objective presentation of the Gudger life, he changes the stance toward reality of American modernist writing.

One of the reasons this change is effective is that the Evans' photographs keep the reader at what seems to be a surface level, their power all the stronger for being distanced. The viewer enters the art with confidence in his or her own ability to read the intent of the pictures. With an aesthetic that has operated in much modernist writing Agee also focuses on stark detail—"freshly laundered cotton print dress held together high at the throat with a ten-cent brooch" (Agee 228)—but he then places that detail in a section called "Clothing," comprised of lists of attire for each family member, by day of the week. The contrast between either Saturday, the day the family goes to town, or Sunday, church day if the family attends, and the weekdays is poignant: much of their clothing is not fit to wear outside the house. The details of this long section blur as Agee takes the reader from one person to another, repeating faces in the same quiet voice throughout, but it also has moments of comedy. One of these is the section "Overalls" ("They are pronounced overhauls"). Agee describes the shape, construction, and purpose of such a garment, the laborer's uniform, with a mock heroic tone that turns to high praise at the ending:

> And on this façade, the cloven halls for the legs, the strong-seamed, structured opening for the genitals, the broad horizontal at the waist, the slant thigh pockets, the buttons at the point of each hip and on the breast, the geometric structures of the usages of the simpler trades—the complexed seams of utilitarian pockets which are so brightly picked out against darkness when the seam-threadings, double and triple stitched, are still white, so that a new suit of overalls has among its beauties those of a blueprint; and they are a map of a working man.
>
> *Agee 234–5*

Agee's incremental sentences suggest the writing of both Thomas Wolfe and, more directly, Walt Whitman.

This sense of uninterrupted voicing also comes to dominate much of the poetry written during the 1930s, as if some kind of people's voice worked constantly against the perfection of shape Imagism had conveyed. Whether it be in Tillie Lerner Olsen's "I Want You Women up North to Know," written in 1934 or Kay Boyle's 1937 "A Communication to Nancy Cunard," or many of Kenneth Fearing's precise poems, or various Langston Hughes's works, many illustrated with his drawings, poets in their anger seemed unable to keep their language from flowing.

Kay Boyle chooses many different stanza forms as she tells the story of the Scottsboro case, in which nine young black men were executed after they were convicted of raping two Alabama women.

> It begins in the dark on a box-car floor, the groaning timber
> Stretched from bolt to bolt above the freight-train wheels
> That grind and cry aloud like hounds upon the trail, the breathing weaving
> Unseen within the dark from mouth to nostril, nostril to speaking mouth.
> This is the theme of it, stated by one girl in a box-car saying:
> "Christ, what they pay you don't keep body and soul together."
> "Where was you working?" "Working in a mill-town." . . . .
>
> *Boyle N 542*

Tillie Olsen attacks the "women up north" who buy the handiwork ("dainty children's dresses you buy/at macy's, wanamakers, gimbels, marshall fields,") stained with the workers' blood, "stitched in wasting flesh,/ down in San Antonio" (Olsen N 652).

Many of the 1930s poems are laments, as is Horace Gregory's 1935 "Chorus for Survival," speaking for the country in its unresolved pain:

> This is thy heritage, America,
> Scaffold of iron deep in stone.
>> Destroy the ruins,
> This is the place; wreck here and build again.
>
> Tell us that love
>> Returns,
> Not soft nor kind,
> But like a crystal turning in the mind,
> Light where the body is . . .
>
> This is thy memory, America,
> The tenuous marriage of disunited blood,
> Captain and slave one bed,
>> in dust until the wind
> Stirs dust to life again . . .
>> and walking here,
> Conquered and conqueror
> (The apple blossoms white in midnight hair) . . . .
>
> *Gregory "Chorus" S 361*

Muriel Rukeyser writes laments (as in her 1938 "The Book of the Dead"), strident politically motivated works, and lyrics. Winner of the 1935 Yale Younger Poets prize for her first collection, *Theory of Flight*, she became famous for her keen ability to choose poetic form that underscored her political vision. While *U.S. 1* (her 1938 collection) may be her most read work, the 1940 long poem, "The Soul and Body of John Brown," is her most visionary. She writes in "Arthur Peyton," one part of "The Book of the Dead," about the engineer at the Hawk's Nest tunnel, dying from silicosis:

> Consumed. Eaten away. And love across the street.
> I had a letter in the mail this morning
> Dear Sir . . . pleasure . . . enclosing herewith our check . . .
> payable to you, for $21.59
> being one-half of the residue which
> we were able to collect in your behalf
> in regard to the above case . . .
>
> After collecting
> the dust   the failure   the engineering corps
> O love   consumed eaten away   the foreman laughed
> they wet the drills when the inspectors came . . . .
> Rukeyser "Arthur Peyton" N 674

Like the changes to both poetry and reportage, fiction of the decade made effective use of the painful phenomenon of hope, coming as it did in the midst of despair.

Erskine Caldwell's short stories, such as "Rachel" and "Daughter," marked him for a kind of fame different from the low comedy of his early novels, *God's Little Acre* and *Tobacco Road*. The proud child who dies after eating poisoned food from her boyfriend's family's garbage can hovers in readers' memory, as does the jailed father who has killed his child with a shotgun: "Daughter said she was hungry, and I just couldn't stand it no longer. I just couldn't stand to hear her say it." The context Caldwell works into this brief story lets Jim, a man respected by his community, explain further:

> I've been working all year and I made enough for all of us to eat . . . . I made enough working on shares, but they came and took it all away from me . . . . They just came and took it all off. Then daughter woke up again this morning saying she was hungry, and I just couldn't stand it no longer . . . . I just couldn't stand it to longer.

Jim's deranged anger—his need to stop his child's misery and his own—is a variation on a narrative common to the 1930s: that of men who cannot understand why they have failed. The paternalistic culture which assumed the male would be the breadwinner, coupled with the materialism undergirding the American dream of success, created the trap that Jim, and others like him, experienced Caldwell Complete 103.

Critic Jennifer Williamson points out in her 2014 study, *Twentieth-Century Sentimentalism*, that the qualities of the so-called "proletarian" fiction that remain memorable here in the twenty-first century are those that reflect domestic fiction, particularly narratives that include family life and human relationships—even if those relationships are frustrated by economic conditions. Readers relate more easily when the "unforgiving American landscape" of poverty and deprivation is leavened with sympathy into "an intimate and familiar homescape" (Williamson 88).[14] Using this rationale, texts such as Albert Maltz's story, "The Happiest Man on Earth" becomes more impressive than his novels—*The Underground Stream, The Cross and the Arrow*—because in the character Jesse's pleading with his brother-in-law for a job driving nitroglycerin cross country, even at the risk of his life, readers sympathize with the man's desperate need to provide for his wife and son. Void of all political abstractions, the best of Maltz's stories (and his play, *The Black Pit*) evoke the power of human connection. In "Man on a Road," for example, Maltz makes readers see how brave the lonely miner is as he leaves his wife—taking his diseased body off to die from silicosis so that she will not be burdened with his care. Maltz's reportorial narrative uses the image of hunger to bond the miner as he hitchhikes with the man who has given him a lift. The latter offers him a cup of coffee:

> "Yes," he replied, "thank you, friend."
> The "thank you" told me a lot. I knew from the way he said it that he wanted the coffee but couldn't pay for it; that he had taken my offer to be one of hospitality and was grateful. I was happy I had asked him.
> We went inside. For the first time since I had come upon him . . . he seemed human. He didn't talk, but he didn't slip inside himself either. He just sat down at the counter and waited for his coffee. When it came, he drank it slowly, holding the cup in both hands as though to warm them.
> When he had finished, I asked him if he wouldn't like a sandwich. He turned around to me and smiled. It was a very gentle, a very patient smile. His big, lumpy face seemed to light up with it and become understanding and sweet and gentle.
> The smile shook me all through. It didn't warm me—it made me feel sick Inside.
>
> *Maltz* Strenuous Decade *245–6*

In Maltz's hands, the reader fuses with the driver—better off financially, both are unable to understand the miner's reticence. Finally, the hitchhiker asks the driver to copy his letter to his wife, a letter in which he explains why he is leaving her so as not to burden her with his death. There is no self-pity. There is no recrimination about the unsafe labor practices the owners of the mine chose to use. There is only his recognition that life as a mine worker has given him no recourse.

Hopeless narratives writ large comprise such novels from throughout the 1930s. Pietro Di Donato wrote the story of his father's death as a construction worker in New York, published that and expanded it to novel form. As *Christ in Concrete*, the book was the primary selection of the Book-of-the-Month Club, surging past Steinbeck's *The Grapes of Wrath*. In the detailed account of shoddy construction practices, pointed particularly at abuses—both conscious and innocent—aimed at

---

EXCERPT FROM CHARLES REZNIKOFF'S "TESTIMONY"

Amelia was just fourteen and out of the orphan asylum; at her
    first job—in the bindery, and yes sir, yes ma'am, oh, so
    anxious to please.
She stood at the table, her blonde hair hanging about her
    shoulders, "knocking up" for Mary and Sadie, the stitchers
    ("knocking up" is counting books and stacking them in piles to
    be taken away) . . . .
as each stitcher put her work through the machine,
she threw it on the table. The books were piling up fast . . . .
three or four had fallen under the table
between the boards nailed against the legs.
She felt her hair caught gently;
put her hand up and felt the shaft going round and round
and her hair caught on it, wound and winding around it,
until the scalp was jerked from her head,
and the blood was coming down all over her face and waist.

---

the Italian American workers who were employed in the large city construction project, Di Donato indirectly promoted reformist agendas for the building industry. Similar in intent were William Attaway's novels. His *Let Me Breathe Thunder* gives the reader the hobo life of two tramps as they try to care for a young Mexican boy while they ride the rails; his *Blood on the Forge*, published two years later in 1941, describes the hardships of southern black workers as they try to get, and keep, jobs in northern steel mills. Grouped as "protest" novels coming here at the end of the Depression, each of these books is a testimony to American racist and classist behavior.

Nelson Algren's *Somebody in Boots* set an earlier standard for the accurate and generally unsentimental depictions of the hobo. He dedicated his novel to "[t]hose innumerable thousands: the homeless boys of America." Serving to expose the innocence of many of these hard-luck characters, Algren's book is structured as a sequence of stories about male characters who see themselves as unable, frustrated as they are by systems that give them no work. Men as both fathers and sons face responsibilities they have no way to meet. Some go crazy. Most die from the effects of their inhuman labor—whether in mines, mills, or factories, as well as on farms.

Algren's novel begins in a Mexican border town (with Part I ironically titled "The Native Son"); the fall of Stub McKay, head of his motherless family, is dictated by his geographic placement. "Good" Americans are not supposed to live in bestial, uncivilized places. Filled with racial epithets and various scenes of sheer despair, *Somebody in Boots* may be true to the conditions of Algren's down-and-out characters, but it also does its share of socialistic proselytizing.

One of the most interesting writers of the 1930s, and one whose fame was as short-lived as his health—because of his own work-induced illness, tuberculosis—was Tom Kromer. Kept by poverty from finishing his degree at the University of West Virginia, thoroughly versed in the hard life of mine workers, Kromer wrote *Waiting for Nothing*, which Knopf published in 1935. Gone is any optimism that the Depression will end soon. Kromer's book is about life among the drifters; originally titled *Three Hots and a Flop*, it draws on his two years as a hobo.

As its original title suggests, Kromer's novel is built almost entirely around episodes of hunger. So starved that he is driven to plan robbery, as well as the begging ("dinging") that is his perpetual way of life, the protagonist in this first-person fiction explains rarely, and then in sentences as short as his pseudo-macho statements:

> I have lost my nerve. I walk until I am on the main stem. Never have I been so hungry. I have got to get me something to eat. I pass a restaurant. In the window is a roast chicken. It is brown and fat. It squats in a silver platter. The patter is filled with gravy. The gravy is thick and brown. It drips over the side, slow. I stand there and watch it drip. Underneath it the sign says: "All you can eat for fifty cents." I lick my lips.
>
> *Kromer 6*

Kromer's fiction maintains this comic undercurrent. As the protagonist moves closer to the window, he focuses on a well-dressed couple who are eating the advertised chicken: "I stare in at the window. Maybe they will know a hungry man when they see him. Maybe this guy will be willing to shell out a couple of nickels to a hungry stiff." Angry that the couple seems to be "nibbling . . . they are not even hungry," the protagonist continues his monologue: "I am starved. That chicken was meant for a hungry man. I watch them as they cut it into tiny bits. I watch their forks as they carry them to their mouths."

Each segment of the book recounts a different episode, but the net effect is a tapestry of vivid hunger: always without adequate work, always hungry, the narrator can see no end to the misery that surrounds him. *Waiting for Nothing* is filled with cryptic narratives of men stealing food, and risking their lives to do so; of women leaving infants on benches so that they can be sheltered and cared for; of boys jumping trains—dying with injuries—and many other deaths. Kromer's static plot emphasizes the novel's theme: there is no reason to hope. Why write a story with a chronology when for these despairing lives, time doesn't matter. A man is as hungry today as he was yesterday—and as he will be tomorrow.

And so is a woman, as Kromer draws her. His women in soup lines are pathetic, and moving, stereotypes:

> I look at their . . . deep eyes. They are sunk in deep hollows. The hollows are rimmed with black. Their brows are wrinkled and lined from worry. They are stoop-shouldered and flat-chested. They have a look on their face. I have

seen that look on the faces of dogs when they have been whipped with a stick. They hold babies in their arms, and the babies are crying. They are always crying . . . because they are hungry.

Kromer 66

Strangely without gender markings, Kromer's characters fill an abstracted landscape of city street, lonely train station, bleak farmhouse.

Waiting for Nothing ends with an ambulance called to another mission flop house, this time to retrieve the body of an unknown man who has died, alone, on a cot, covered with a thin blanket. In its structure as in its powerful yet undifferentiated characters, *Waiting for Nothing* underscores all parts of its theme. And in case the reader has missed that implicit sorrow, Kromer has his protagonist meditate as he waits for the ambulance,

I try to think back over the years that I have lived. But I cannot think of years any more. I can think only of the drags I have rode, of the bulls that have sapped up on me, and the mission slop I have swilled . . . whatever is gone before is gone . . . . My life is spent before it is started.

Kromer 128

The literature of work

Just as many readers did not want to focus on the deprivations of the poor during the 1930s, a great many others did not want to scrutinize the lives of working-class characters. Literature—good, moral, respectable literature—was meant to be ennobling. It bore little resemblance to sociological studies. At its best, even when it dealt with working-class characters, it found ways to describe the manner in which doing expert work brought positive emphasis to the characters involved; it also served as a means of showing the heroic qualities of those working-class people. Eric Schocket, in his 2006 study *Vanishing Moments: Class and American Literature*, uses the term "the economic novel" to broaden the above category. He begins with the novels of Rebecca Harding Davis and Herman Melville, and he avoids using an adjective such as *political*. He instead dwells on the role of laborers' use of the strike as a mechanism for supporting class insurrection, as well as that act being "a social action whose meaning was anxiously debated by nonstriking observers, managers, and capitalists" (Schocket 71). Detailing the strike (and the strikers who created it) was a way of exploring working class culture, "particularly inasmuch as working class culture is a culture of struggle." Schocket starts from a number of presumptions—among them, mentioning that the decade of the 1880s saw more than 7,000 strikes in the United States alone—as he builds his argument that the existence of the strike was pervasive: all working-class people were affected by strikes and were invested in their outcomes. Perhaps more significantly, in the philosophy of making it in America, strikes "embodied the germ of an alternate social organization—founded on cooperation rather than competition" (Schocket 73).

This critic takes the importance of the strike far beyond most observers of the 1930s when he suggests that the concept of the strike not only gave the working-class a positive articulation of their power but also that it provided a language for the workers:

> In an era when successive groups of non-English speaking immigrants repeatedly reconstituted the working class, the strike was an especially important cross-lingual expression of collectivity.
>
> *Schocket 73*

An essential part of the modernist struggle, as we have seen, as well as the working-class efforts to gain equality, this focus on the vernacular—indeed, on a kind of creation of new language—became a way of challenging "the strictures of genteel English" (Schocket 152).

Then a student at the University of Chicago, James T. Farrell understood the reach of profanity, intentionally bad grammar, and a strident poverty of introspection. When in 1933 he published *Gas-House McGinty*, a novel soon to be followed by the three books of his *Studs Lonigan* trilogy, Farrell used the trappings of the uneducated, the tough, the prickly and sometimes shudderingly real character to create a new kind of market for readers.

Farrell draws constantly on the theme that class differences are inescapable. When he introduces his "successful" protagonist Ambrose J. McGinty as a man with a "blown-out gut," "convict haircut," and "fatty, but still muscular, neck," he takes on reader assumptions about heroism. Sitting at a saloon bar, Gas-House has just spit tobacco juice and "missed the spittoon." Cramming down the free lunch, McGinty muses on the grief his job—dispatching express trucks, i.e. gas cars—causes him; his unspoken monologue is peppered with "Goddamn'em!" "Christ!" and "Hell . . . them bastards." Hardly suave and well-born, McGinty speaks a crude language designed expressly to offend Farrell's readers. "I don't trust them bastards none," he says later about the men who work for him (Farrell *McGinty* 21, 27).

What may be even more objectionable are McGinty's comments about women—"Goddamn hag! Two-bit whore with enough clap and syphilis to infect the whole Japanese army"—and the names he uses to refer to the foreign workers (in this case the non-Irish): "Jews," "garlic-eatin' spaghetti guzzlers," "Bohunks," "goddamn Mexs." As the narrative progresses, McGinty develops "piles," has anxiety over a speech he must give, and then worries about losing his job. Rather than being McGinty's story, however, the novel is a mélange of voices—those of men at work, at the bar, and on the street, repetitively insulting, discussing, and gossiping as they live from day to day.

To avoid being persecuted by the Comstock laws for Farrell's language, his first *Studs Lonigan* novel—*Young Lonigan*, 1932—is advertised "for doctors only." Filled as the book is with a teenager's angst, rejecting as Studs does his parents' wisdom, eager as he is to have sex with his girlfriends, confused as he is by his buddies' bragging about sexual and physical things he knows they are lying about, Farrell's Lonigan novels are

comparatively slow and plodding; they engage the reader partly because of their blatant language, but the language is often a mask for the innocence of the characters.
After a long stretch of fumbling attempts, Studs finally rapes a woman—unfortunately,
Farrell intends his act to be a denouement, and critically it has been. In these decades
of gender self-consciousness, Studs' brutal act has kept readers from seeing beyond this
scene. To posit that Farrell's Studs trilogy parallels James Joyce's first novel, *A Portrait of
the Artist as a Young Man*, after this scene, would fall on unsympathetic ears.

Set as Studs' rape of Irene is at a New Year's party, in the midst of a kaleidoscope
of confused and loud speech, the act passes almost unnoticed. Studs tackles Irene
as she runs to escape him, and throws her to the floor ("'Will you come across now,'
he said"). He gags her, twists her arm, "gave her an uppercut," attacks her (saying
simultaneously, "I won't hurt you. For Christ sake, cut out the stalling"), knees her
in the stomach, slaps her "viciously," punches her, and "carried her unconscious to
the bed." When the police arrive the next morning, "Her face was black and blue,
and her coat thrown over her torn dress. She winced with each step, sobbed hys-
terically, shook all over." Questioned by the officer, Studs responds that "she ain't
got no kick. She only got that much!" (Farrell *Studs* 409–11).

James T. Farrell knew that his books about Studs were objectionable. His point
as a young writer was that the Irish-Catholic neighborhood in Chicago (his own
neighborhood) had declined, had failed its occupants. Studs' lack of promise, his
death from double pneumonia brought on by general dissipation, is not ever meant
to be heroic: Farrell studied that Chicago neighborhood as if he were an anthro-
pologist. Ranked next to the scandalous novels of Henry Miller, Farrell's *Studs* was
intended to be "a dirty book, of the sort which schoolchildren index and pass from
hand to hand" (Klein 207). In creating a modern-day naturalism, Farrell was not
writing a proletarian novel: he did not see his, and Studs', Chicago neighborhood
as a slum, and he was not interested in economic deprivation *per se*. His *bildungsroman* was a spiritual quest of sorts, but he gave Studs no real father and uses his
admiration for Johnny O'Brien's father to convey the values of the tribe. In Marcus
Klein's assessment, "To be true to the heritage is to be skilled in battle, and vice
versa" (Klein 210). This is a sample of O'Brien's advice:

> They didn't have fighters like that nowadays. None of 'em were no-fight
> champions like Jess Willard, and most of them were real Irish, lads who'd
> bless themselves before they fought; they weren't fake Irish like most of the
> present-day dagoes and wops and sheenies who took Hibernian names . . . .
> "But I ain't so much interested in sport as I used to be. Baseball's the only
> clean game we got left. The Jews killed all the other games. The kikes dirty
> up everything. I say the kikes ain't square. There never was a white Jew, or a
> Jew that wasn't yellow . . . . And now I'll be damned if they ain't comin' in
> spoiling our neighborhood. It used to be a good Irish neighborhood, but
> pretty soon a man will be afraid to wear a shamrock on St. Patrick's Day,
> because there are so many noodle-soup drinkers around.
>
> *Farrell* Young *82–4*

Unlike Farrell, William Carlos Williams placed his stories in the most radical of magazines—*New Masses* and *Blast*—yet his own position as a physician and a friend of many modernists (both artists and writers) saved him from the incipient shame of being working-class. Known primarily as a poet and an essayist, Williams wrote about "the plight of the poor in a rich country. I wrote it down as I saw it. The times—that was the knife that was killing them." (His story collections—*The Knife of the Times*, 1932, and *Life along the Passaic River*, 1938—portrayed these characters, many of them the patients in his New Jersey practice, seen often through the eyes of the pitying, caring doctor. His brusque voice, and the economical, almost nonliterary style of the stories, helped to save Williams's fiction from the charge of sentimentality, though that charge could certainly have been made about such stories as "Jean Beicke," "The Girl with a Pimply Face," and "A Face of Stone.")

A key consideration in comparing Williams' fiction of the early thirties with that written by James T. Farrell is the author's aesthetic belief about the purpose for his language choices. Farrell is playing camera: he tries to replicate the diction he literally hears. For Williams, however, he is attempting to create an "economic" fiction, a text that draws from the mnemonic in order to make a larger point. In a retrospective essay, Williams wrote,

> I lived among these people. I know them and saw the essential qualities (not stereotype), the courage, the humor (an accident), the deformity, the basic trag-edy of their lives—and the *importance* of it. You can't write about something unimportant to yourself. I was involved. That wasn't all. I saw how they were maligned by their institutions of church and state—and "betters." I saw how all that was acceptable to the ear about them maligned them. I saw how stereotype falsified them. Nobody was writing about them, anywhere, as they ought to be written about. There was no chance of writing anything acceptable, certainly not salable, about them. It was my duty to raise the level of consciousness, not to say discussion, of them to a higher level, a higher plane. Really to tell ....
>
> *Williams* Essays *300*

As he did in his short fiction, Williams depended on the realistic and convincing detail, the language that spoke honestly of the times and of the people he knew living through those times, in his longer works. *White Mule*, the first volume of his story of his in-laws' lives as working-class Americans, begins with his wife's birth: Flossie, caught in the gendered bias of her culture, becomes the true American hero. A trilogy centered in this common and often woman-centered life of the early twentieth century brought Williams little notice but as with all his writing from the 1930s, his 1937 novel spoke volumes about the actuality of living American.

Given the most usual lens for judging the political beliefs of these 1930s writers, one would have to fault both Farrell and Williams as finding more interest in aes-thetics than in either socialism or Communism. Decades later, Williams saw his appointment as Consultant in Poetry to the Library of Congress taken away from him, a rejection that occurred because *The Golden Goose*, a little magazine sponsored

EXCERPTS FROM FRANKLIN DELANO ROOSEVELT, FIRST AND SECOND INAUGURAL ADDRESSES

This is preeminently the time to speak the truth, the whole truth, frankly and boldly. Nor need we shrink from honestly facing conditions in our country today.

This great nation will endure as it has endured, will revive and will prosper. So, first of all, let me assert my firm belief that the only thing we have to fear is fear itself—nameless, unreasoning, unjustified terror . . . .

I see millions of families trying to live on incomes so meager that the pall of family disaster hangs over them day by day.

I see millions whose daily lives in city and on farm continue under conditions labeled indecent by a so-called polite society half a century ago.

I see millions denied education, recreation, and the opportunity to better their lot and the lot of their children.

I see millions lacking the means to buy the products of farm and factory and by their poverty denying work and productiveness to many other millions.

I see one-third of a nation ill-housed, ill-clad, ill-nourished . . . .

by Ohio State University, had published his poem "The Pink Church."[15] Media attention was evidently alerted by the color, because the early 1950s had become the starkly oppressive period of the McCarthy investigations, the HUAC committee, the Hollywood Ten (of which Albert Maltz was a member), and other rigorously punitive stages in public persecution.

Similarly, James T. Farrell, although he did identify with left-wing causes, "defined himself as a writer." Marcus Klein points out that in the third volume of the *Studs* trilogy, Farrell mentions both *Jews Without Money* and *Bottom Dogs*. In this critic's assessment, "Apparently Farrell could not discover the coherence he wanted in either socialism or Lawrentianism, or in any idea extraneous to the given materials" (Klein 214).

In 1932 the election of Franklin Delano Roosevelt to the Presidency of the United States showed beyond any doubt that America was in grave trouble. The dissonance within the fabric of the country's millions of citizens meant that some Americans were, indeed, looking to other than democratic systems for choices. Many United States citizens did join the American Communist Party; others became fellow travelers; others moved to Russia. Considering the disaffection of the people in the United States in 1932, the literature written in the early 1930s is surprisingly apolitical.

The dissonance was not only economic. The lack of parity in salaries was only a starting point for the essential dissatisfaction with allotment of powers. As Jonathan Alter summarized the economic situation the weekend of Roosevelt's Inauguration (March 3, 1933):

the New York Stock Exchange suspended trading indefinitely and the Chicago Board of Trade bolted its doors for the first time since its founding in 1848. The terrifying 'runs' that began the year before on more than five thousand failing banks had stripped rural areas of capital and now threatened to overwhelm American cities . . . the governors of New York, Illinois, and Pennsylvania signed orders closing the banks in those states indefinitely, which meant that thirty-four out of forty-eight American states, including the largest ones, now had no economic pulse . . . . The official national unemployment rate stood at 25 percent, but that figure was widely considered to be low. Among non-farm workers unemployment was more than 37 percent, and in some areas, like Toledo, Ohio, it reached 80 percent. Business investment was down 90 percent from 1929.

Alter 2

To chart the amazing reforms that Roosevelt was able to enact early in his first term—those memorable *100 days*—is to see a quick mind taking the advice of a myriad of keen advisors—involving the highest-placed non-political strategists as well as a cadre of fine political minds (known as FDR's "Brain Trust"). Roosevelt knew the times were dire; he knew he must act, and yet he understood enough psychology to understand that he needed to keep the condition of the United States to himself. So he comforted his listeners. Ironically, the key phrase from his first Inaugural Address, "The only thing we have to fear is fear itself" was overlooked by most newspapers covering the speech.

It seems somewhat disrespectful to comment on only a few of the bills and proposals that Roosevelt created during those first 100 days, and the first few years of his Presidency—the Tennessee Valley Authority, the repeal of Prohibition, the Tydings-McDuffie Act, the Works Progress Administration, the National Labor Relations Board, the Social Security Act. For all their impact—saving the United States economy, and saving as well the position of the United States within the world of nations—they didn't change much about the way workers in South Chicago or farmers in Iowa or mechanics in Detroit or nurses in Manhattan viewed American life. Ticking off items that he felt were necessary not only in the early days of his first term in office, but in the subsequent terms—until his death on April 12, 1945—Roosevelt (aided by his intensely bright wife, Eleanor, a woman perhaps even more beloved than he) served his country, and its people, extraordinarily well.

One of the most distinguished of America's 1930s writers was himself nearly apolitical. Trained to be an observant journalist, John Steinbeck followed Roosevelt's choices and career, as did much of the United States population, but he poured every ounce of his personal energy into his writing. Somewhat ironically, because he had begun his writing career with romantic books, or with collections of fiction about the down-and-out in Monterey, California, Steinbeck came slowly to any kind of protest fiction. Writing about the poor gave him one foot in an interesting set of conventions; his 1935 book, *Tortilla Flat*, was his first best-seller. It was followed in 1936 by a work he conceived of as journalism; *In Dubious Battle* grew from Steinbeck's friendship with union organizers for the AWIU (the Agricultural Workers' Industrial Union) trying to win justice from the huge California farming conglomerates. As he wrote *In Dubious*

> ## EXCERPT FROM JOHN STEINBECK'S *THE GRAPES OF WRATH*
>
> . . . The dawn came, but no day. In the gray sky a red sun appeared, a dim red circle that gave a little light, like dusk; and as that day advanced, the dusk slipped back toward darkness, and the wind cried and whimpered over the fallen corn.
>
> Men and women huddled in their houses, and they tied handkerchiefs over their noses when they went out, and wore goggles to protect their eyes.
>
> When the night came again it was black night, for the stars could not pierce the dust to get down, and the window lights could not even spread beyond their own yards. Now the dust was evenly mixed with the air, an emulsion of dust and air. Houses were shut tight, and cloth wedged around doors and windows, but the dust came in so thinly that it could not be seen in the air, and it settled like pollen on the chairs and tables . . . .

Battle, which he called a "brutal" story, Steinbeck finds the pattern that will shape both this strike novel and his monumental *The Grapes of Wrath*: in Steinbeck's hands, readers sympathize with the angry, starving fruit pickers, and their emotional response turns them as lawless as the strikers.

Often described as a scientist (after studies in marine biology and his long-lasting friendship with Ed Ricketts), Steinbeck at times relied on paralleling human interests with natural ones. That was the alternation that made *The Grapes of Wrath* so effective: the Joad family story takes on characteristics of an Everyman plot.

Drawing from his wide-ranging knowledge, Steinbeck found in the debacle of the Oklahoma farmers being driven west by Dust Bowl conditions an even more dynamic situation than he had portrayed in Jim's union activities throughout *In Dubious Battle*. There, Jim, as a single man, standing with his union peers, took on large corporate interests, hopefully engaging the capitalist structure in asking that amends be made to the industry workers. Steinbeck's slim novel drew from the classic strike situation Schocket describes. *In Dubious Battle*, however, fails to present what Schocket calls "the germ of an alternate social organization." Jim's death does not have the power to effect change.

By the time of *The Grapes of Wrath*, one entire segment of the United States was traumatically uprooted: the displaced Oakies had lost their farms, and were trying to reach the advertised work opportunities in California, traveling by any means possible. As Steinbeck worked on the interviews and journalism about the plight of the Oklahoma farmers, he saw what an immense undertaking writing about this tragic exodus would become. What saved Steinbeck from relying too heavily on facts, and what became the skeletal structure of the novel, was his belief in a story that drew from a human endeavor that was much larger than the farmers' displacement. *The Grapes of Wrath* showed to full advantage Steinbeck's innate understanding of, and sympathy with, the poorest of human beings—some American, some Mexican, others immigrant.

Steinbeck's truly original sympathy in telling the Joads' story, both of the family and its larger incarnation as the family of man, gave him a way of reaching millions of readers. It had become a given that many authors during the 1930s and 1940s were class-blind: the poor seemed to be of little interest. *The Grapes of Wrath* provided an almost systematic expose of poverty, again drawing from good journalism. Even as observers of the United States did not want to believe that so much poverty existed in America, the truth has always been that more poverty, despite hard work and frugal living, marks the United States than it does many other civilized countries. In his pervasive concern with the lower class, Steinbeck also dealt with issues of gender and religion, sometimes expressing attitudes well beyond the reach of the work's publication date of 1939.

In the purposefully-chosen Biblical rhythms of the novel's interchapters, Steinbeck soothed his readers, just as he did with his metaphors of flowers, fruits, and animal life. The solace provided by the steadfast turtle as it crosses the highway goes a long way toward reassurance. Steinbeck's title, with all its bitter irony of promise in the American dream now rotted to the wrath of the displaced farmers, parallels the kind of irony Hemingway and Fitzgerald had earlier achieved. And Steinbeck's insistence on the real dominance of women—as creators and nurturers of the race—links *The Grapes of Wrath* more closely to other writing of the 1930s by such women authors as Meridel Le Sueur, Josephine Herbst, Clara Weatherwax, and Tillie Olsen. After reading Steinbeck's *The Grapes of Wrath*, alongside Richard Wright's *Native Son*, Ernest Hemingway wrote somewhat apologetically to his editor about his own 1940 novel, *For Whom the Bell Tolls*. As he compared *The Grapes of Wrath* to *The Brothers Karamazov*, *Madame Bovary*, and *Native Son*, Hemingway noted that his book "was not in that class" (Kennedy Library Archive, to Charles Scribner).

Notes

1 Critic Barbara Foley explains that "the term 'proletarian novel' is most applicable to a grouping of approximately 100 novels that were produced during the years 1929–1941" (Foley Matthews 353).
2 Werner Sollors noted about the "dream,"

> the new wisdom seemed to be that the dream was destined to be completed in the multiethnic, nontotalitarian United States and not anywhere else; in Massachusetts and Delaware, and not in Rome, Berlin, or Moscow. American culture was being viewed as vital because it was the culture of democracy, of process, of mobility, and of plenty.
>
> *Sollors 524*

3 Minter lists

> the accumulation of brutal scenes, a literary equivalent of stockpiling, calculated to make readers pity the victims of a brutal political economy. Their language, which comes from ghetto streets, slums, mineshafts, and factories, seems almost as misshapen as the lives of the people who speak it.
>
> *Minter 231*

4 Foley notes that her inclusion of Wright's *Native Son* is unusual. The book is "not routinely read as a proletarian novel, but in fact it is a key text of the genre" (Foley Matthews 361).

5 Among the books now available from the University of Illinois Press series are John Sanford's *The People from Heaven*, Phillip Bonosky's *Burning Valley*, Alfred Maund's *The Big Boxcar*, Anzia Yezierska's *Salome of the Tenements*, Abraham Polonsky's *The World Above*, Alexander Saxton's *The Great Midland*, Ira Wolfert's *Tucker's People*, and better-known novels by Grace Lumpkin, Myra Page, Josephine Herbst, and Jack Conroy.

6 Walker Evans's term for the inclusion of photographs was "lyric documentary" (Orvell 108).

7 Assessing the hundreds of WPA projects, particularly the "American Guide" series, Klein notes that many "of the researchers and writers ... were immigrants or were the children of immigrants, or were black" (Klein 183).

8 Odets was born in a middle-class Philadelphia family, but grew up in a Jewish area of the Bronx. He joined the Communist party briefly in the mid-thirties but, aside from being influenced by friends and by associations with the Group Theatre, seemed to have few political allegiances. His other well-known plays, *Golden Boy*, 1937, and *The Country Girl*, 1950, led to years of successful writing for Hollywood.

9 Dos Passos's third play, the 1933 *Fortune Heights*, was divided into 41 separate scenes (titled as vaudeville acts, for example, "Detroit: City of Leisure," a scathing indictment of Midwestern unemployment) and may have given Odets the idea for organization by scene.

10 Orvell states flatly that racism against African Americans went unquestioned: "If blacks were tolerated in the southern town, they were restricted by Jim Crow practices to their own distinct places. In the small towns of the Midwest, North, and West, there was more typically no place at all for blacks." Racism in these so-called idyllic small towns was "virtually invisible to residents (Orvell 134).

11 The significance of all Fitzgerald's carefully-chosen names of guests at Gatsby's parties parallels the intentionality of T. S. Eliot's choice of the name "Sweeney" (to indicate an Irishman) and "Bleistein" (to indicate a Jew) within his poems.

12 Leslie Fiedler comments on the number of Jewish writers becoming prominent in this decade (his attention falls on Daniel Fuchs, Henry Roth, and Nathanael West), saying

> Jews seem not only peculiarly apt at projecting images of numinous power for the unchurched, but are skillful, too, at creating myths of urban alienation and terror. The thirties ... is a period especially favorable for the Jewish writer bent on universalizing his own experience into a symbol of life in the Western world.
>
> *Fiedler 493*

13 In John Lavelle's *Blue Collar, Theoretically*, he notes that years later, when Studs Terkel's *Working* was published, people responded to what Terkel presented as "a continuum of happiness." People are united, whether fulfilled or unfulfilled (Lavelle 140).

14 Williamson uses the fact that Steinbeck's *The Grapes of Wrath* illustrates his use of family to create this "homescape." ("By drawing the Joads as an 'Everyfamily,' Steinbeck crosses class boundaries to create sympathy for the working class and promotes a humanist argument for collective caretaking and survival" (88)).

15 "The Pink Church" is about the human body, not about anything Russian, or Socialist, or political.

Suggested further reading

Daniel Aaron. *Writers on the Left*. Harcourt, Brace, 1961.

Michael Denning. *The Cultural Front: The Laboring of American Culture in the 20th Century*. Verso, 1996.

Barbara Foley. *Radical Representations: Politics and Form in U.S. Proletarian Fiction, 1929–1941*. Duke UP, 1994.

Jennifer Haytock. *The Middle Class in the Great Depression: Popular Women's Novels of the 1930s*. Palgrave, 2013.

8

1940s WRITING

There is some resonance to be gained by beginning a discussion of the decade of the American 1940s with scrutiny of this triumvirate:

Steinbeck's *The Grapes of Wrath* won the 1939 Pulitzer Prize for Fiction and was soon made into a well-distributed if controversial film. Copies of it were burned in California, where large farm organizations feared erupting protests; there were plots against Steinbeck's life as he traveled the country.

Richard Wright's ironically-titled *Native Son* was the first African American novel to be a Book-of-the-Month Club Selection and even though most readers were shocked by the author's use of Bigger Thomas's murders—and his character's lack of contrition about the deaths of the two women who were his victims—the novel became the most significant study of class and race oppression in publishing history.

Without appearing to be "literary," *Native Son* was exceptionally so. It drew on an earlier factual narrative, much as had Theodore Dreiser's *An American Tragedy* (Wright was using the Chicago papers as they followed the route of a man suspected of murder). It posed a number of questions about the American family—as had Faulkner's *The Sound and the Fury*—and about "success" in this country, as had Fitzgerald's *The Great Gatsby* and Lewis's *Babbitt*. It played with the issue of shades of blackness, designating personal values in accordance with the color of a character's skin, and with the pervasive imagery of threatening whiteness. It featured an ironic and explosive emphasis on the role of the young male in American culture, as sexually powerful, that sexual prowess to become financial power in the best of circumstances. In Bigger Thomas, the reader sees that the size, and the ability to become "bigger" in some phallic sense, means nothing. And with the play on Bigger's name—"Bigger Thomas" echoes "Nigger Tom," with its suggestion of Uncle Tomism, and the original *Uncle Tom's Cabin*—Wright had titled his 1938 book of long stories *Uncle Tom's Children*. By emphasizing Bigger's name, Wright set up the ambivalence that haunts the entire novel, ambivalence about education, law, class, race, and morality.

In both Steinbeck's novel and Wright's, a great many American premises are treated with ambivalence. In both books the "answers" given as conclusions are unacceptable to nearly every reader: sheer optimism cannot solve the myriad social problems that the 1930s revealed. The Joad family's retreat to the barn at the start of California's rainy season is only a temporary answer, and Steinbeck's text gives the reader nothing but such temporizing. The literary progress of having the Joads leave the dessication of the Dust Bowl (with its echoes of Eliot's *The Waste Land*) and end in a deluge of rain, implying that the Fisher King has come, must be read as either irony or despair.

Ernest Hemingway's 1940 *For Whom the Bell Tolls*, a novel set during the Spanish Civil War, won no prizes, though the fact that it did not receive the Pulitzer—nor did any novel of that year—became a kind of commendation. It did become a popular film; more importantly, the novel moved American letters out of the United States and onto the world scene. As one forerunner to World War II, the conflict in Spain—in which many Americans had participated—brought understanding of coercive military force, rooted in whatever politics seemed appropriate, into literature.

In all three of these novels, modernist techniques were plain: metaphoric and wide-reaching titles that encapsulated many of the works' themes, often ironically; action dominated by scenes and dialogue, leaving gaps in the books' import to be filled in by readers; significance hanging by small details which also needed to be "read" correctly by enlightened readers—for all the length of each of these novels, in many instances and on many pages the writing operated as if it were poetic. *Modernism* underlay the comparative successes of not only these three novels, but the *oeuvre* of each of these three writers. Whereas Steinbeck had not begun his writing career as a poet, both Wright and Hemingway had. The rubric that *Poetry* magazine had used to describe Hemingway, "A young Chicago poet," could also have been used to describe Wright; and the centrality of the Midwestern city itself, for not only American literature but also for Modernism, is reified once again.

Each of these three novels was instructive for readers. They helped people understand class issues: what damage poverty—both collectively and individually—does to a culture. Not only Wright's Bigger Thomas but Hemingway's Pablo is marked by the suffocating awareness of being powerless as well as "other." Steinbeck leaves the entire Joad family to mourn not only Jim Casey but also neighbors and family members, forcing themselves to continue a search for the barest of livings. Part of the sympathy Steinbeck evokes for the Joads comes from the fact that they were land owners, *moral* members of families, and white. As he crosses the line from seeing the Joads as a family headed by a father to showing the power of that family's indefatigable women, Steinbeck breaks a much less visible boundary than does Richard Wright.

Different as these books seemed to be, each forced readers to look at the poverty that ruled throughout the world. Poverty rather than political allegiances was the link among the works, and Steinbeck's depiction of what personal poverty meant made *The Grapes of Wrath* the most innocent: the anger that the title signified was, and remained, remote from the lives the Joad family members had to endure.

In reading all three of these novels, readers came to realize that literary aims had changed: the parochialism of dominant aesthetic concerns had given way to real-world anxieties. The questions for readers here at the beginning of the 1940s were, Who would save millions throughout the world from the unrelieved ravages of poverty? Who would control the outcomes of both military and political force on the international scene?

Late 1930s literature tended to fuse the question of these poignant outcomes. In 1938 William Carlos Williams published such a wide-ranging poem, titled simply "These":

These

are the desolate, dark weeks
when nature in its barrenness
equals the stupidity of man.

The year plunges into night
and the heart plunges
lower than night

to an empty, windswept place . . . .

Similarly, Robinson Jeffers' "The Answer" forces the questioning that revealed an anxiety new to the United States. The Jeffers' poem opens,

Then what is the answer?—Not to be deluded by dreams.
To know that great civilizations have broken down into violence, and
   their tyrants come, many times before.
When open violence appears, to avoid it with honor or choose the least
   ugly faction; these evils are essential . . . .

S 234

As Leslie Fiedler pointed out decades ago, American writing

is a product of the age as it worked on writers beneath the level of conscious-ness. This is the *tone* of the proletarian novel: the note of sustained and self-satisfied hysteria bred, on the one hand, of Depression years' despair and, on the other, of the sense of being selected as brands to be snatched from the fire.

Fiedler 488

World War II

During the later years of the American Depression, United States poverty was not the complete story: Europe was being shattered by the powerful aggression of what would eventually become the Axis. In October of 1933, Germany withdrew from the League of Nations; a year later Italy invaded Ethiopia and in March, 1936, Germany occupied the Rhineland. In October, 1936, Hitler and Mussolini signed the Rome-Berlin Axis agreement and in April, 1937, Germany bombed Guernica. Despite the Munich Pact between England and Germany, Germany allowed anti-Semitic riots and *Kristallnacht* occured in November, 1938. September 1, 1939, Germany invaded Poland and two days later, England declared war on Germany. June, 1940, Germany invaded the Soviet Union and less than a month later, the German "Blitz" of England began. On December 7, 1941, the United States was drawn into World War II when the Japanese bombed U.S. troops and ships at Pearl Harbor.

With the military draft in process, and industries changing over to manufacture war supplies rather than civilian products, the United States found little time to create literature about the war: energies that had been devoted to finding panaceas for poverty were quickly absorbed in the needs of a largely unexpected war.

Between 1940 and 1947, most war fiction is tightly focused; it is miniaturized in some respects. It deals with the lives of only a few soldiers, with the Italian front, with French resistance, with the Germans in Norway, with civilian life at home (John Steinbeck's *The Moon Is Down,* Albert Halper's *Sons of the Fathers,* Albert Maltz's *The Cross and the Arrow,* John Hersey's *A Bell for Adano,* and, later, his *The War Lover,* Harry Brown's *A Walk in the Sun,* Carlos Bulosan's *The Voice of Bataan,* Kay Boyle's *Primer for Combat,* Martha Gellhorn's *A Stricken Field,* Saul Bellow's *Dangling Man* and later, *The Victim,* Thomas Heggen's *Mr. Roberts,* Vance Bourjaily's *The End of My Life,* John Horne Burns's *The Gallery,* James A. Michener's *Tales of the South Pacific,* and others, augmented by Lillian Hellman's plays *Watch on the Rhine* and *The Searching Wind* as well as Gertrude Stein's *Wars I Have Seen* and *Brewsie and Willie*).

Some of the most effective "war writing" occurred in great modernist poems. Both H.D. and T. S. Eliot, living as they were then in England, created anguished observations, long stanzas in suites in both Eliot's *Four Quartets* and H.D.'s war trilogy, "The Walls Do Not Fall," "Tribute to the Angels," and "The Flowering of the Rod." Each a book-length poem, the myriad images that the lines encompass define a human consciousness beset by terror as well as joy. H.D. creates for the reader

> . . . ruin everywhere, yet as the fallen roof
> leaves the sealed room
> open to the air,
>
> so, through our desolation
> thoughts stir, inspiration stalks us
> through gloom . . . .
>
> $\qquad$ *N 241*

Using a journey-quest motif in her "The Walls Do Not Fall," H.D. describes the struggle,

> . . . we pass on
>
> to another cellar, to another sliced wall
> where poor utensils show
> like rare objects in a museum;
>
> Pompeii has nothing to teach us,
> we know crack of volcanic fissure,
> slow flow of terrible lava,
>
> pressure on heart, lungs, the brain
> about to burst its brittle case
> (what the skull can endure!):
>
> over us, Apocryphal fire,
> under us, the earth sway, dip of a floor,
> slope of a pavement . . . .
>
> *N 241*

As the poet has throughout her career as Imagist, she here forces the reader to slow down into the crawl that the nighttime bombings mandate: the human figure is always wary of that "slow flow of terrible lava," the rubble of the broken streets, the impact of the mangled human body.

In much of T. S. Eliot's *Four Quartets*, his anguish is more intellectual than it is physical, but the pain still continues. Famous for clusters of his unusually long lines ("At the still point of the turning world. Neither flesh nor fleshless,/Neither from nor towards: at the still point there the dance is"), the first part of the poem, "Burnt Norton," creates a sonorous meditation on knowledge, on human understanding, on what human beings can do to each other.

> IV
> Time and the bell have buried the day,
> The black cloud carries the sun away.
> Will the sunflower turn to us, will the clematis
> Stray down, bend to us; tendril and spray
> Clutch and cling?
> Chill
> Fingers of yew be curled
> Down on us? After the kingfisher's wing
> Has answered light to light, and is silent, the light is still
> At the still point of the turning world.
>
> *N 310*

While William Carlos Williams continued writing short war poems and Pound—despite his being incarcerated for his seemingly treasonous radio broadcasts from Italy—eventually wrote his magisterial "The Pisan Cantos,"[1] other modernist poets were also writing powerfully. When Robinson Jeffers said flatly in "Watch the Lights Fade," "Hate and despair take Europe and Asia/And the sea-wind blows cold," the year is 1941 and every reader in the Western world would recognize this reference. A later segment of that short poem states,

> The world is not changed, only more naked:
> The strong struggle for power, and the weak
> Warm their poor hearts with hate.
> *S 235*

Such younger poets, many of them veterans of World War II, were also creating powerful works—Karl Shapiro, Richard Eberhart, Randall Jarrell, Richard Wilbur were among the prize-winning poets of the next decade.

With the publication in 1948 of Norman Mailer's *The Naked and the Dead*, a prize-winning novel and the entry point for one of the last century's most esteemed (and always experimental) writers, war writing became a steady and important force in the development of American letters. Gordon Hutner makes the comment, as he looks ahead to the primacy of Ralph Ellison's 1952 novel *Invisible Man* and aligns that African American work with Richard Wright's *Native Son*, that the 1940s seemed strangely empty:

> The idea seems to have been that between Richard Wright's *Native Son* (1940) and Ralph Ellison's *Invisible Man* (1952), the only novel that counted was Norman Mailer's *The Naked and the Dead* (1948), as if the era were divided into two monolithic periods—the war and the postwar.
> *Hutner 194*

What most readers consider "war literature" does seem to start with the Mailer novel—its wide canvas, exacting descriptions, implementation of human needs

---

EXCERPT FROM RANDALL JARRELL'S "LOSSES"

It was not dying: everybody died.
It was not dying: we had died before
In the routine crashes—and our fields
Called up the papers, wrote home to our folks,
And the rates rose, all because of us.
We died on the wrong page of the almanac,
Scattered on mountains fifty miles away;
Diving on haystacks, fighting with a friend,
We blazed up on the lines we never saw . . . .

other than survival, and sometimes ironic realism made for both fascinating reading and good watching after it became a film. James Jones' *From Here to Eternity*
was as big a money-maker (and film) but in the cascade of novels that dealt with
World War II, William Styron's *The Long March*, Herman Wouk's *The Caine
Mutiny*, Irwin Shaw's *The Young Lions*, John Hawkes's *The Cannibal*, Ross
MacDonald's *The Moving Target*, Kurt Vonnegut's *Player Piano*, and others marked
the gripping necessity of trying to wrap imaginations around the millions of stories the war unleashed. After atomic bombs were dropped on Nagasaki and
Hiroshima and the war ended, a more graphic and inescapable narrative came into
play—and once the full discovery of the Nazi concentration camps, and the existence of the Holocaust, was made, even more urgent writing had to be undertaken.
(The comic relief of two of the more famous World War II sagas—Ken Kesey's
One Flew Over the Cuckoo's Nest and Joseph Heller's *Catch-22*—lightened the early
1960s and proved that even the most indelible of wartime horrors could be treated
sympathetically.)

To focus only on literature about war obscures the appearance of new writers, new
strategies, new themes to help characterize the 1940s. Given that publishers were
limited by having little paper on which to print books, and that the American people
were extraordinary busy once war had been declared, publishers still found ways to
flourish. They were also surprisingly open to new categories of writers and their
works, although they still accepted very few works by women. As Hutner explains,

> American women writers would be slighted in the years that followed for
> not being veterans of the recent war. Thus, their contributions were typically
> considered less important than those of the male writers who were them-
> selves under critical indictment for not having written novels worthy of
> Fitzgerald, Hemingway, and Faulkner . . . . So much of the historiography of
> the postwar era is a narrative of omission and neglect . . . .
>
> *Hutner 268*

After the war

Probably one of the most prominent 1940s novels came from an unexpected quarter. Robert Penn Warren's 1946 *All the King's Men* was a "war" novel only in the
way state and national politics had the power to usurp the rights of private citizens.
In a temper of acquiescence to the times, jumping with both feet into an exploration of authoritarian militarism, Warren's tripartite narrative covers three significant
points of view: Jack Burden, the young well-educated narrator; the politician Willie
Stark; and the embedded story of Cass Mastern's betrayal of his friend, the husband
of his lover, Annabelle Trice. In a network of relationships that stretches through
recent southern history, Warren does much more than rehearse Huey Long's career
as Louisiana demagogue—he investigates the way society allows itself to be used
by Long/Starks. Under the guise of benefiting his state, Starks abuses the power
people had given him. But so too does the seemingly more innocent Judge Irwin,

EXCERPT FROM ADRIENNE RICH'S "DIVING INTO THE WRECK"

I came to explore the wreck.
The words are purposes.
The words are maps.
I came to see the damage that was done
And the treasures that prevail.
I stroke the beam of my lamp
Slowly along the flank
Of something more permanent
Than fish or weed

The thing I came for:
The wreck and not the story of the wreck
The thing itself and not the myth
The drowned face always staring
Toward the sun . . . .

the man who is Jack's true father. And—Warren makes clear—so does Jack himself, particularly in his friendships with his childhood friends, the Stantons.

A novel about betrayal, this Pulitzer-Prize winning book reflected the lost idealism of the Italians, betrayed by Mussolini, and the Germans, equally betrayed by Hitler, but it also showed the way faulty allegiances could warp all intimate relationships. *All the King's Men* is also a 1930s novel. Told in the distinctive idiom of the young Burden, the male-identified account of life on the run reads like a tale of poverty or displacement or hunger. The book opens,

MASON CITY.

To get there you follow Highway 58, going northeast out of the city, and it is a good highway and new. Or was new, that day we went up it. You look up the highway and it is straight for miles, coming at you, with the black line down the center coming at and at you, black and slick and tarry-shining against the white of the slab, and the heat dazzles up from the white slab so that only the black line is clear, coming at you with the whine of the tires, and if you don't quit staring at that line and don't take a few deep breaths and slap yourself hard on the back of the neck you'll hypnotize yourself and you'll come to just at the moment when the right front wheel hooks over into the black dirt shoulder off the slab.

Warren 3

The use Warren makes of elements from 1930s fiction aligns with the critique of Chester E. Eisinger, as well as Joseph J. Waldmeir, that

The rebellion against mindless, arbitrary authority, which had been directed against the police in the thirties, was directed, in the war novels, against the officer class . . . . The war novelist was sensitive to injustice and compassionate toward those who were wronged or victimized by the military machine. The engagement of his mind and his emotions with the problems of what have been called the ritualistic victims of our culture—Negroes and Jews— is a mark of his indebtedness to the thirties.

Eisinger 27

Norman Mailer's *The Naked and the Dead* draws from that same kind of thinking, perhaps intensified because Mailer himself was Jewish. He creates an epic format so that he could draw a panorama of men, all caught in a military action he labels futile from the start: Mailer forces the reader to question the premises of not only war, but of war fiction. Recounting the stories of what he calls the "bunch of dispossessed" men in the military is not pleasant in any way. His subjective "Time Machine" biographies speak for a wide array of men—Brooklyn Jews, Polish Chicagoans, Boston Irish, Mexicans, Texans, poor southerners. Regardless of their place of origin, education, incomes, ethnicity, politics, if they were enlisted men, they were all headed for tragedy. Taking orders is what they are trained to do, and in the Pacific theater of World War II, death seemed inevitable. While readers savored the cynicism, reviewers made charges that Mailer bordered on the "un-American." Ann Petry's 1946 novel *The Street* was cut from the same cloth—unpleasant racial narratives focused here on a woman protagonist who thinks to better her life and that of her growing son through becoming a nightclub singer. African American works had not grown in popularity since the shocking debut of Richard Wright's *Native Son* at the start of the decade; yet once again, the Book-of-the-Month Club chose a novel about black life on the streets. Lutie Johnson, for all her admirable qualities, cannot make it in the city: her life is a series of financial shocks.

Married to a spouse who loses his job, she then works as a live-in maid, to keep their house in the suburbs—separated from Bub, her own little boy, she exists in misery. Eventually she and Bub constitute the household, and then the sexual and violent perils of being a black woman come into play. Neither the white club owner nor Boots, the black band leader, respects Lutie's boundaries; they prey on her body as well as her independence. *The Street* is not a war novel, but the life Lutie has chosen leads only to defilement and death.

It may be the contrast between this energy of violence—whether in actual war novels or in such major 1940s books as *All the King's Men*, *The Street*, or Wallace Stegner's *Big Rock Candy Mountain*, Harriette Arnow's *Hunter's Horn* and her better-known *The Dollmaker*, and Nelson Algren's *The Man with the Golden Arm*—that led to the awarding of the Nobel Prize in Literature to both William Faulkner (in 1949) and Ernest Hemingway (in 1954). What each modernist writer had achieved here, after the conviction of modernist aesthetics had modulated in his later work, brought him renewed attention from the world of letters.

In the case of William Faulkner, part of that attention came from his "The Bear," a long story of near-novella length, published both separately and then as a chapter in his 1942 novel, *Go Down, Moses*. In the case of Ernest Hemingway, the attention came from the publication, as a special issue of *Life* Magazine, of his 1952 novella *The Old Man and the Sea*. Each work was archetypal: each posited man against the earth and its creatures, each included a young boy growing into the manhood expected of him as he faced adversity, each struck readers with parabolic force. In the pruning away of flamboyant juxtapositions and ellipses, in clarifying both plot and character, each of these novelists gifted readers with texts that went immediately from page to heart. As Werner Sollors admits, "By 1944, virtually all of Faulkner's seventeen books had slipped out of print . . . ultimately the most significant American prose writer of the century, [Faulkner] wrote his most important works from 1929 to 1942 to mixed reviews and a small audience" (Sollors 358-9). In the case of Faulkner's *Go Down, Moses*, a book that exposed deep-seated and inexhaustible racial prejudice throughout the southern culture the author knew so well, its reception by American readers—along with the novel that followed it, *Intruder in the Dust*—would not come for decades.

French readers had always followed the works of William Faulkner, however, and living through the enormity of their country's destruction during World War II had created even more empathy for Faulkner's South. In the ever-growing body of existential fiction—grouped around the novels of Albert Camus, most often his *L'Étranger*—uncompromising American novels, specifically those of Faulkner, were in alignment. Readers respected the conviction that modern life had become increasingly inhumane; the brutality of war only mirrored other of life's disappointments. Tonally, there was little relief from the serious.[2]

A kind of perverse satisfaction with finding holes in the fabric of the long-enduring American dream (a theme that both Faulkner's "The Bear" and Hemingway's *The Old Man and the Sea* avoided as they stretched beyond the present and the immediate) dominated readers' tastes. What people were most interested in, probably because of the impact of existentialism on literature throughout the world, was the depiction of the loss of innocence. Resurgent sales of Hemingway's *The Sun Also Rises* and Fitzgerald's *The Great Gatsby* reflected that fascination; but the clearest testimony to the self-conscious need to question accepted national values was in the writing of a new generation of writers.

Such writers as Truman Capote, Gore Vidal, Carson McCullers and other southerners (Peter Taylor, Eudora Welty, Elizabeth Spencer, Flannery O'Connor, Shirley Ann Grau) may have been alienated from mainstream culture because of sexual preference or agnosticism. (James Baldwin was taking a similar path among African American writers.) For what biographical reasons, these authors' fiction during the 1940s and the 1950s created a new category of American letters—that of the minority viewpoint (though white), the literature of the anti-dream. Expressing themselves in nonrealistic, or at least unconventionally structured, works, these newer writers insisted on the dreamlike (or, sometimes, hallucinatory) quality of much human experience. At their most ephemeral, novels by these visionary if fragile writers were written to disguise the bleakness of the stories being told.

Capote's *Other Voices, Other Rooms* (1948) illustrates how a text can antagonize mainstream readers. In its beginning, Capote appears to be writing the Horatio Alger, boy-as-orphan tale. Joel Harrison Knox is presented as a young teenager, a "delicate" boy marked by "a girlish tenderness," motherless, living with his aunt. His prayer as he travels to the home of his long-lost father on the forbidding Skully's Landing is "God, let me be loved." Capote's novel is not a lost-boy text, however; it is the story of Randolph Skully, cross-dressing transvestite, who has plotted for young Joel to come to the house, even though his father is paralyzed because of Randolph's sinister love life.

Gore Vidal's *The City and the Pillar* was published earlier that same year, and includes offensive homosexual initiation scenes; it lacks the psychological depth of Capote's work. Often grouped with these two writers is Carson McCullers, whose *The Heart Is a Lonely Hunter* implies sexual difference without detailed exposition. Her 1940 novel treated with dignity and love a group of classic misfits, related only through human sympathy. In 1941, McCullers' *Reflections in a Golden Eye* extended the first book's themes, but in 1946 her *The Member of the Wedding* created the lonely adolescent girl prototype that would be reified through the next decades, as feminism took over publishing houses and women characters became the mainstay of literary criticism.

The American stage was taken over by a variety of playwrights, among them Arthur Miller (whose second play, *Death of a Salesman*, won the Pulitzer Prize for Drama in 1949—following his first Broadway success, *All My Sons* in 1947). It would be Miller's 1953 *The Crucible*, his rewriting of the New England witch hunts reflective of the 1950s HUAC investigations, that would make him world-famous. Appearing simultaneously, though avoiding realistic stage settings, was Tennessee Williams with countless provocative plays: his *The Glass Menagerie* in 1944, *A Streetcar Named Desire* in 1947, *Summer and Smoke* in 1948, *Cat on a Hot Tin Roof* in 1955—winning his own first Pulitzer. Beginning in the early 1950s was a stunning set of plays from the Midwestern playwright William Inge, starting with *Picnic* in 1953, another Pulitzer Prize winner. His other long-running works, all during that decade, were *The Dark at the Top of the Stairs, Bus Stop*, and *Come Back, Little Sheba*.

In 1949 the Soviet Union detonated its first atomic bomb; from that time on, détente and its Cold War occupied the mood of the observing world. In 1952 Dwight D. Eisenhower was elected President of the United States, and in choosing the former general, American citizens may have been creating a psychological fortress around their steadily-recovering country. Whereas some economic recovery had occurred, America was still a land of "haves" and "have-nots," and economic divisions all too often ran along racial lines.

Prejudice ran rampant, and some of the disavowals about the German treatment of Jews, homosexuals, and gypsies, among others—categorized in the 1950s as the Holocaust—stemmed from mainstream indifference to the world's dead. Between the incipient Vietnam War, and the still tentative writing about the

EXCERPT FROM DENISE LEVERTOV'S POEM "LIFE AT WAR"

. . . We are the humans, men who can make;
whose language imagines *mercy*,
lovingkindness; we have believed one another
mirrored forms of a God we felt as good—

who do these acts, who convince ourselves
it is necessary; these acts are done
to our own flesh; burned human flesh
is smelling in Vietnam as I write.

Yes, this is the knowledge that jostles for space
in our bodies along with all we
go on knowing of joy, of love;

our nerve filaments twitch with its presence
day and night,
nothing we say has not the husky phlegm of it in the saying,
nothing we do has the quickness, the sureness,
the deep intelligence living at peace would have.

Holocaust, readers could not shake the dark tone of even comic American writing. When J. D. Salinger wrote his supposedly humorous *The Catcher in the Rye* (1952), followed by Sylvia Plath's *The Bell Jar*, a stolid acknowledgment of the tone of dis-ease throughout the United States seemed evident.

As Elie Wiesel said in his new introduction to his classic *Night*, when his testimonial memoir appeared in the late 1950s, "the book sold poorly. The subject was considered morbid and interested no one." He is pleased that times have changed, speaking for people's humanity and their capacity to accept learning about such horrors. "What I do know is that there is 'response' in responsibility. When we speak of this era of evil and darkness, so close and yet so distant, 'responsibility' is the key word" (Wiesel xiv–xv).

In this shift away from scrutiny of a writer's aesthetic principles—as would have been the case in any study of American modernist writing—to an overarching insistence on all dimensions of the writer's work (characters, themes, structures, plot, metaphors, language choices and effects) lies one difference between the way readers have apprehended Modernism in the past, and the way their demands about excellent writing have become more related to their immediate lives, their own experiences, their valid reactions to what writers are coming to write about. It was never easy to categorize what was happening throughout the world of literature, and in that categorizing, reductionism may have occurred. Even in retrospect, the task is not easy. One hopes, however, that the gift of reading from the pages of the American modernists brings not only information and interest, but its own creative joy.

Notes

1 Among Pound's last notes toward his *Cantos* is the prayerful evocation, "To be men not destroyers" (N 231).
2 Publishers tried to bring readers back into the "gallows" humor of Nathanael West's *The Day of the Locust* (1939), and Shirley Jackson always brought smiles to readers who loved the gothic, but the tone of American fiction remained somber. For every *Henderson the Rain King*, there was a Lillian Smith's *Strange Fruit*.

Suggested further reading

David Minter. *A Cultural History of the Modern American Novel. The Cambridge History of American Literature VI.* Ed. Sacvan Bercovitch. Cambridge UP, 2002.
Miles Orvell. *The Death and Life of Main Street.* U of North Carolina P, 2012.
Robert Scholes. *Paradoxy of Modernism.* Yale UP, 2006.
Vincent Sherry. *Modernism and the Reinvention of Decadence.* Cambridge UP, 2015.

BIBLIOGRAPHY

Aaron, Daniel. *Writers on the Left*. New York: Harcourt, Brace, 1961. Print.

Abrahams, Edward. *The Lyrical Left*. Charlottesville: UP of Virginia, 1986. Print.

Agamben, Giorgio. *Remnants of Auschwitz: The Witness and the Archive*. New York: Zone, 2002. Print.

Agee, James, with Walker Evans. *Let Us Now Praise Famous Men*. Boston: Houghton Mifflin, 1941. Print.

Algren, Nelson. *Somebody in Boots*. New York: Vanguard, 1935.

Allen, Frederick Lewis. *Only Yesterday*. New York: Harper, 1931. Print.

Allen, Nicole and David Simmons, eds. *Reassessing the Twentieth-Century Canon: From Joseph Conrad to Zadie Smith*. New York: Palgrave Macmillan, 2014. Print.

Alter, Jonathan. *The Defining Moment: FDR's Hundred Days and the Triumph of Hope*. New York: Simon & Schuster, 2006. Print.

Altieri, Charles. *The Art of Twentieth-Century American Poetry: Modernism and After*. Malden, Massachusetts: Blackwell, 2006. Print.

Anderson, Benedict. *Imagined Communities: Reflections on the Origin and Spread of Nationalism*. London: New Left, 1983. Print.

Anderson, Sarah Wood. *Readings of Trauma, Madness, and the Body*. New York: Palgrave, 2012. Print.

Anderson, Sherwood. *The Portable Sherwood Anderson*. New York: Viking, 1949. Print.

———. *Winesburg, Ohio: A Group of Tales of Ohio Small Town Life*. New York: Huebsch, 1919. Print.

Anon. "Stein's *Three Lives*," *The Nation* (January 20, 1910):371–2. Print.

Anon. "Three Lives," *Washington Herald* (December 12, 1909). Print.

Armstrong, Tim. *Modernism, Technology and the Body: A Cultural History*. New York: Cambridge UP, 1998. Print.

Aronoff, Eric. *Composing Cultures: Modernism, American Literary Studies, and the Problem of Culture*. Charlottesville: UP of Virginia, 2013. Print.

Ashton, Jennifer. *From Modernism to Postmodernism: American Poetry and Theory in the Twentieth Century*. Cambridge: Cambridge UP, 2005. Print.

Axelrod, Steven Gould, Camille Roman, Thomas J. Travisano, eds. *The New Anthology of American Poetry*, Vol. 2. New Brunswick, New Jersey: Rutgers UP, 2003. Print.

Baker, Houston A., Jr. *Modernism and the Harlem Renaissance.* Chicago: U of Chicago P, 1987. Print.

Beach, Sylvia. *Shakespeare and Company.* New York: Harcourt, Brace, 1959. Print.

Becker, George Joseph, ed. *Documents of Modern Literary Realism.* Princeton, New Jersey: Princeton UP, 1963. Print.

Beebe, Maurice. "What Modernism Was," *Journal of Modern Literature* 3.5 (July 1974):1065–84. Print.

Beja, Morris. *Epiphany in the Modern Novel.* London: Peter Owen, 1971. Print.

Bell, Bernard W. *The Afro-American Novel and Its Tradition.* Amherst: U of Massachusetts P, 1987. Print.

Bennett, Paula. *My Life a Loaded Gun: Female Creativity and Feminist Poetics.* Boston: Beacon, 1986. Print.

Benstock, Shari. "Expatriate Modernism, Writing on the Cultural Rim," *Women's Writing in Exile.* Ed. Mary Lynn Broe and Angela Ingram. Chapel Hill: U of North Carolina P, 1989:19–40. Print.

——. *Women of the Left Bank, Paris, 1900–1940.* Austin: U of Texas P, 1986. Print.

Bergson, Henri. *An Introduction to Metaphysics,* trans. T. E. Hulme. Indianapolis, Indiana: Liberal Arts Press, 1912, 1955. Print.

Berke, Nancy. *Women Poets on the Left: Lola Ridge, Genevieve Taggard, Margaret Walker.* Gainesville: UP of Florida, 2001. Print.

Bernard, Emily. *Carl Van Vechten and the Harlem Renaissance: A Portrait in Black and White.* New Haven, Connecticut: Yale UP, 2012. Print.

Biers, Katherine. *Virtual Modernism: Writing and Technology in the Progressive Era.* Minneapolis: U of Minnesota P, 2013. Print.

Blackmur, R. P. *Language as Gesture.* New York: Harcourt, Brace, 1952. Print.

Blair, Sara. "Modernism and the Politics of Culture," *The Cambridge Companion to Modernism.* Ed. Michael Levenson. Cambridge, Massachusetts: Cambridge UP, 1999:157–73. Print.

Bogan, Louise. *Achievement in American Poetry, 1900–1950.* Chicago: Henry Regnery, 1951. Print.

Boone, Joseph Allen. *Libidinal Currents: Sexuality and the Making of Modernism.* Chicago: U of Chicago P, 1998. Print.

Boyle, Kay and Robert McAlmon. *Being Geniuses Together, 1920–1930.* San Francisco: North Point, 1968, 1984. Print.

Braudy, Leo. *The Frenzy of Renown: Fame and Its History.* New York: Oxford UP, 1986. Print.

Brown, Bill. *The Material Unconscious: American Amusement, Stephen Crane, and the Economies of Play.* Cambridge, Massachusetts: Harvard UP, 1996. Print.

——. *A Sense of Things: The Object Matter of American Literature.* Chicago: U of Chicago P, 2003. Print.

Buell, Lawrence. *The Dream of the Great American Novel.* Cambridge, Massachusetts: Harvard UP, 2014. Print.

Cadle, Nathaniel. *The Mediating Nation: Late American Realism, Globalization, and the Progressive State.* Chapel Hill: U of North Carolina P, 2014. Print.

Caldwell, Erskine. *The Complete Stories of Erskine Caldwell.* Boston: Little, Brown, 1941. Print.

Calinescu, Matei. *Five Faces of Modernity: Modernism, Avant-Garde, Decadence, Kitsch, Postmodernism.* Durham, North Carolina: Duke UP, 1987. Print.

Cambon, Glauco. *The Inclusive Flame: Studies in American Poetry.* Bloomington: Indiana UP, 1963. Print.

Capetti, Carla. *Writing Chicago: Modernism, Ethnography, and the Novel.* New York: Columbia UP, 1993. Print.

Casey, Janet Galligani, ed. *The Novel and the American Left: Critical Essays on Depression-Era Fiction*. Iowa City: U of Iowa P, 2004. Print.

Castle, Terry. *The Apparitional Lesbian: Female Homosexuality and Modern Culture*. New York: Columbia UP, 1993. Print.

Cather, Willa. *One of Ours*. New York: Knopf, 1922. Print.

Cawelti, John G. *Adventure, Mystery and Romance: Formula Stories as Art and Popular Culture*. Chicago: U of Chicago P, 1976.

Chesler, Phyllis. *Women & Madness*. New York: Doubleday, 1972. Print.

Childs, Peter. *Modernism*. New York: Routledge, 2008. Print.

———. *Modernist Literature: A Guide for the Perplexed*. New York: Continuum, 2011. Print.

Christ, Carol. *Diving Deep and Surfacing: Women Writers on Spiritual Quest*. Boston: Beacon, 1980. Print.

Christian, Barbara. *Black Women Novelists: The Development of a Tradition, 1892–1976*. Westport, Connecticut: Greenwood, 1980. Print.

Clark, Suzanne. *Sentimental Modernism: Women Writers and the Revolution of the Word*. Bloomington: Indiana UP, 1991. Print.

Coffman, Stanley K., Jr. *Imagism: A Chapter for the History of Modern Poetry*. Norman: U of Oklahoma P, 1951. Print.

Cohen, Milton A. *Beleaguered Poets and Leftist Critics: Stevens, Cummings, Frost and Williams in the 1930s*. Tuscaloosa: U of Alabama P, 2010. Print.

Condor, John J. *Naturalism in American Fiction: The Classic Phase*. Lexington: UP of Kentucky, 1984. Print.

Conn, Peter. *The American 1930s*. Cambridge, UK: Cambridge UP, 2009.

Connerton, Paul. *How Societies Remember*. New York: Cambridge UP, 1989. Print.

Conroy, Jack. *A World to Win*. Urbana: U of Illinois P, 1935, 2000.

Cooperman, Stanley. *World War I and the American Novel*. Baltimore, Maryland: Johns Hopkins UP, 1967. Print.

Cowley, Malcolm. *Exile's Return*. New York: Penguin, 1951, 1994. Print.

———. *A Second Flowering*. New York: Viking, 1973. Print.

Crowley, John W. *The White Logic, Alcoholism and Gender in American Modernist Fiction*. Amherst: U of Massachusetts P, 1994. Print.

Davis, James. *Eric Walrond: A Life in the Harlem Renaissance and the Transatlantic Caribbean*. New York: Columbia UP, 2015. Print.

Davis, Thadious M. *Games of Property*. Durham, NC: Duke UP, 2003. Print.

———. *Southscapes*. Chapel Hill: U of North Carolina P, 2011. Print.

DeGuzman, Maria. *Buenas Noches, American Culture*. Bloomington: Indiana UP, 2012. Print.

———. *Spain's Long Shadow: The Black Legend, Off-Whiteness, and Anglo-American Empire*. Minneapolis: U of Minnesota P, 2007. Print.

DeKoven, Marianne. *Rich and Strange: Gender, History, Modernism*. Princeton, New Jersey: Princeton UP, 1991. Print.

Dembo, L. S. *Conceptions of Reality in Modern American Poetry*. Berkeley: U of California P, 1966. Print.

Denning, Michael. *The Cultural Front, The Laboring of American Culture in the 20th Century*. New York: Verso, 1996. Print.

Dettmar, Kevin J. H. and Stephen Watt, eds. *Marketing Modernisms: Self-Promotion, Canonization, Rereading*. Ann Arbor: U of Michigan P, 1996. Print.

Deutsch, Babette. *Poetry in Our Time*. New York: Columbia UP, 1956. Print.

Dimock, Wai Chee. *Residues of Justice: Literature, Law, Philosophy*. Berkeley: U of California P, 1996. Print.

——. *Through Other Continents: American Literature Across Deep Time*. Princeton, New Jersey: Princeton UP, 2006. Print.

Dolan, Marc. *Modern Lives: A Cultural Re-Reading of "The Lost Generation"*. West Lafayette, Indiana: Purdue UP, 1996. Print.

Donaldson, Scott. *Hemingway vs. Fitzgerald: The Rise and Fall of a Literary Friendship*. Woodstock, New York: Overlook P, 1999. Print.

Donaldson, Susan V. "Writing the Modern South," *A Companion to the Modern American Novel, 1900–1950*. Ed. John T. Matthews. Malden, Massachusetts: Wiley-Blackwell, 2009:266–81. Print.

Donoghue, Denis. *The Ordinary Universe: Soundings in Modern Literature*. New York: Macmillan, 1968. Print.

Doody, Terrence. *Confession and Community in the Novel*. Baton Rouge: Louisiana State UP, 1980. Print.

Dore, Florence. *The Novel and the Obscene: Sexual Subjects in American Modernism*. Stanford, California: Stanford UP, 2005. Print.

Dos Passos, John. *The Best Times*. New York: New American Library, 1966. Print.

——. *Occasions and Protests*. New York: Henry Regnery, 1965. Print.

——. *One Man's Initiation—1917*. New York: Philosophical Library, 1945 (1917). Print.

——. *A Pushcart at the Curb*. New York: George H. Doran, 1922. Print.

——. *U.S.A.* New York: Library of America, 1996. Print.

Douglas, Ann. *Terrible Honesty: Mongrel Manhattan in the 1920s*. New York: Farrar, Straus, 1995. Print.

Dow, William. *Narrating Class in American Fiction*. New York: Palgrave, 2009. Print.

Doyle, Laura. *Bordering on the Body: The Racial Matrix of Modern Fiction and Culture*. New York: Oxford UP, 1994. Print.

Driscoll, Catherine. *Modernist Cultural Studies*. Gainesville: UP of Florida, 2010. Print.

Drowne, Kathleen. *Spirits of Defiance, National Prohibition and Jazz Age Literature, 1920–1933*. Columbus: Ohio State UP, 2005. Print.

Duberman, Martin, Martha Vicinus, and George Chauncey, Jr., eds. *Hidden From History: Reclaiming the Gay and Lesbian Past*. New York: NAL, 1989. Print.

Duck, Leigh Anne. *The Nation's Region: Southern Modernism, Segregation, and United States Nationalism*. Athens: U of Georgia P, 2006. Print.

DuPlessis, Rachel Blau. *Writing beyond the Ending: Narrative Strategies of Twentieth-Century Women Writers*. Bloomington: Indiana UP, 1985. Print.

Eby, Carl P. "Literary Movements," *Ernest Hemingway in Context*. Ed. Debra A. Moddelmog and Suzanne Del Gizzo. New York: Cambridge UP, 2013:173–82. Print.

Eckman, Frederick. *Cobras and Cockle Shells: Modes in Recent Poetry*. Flushing, New York: Sparrow P, 1958. Print.

Eisinger, Chester E. *Fiction of the Forties*. Chicago: U of Chicago P, 1963. Print.

Eliot, T. S. *The Waste Land: A Facsimile and Transcript of the Original Drafts*. Ed. Valerie Eliot. New York: Harcourt, Brace, 1971.

Elliott, Emory, ed. *Columbia Literary History of the United States*. New York: Columbia UP, 1988. Print.

Ellmann, Richard and Charles Feidelson, Jr., eds. *The Modern Tradition: Backgrounds of Modern Literature*. New York: Oxford UP, 1965. Print.

English, Daylanne. *Unnatural Selections: Eugenics in American Modernism and the Harlem Renaissance*. Chapel Hill: U of North Carolina P, 2004. Print.

Entin, Joseph. *Sensational Modernism: Experimental Fiction and Photography in Thirties America*. Chapel Hill: U of North Carolina P, 2007. Print.

Evans, Brad. *Before Cultures: The Ethnographic Imagination in American Literature, 1865–1920.* Chicago: U of Chicago P, 2005. Print.

Eysteinsson, Astradur. *The Concept of Modernism.* Ithaca, New York: Cornell UP, 1990. Print.

Farrell, James T. *Gas-House McGinty.* New York: Vanguard, 1933. Print.

——. *Studs Lonigan.* New York: Vanguard, 1935. Print.

——. *Young Lonigan.* New York: Vanguard, 1932. Print.

Faulkner, William. *Absalom, Absalom!* New York: Random, 1936. Print.

——. *Early Prose and Poetry.* Ed. Carvel Collins. Boston: Little Brown, 1962. Print.

——. *Essays, Speeches and Public Letters.* Ed. James B. Meriwether. New York: Random, 1965. Print.

——. *Light in August.* New York: Random, 1932. Print.

——. *Lion in the Garden.* Ed. James B. Meriwether and Michael Millgate. New York: Random, 1968. Print.

——. *The Marble Faun and A Green Bough.* New York: Random, 1965. Print.

——. *Soldiers' Pay.* New York: Boni & Liveright, 1926. Print.

——. *The Sound and the Fury.* New York: Random, 1929. Print.

Fetterley, Judith. *The Resisting Reader: A Feminist Approach to American Fiction.* Bloomington: Indiana UP, 1977. Print.

Fiedler, Leslie A. *Love and Death in the American Novel.* New York: Stein and Day, 1966. Print.

Fitzgerald, F. Scott. *The Great Gatsby.* New York: Scribner's, 1925. Print.

Foley, Barbara. "The Proletarian Novel," *A Companion to the Modern American Novel, 1900–1950.* Ed. John T. Matthews. Malden, Massachusetts: Wiley-Blackwell, 2009:353–66. Print.

——. *Radical Representations: Politics and Form in U.S. Proletarian Fiction, 1929–1941.* Durham, NC: Duke UP, 1994. Print.

Foucault, Michel. *The History of Sexuality,* vol. 1, trans. Robert Hurley. New York: Random, 1978. Print.

Frank, Joseph. *The Idea of Spatial Form.* New Brunswick, New Jersey: Rutgers UP, 1991. Print.

Freedman, Ralph. *The Lyrical Novel.* Princeton, New Jersey: Princeton UP, 1963. Print.

Freud, Sigmund. *The Freud Reader.* Ed. Peter Gay. New York: Norton, 1989. Print.

Fussell, Paul. *The Great War and Modern Memory.* New York: Oxford UP, 1975. Print..

Galow, Timothy W. *Writing Celebrity: Stein, Fitzgerald, and the Modern(ist) Art of Self-Fashioning.* New York: Palgrave, 2011. Print.

Gasiorek, Andrzej. "Class Positions," *The Oxford Handbook of Modernisms.* Ed. Peter Brooker, Andrzej Gasiorek, Deborah Longworth, Andrew Thacker. New York: Oxford UP, 2010:178–98. Print.

Gates, Henry Louis, Jr. *Figures in Black: Words, Signs, and the Racial Self.* New York: Oxford UP, 1987. Print.

——. *The Signifying Monkey,* 25th anniversary edition. New York: Oxford UP, 2014. Print.

Geismar, Maxwell. *Writers in Crisis, The American Novel, 1925–1940.* New York: Dutton, 1971. Print.

Georgakas, Dan and Ernie Brill. "Proletarian and Radical Writers," *Encyclopedia of the American Left,* 2nd edition. Ed. Mari Jo Buhle, Paul Buhle, and Dan Georgakas. New York: Oxford UP, 1998:637–41. Print.

Gerstle, Gary. *American Crucible: Race and Nation in the Twentieth Century.* Princeton, New Jersey: Princeton UP, 2002. Print.

Gifford, James. *Personal Modernisms: Anarchist Networks and the Later Avant-gardes.* Edmonton, Alberta, Canada: U of Alberta P, 2014. Print.

Gilbert, Sandra M. and Susan Gubar. *No Man's Land: The Place of the Woman Writer in the Twentieth Century.* New Haven, Connecticut: Yale UP, 1988–1993. Print.

Gilroy, Paul. *The Black Atlantic: Modernity and Double Consciousness.* New York: Verso, 1993. Print.

Glass, Loren. *Authors, Inc.: Literary Celebrity in the United States, 1880–1980.* Albany: New York UP, 2003. Print.

Gleason, Philip. *Speaking of Diversity: Language and Ethnicity in Twentieth-Century America.* Baltimore, Maryland: Johns Hopkins UP, 1992. Print.

Godden, Richard. *Fictions of Capital, The American Novel from James to Mailer.* Cambridge: Cambridge UP, 1990. Print.

Golden, Jonathan. *Modernism Is the Literature of Celebrity.* Austin: U of Texas P, 2011. Print.

Goldman, June. *Modernism 1910–1945.* New York: Palgrave, 2004. Print.

Gray, Jonathan W. "Harlem Modernism," *The Oxford Handbook of Modernisms.* Ed. Peter Brooker, Andrzej Gasiorek, Deborah Longworth, Andrew Thacker. New York: Oxford UP, 2010:235–48. Print.

Gray, Richard. *A Brief History of American Literature.* Malden, Massachusetts: Wiley-Blackwell, 2011. Print.

H.D. *HERmione.* New York: New Directions, 1980. Print.

Hale, Grace Elizabeth. *Making Whiteness: The Culture of Segregation in the South, 1890–1940.* New York: Pantheon, 1998. Print.

Halper, Albert. *The Chute.* New York: Viking, 1937.

Hapke, Laura. *Labor's Text: The Worker in American Fiction.* New Brunswick, New Jersey: Rutgers UP, 2001. Print.

Harris, Trudier. *Exorcising Blackness: Historical and Literary Lynching and Burning Rituals.* Bloomington: Indiana UP, 1984. Print.

Haslam, Sara and Sue Asbee. *The Twentieth Century.* New York: Bloomsbury, 2014. Print.

Hassan, Ihab. *Contemporary American Literature, 1945–1972.* New York: Frederick Ungar, 1973. Print.

———. *Radical Innocence.* Princeton, New Jersey: Princeton UP, 1961. Print.

Haytock, Jennifer. *At Home, At War: Domesticity and World War I in American Literature.* Columbus: Ohio State UP, 2003. Print.

———. *The Middle Class in the Great Depression: Popular Women's Novels of the 1930s.* New York: Palgrave, 2013. Print.

Hegeman, Susan. *Patterns for America: Modernism and the Concept of Culture.* Princeton, New Jersey: Princeton UP, 1999. Print.

Hemingway, Ernest. *The Collected Poems of Ernest Hemingway.* New York: Haskell House, 1960. Print.

———. *The Complete Short Stories of Ernest Hemingway.* New York: Simon & Schuster, 1987. Print.

———. *In Our Time.* New York: Boni & Liveright, 1925. Print.

———. *The Selected Letters, 1917–1961.* Ed. Carlos Baker. New York: Scribner's, 1981. Print.

———. *The Sun Also Rises.* New York: Scribner's, 1926. Print.

Herring, Scott. *Queering the Underworld: Slumming, Literature, and the Undoing of Lesbian and Gay History.* Chicago: U of Chicago P, 2007. Print.

Hoffman, Frederick J. *The Modern Novel in America: 1900–1950.* Chicago: Henry Regnery, 1951. Print.

———. *The Twenties* (revised). New York: Free P, 1949, 1952. Print.

Homberger, Eric. *American Writers and Radical Politics, 1900–1930: Equivocal Commitments.* New York: St. Martin's, 1987. Print.

Hough, Graham. *Image and Experience: Studies in a Literary Revolution.* London: Duckworth, 1960. Print.

Howard, June. *Form and History in American Literature Naturalism.* Chapel Hill: U of North Carolina P, 1985. Print.

Huggins, Nathan. *Harlem Renaissance*. New York: Oxford UP, 1971.

Hurston, Zora Neale. *Their Eyes Were Watching God*. Urbana: U of Illinois P, 1978. Print.

Hutchinson, George. *The Harlem Renaissance in Black and White*. Cambridge, Massachusetts: Harvard UP, 1995. Print.

Hutner, Gordon. *What America Read: Taste, Class, and the Novel, 1920–1960*. Chapel Hill: U of North Carolina P, 2009. Print.

Huyssen, Andreas. *After the Great Divide: Modernism, Mass Culture, Postmodernism*. Bloomington: Indiana UP, 1986. Print.

Ignatiev, Noel. *How the Irish Became White*. New York: Routledge, 1995. Print.

Irr, Caren. *The Suburb of Dissent: Cultural Politics in the United States and Canada During the 1930s*. Durham, N.C.: Duke UP, 1998. Print.

Izenberg, Gerald N. *Modernism and Masculinity*. Chicago: U of Chicago P, 2000. Print.

Jackson, Kevin. *Constellation of Genius: 1922: Modernism Year One*. New York: Farrar, Straus and Giroux, 2013. Print.

Jackson, Laurence P. *The Indignant Generation: A Narrative History of African American Writers and Critics, 1934–1960*. Princeton, New Jersey: Princeton UP, 2011. Print.

Jacobson, Matthew. *Whiteness of a Different Color: European Immigrants and the Alchemy of Race*. Cambridge, Massachusetts: Harvard UP, 1998. Print.

Jaffe, Aaron. *Modernism and the Culture of Celebrity*. New York: Cambridge UP, 2005. Print.

James, Pearl. *The New Death: American Modernism and World War I*. Charlottesville: U of Virginia P, 2013. Print.

Jameson, Fredric. *The Political Unconscious: Narrative as a Socially Symbolic Act*. Ithaca, New York: Cornell UP, 1981. Print.

Johnson, Josephine. *Now in November*. New York: Simon & Schuster, 1934. Print.

Juhasz, Suzanne. *Naked and Fiery Forms, Modern American Poetry by Women: A New Tradition*. New York: Harper, 1976. Print.

Kadlec, David. *Mosaic Modernism: Anarchism, Pragmatism, Culture*. Baltimore, Maryland: Johns Hopkins UP, 2000. Print.

Kalaidjian, Walter. *The Cambridge Companion to American Modernism*. Cambridge, Massachusetts: Cambridge UP, 2005. Print.

———, ed. *Revisionary Modernism and Postmodern Critique*. New York: Columbia UP, 1993. Print.

Kammen, Michael. *American Culture, American Tastes, Social Change in the Twentieth Century*. New York: Knopf, 1999. Print.

Kaplan, Amy. *The Anarchy of Empire in the Making of U.S. Culture*. Cambridge, Massachusetts: Harvard UP, 2005. Print.

———. *The Social Construction of American Realism*. Chicago: U of Chicago P, 1988. Print.

Kaplan, E. Ann. *Motherhood and Representation: The Mother in Popular Culture and Melodrama*. New York: Routledge, 1992. Print.

Karl, Frederick R. *Modern and Modernism: The Sovereignty of the Artist, 1885–1925*. New York: Atheneum, 1985. Print.

Kazin, Alfred. *On Native Grounds*. New York: Harcourt, Brace, 1942. Print.

———. *Starting Out in the Thirties*. Boston: Little, Brown, 1965. Print.

Keller, Lynn. *Re-making It New: Contemporary American Poetry and the Modernist Tradition*. New York: Cambridge UP, 1987. Print.

Kennedy, David M. *Freedom from Fear: The American People in Depression and War, 1929–1945*. New York: Oxford UP, 1999. Print.

Kennedy, J. Gerald. *Imagining Paris: Exile, Writing, and American Identity*. New Haven, Connecticut: Yale UP, 1993. Print.

Kenner, Hugh. *A Homemade World: The American Modernist Writers*. New York: Knopf, 1975. Print.

———. *The Pound Era*. Berkeley: U of California P, 1971. Print.

Klein, Marcus. *Foreigners: The Making of American Literature, 1900–1940*. Chicago: U of Chicago P, 1981. Print.

Kohlmann, Benjamin. *Committed Styles: Modernism, Politics, and Left-Wing Literature in the 1930s*. New York: Oxford UP, 2014. Print.

Kromer, Tom. *Waiting for Nothing*. New York: Knopf, 1935. Print.

Lacey, Paul A. *The Inner War: Forms and Themes in Recent American Poetry*. Philadelphia: Fortress P, 1972. Print.

Lang, Amy Schrager. *The Syntax of Class*. Princeton, New Jersey: Princeton UP, 2003. Print.

Larsen, Nella. *Quicksand* in *Quicksand and Passing*. New Brunswick, New Jersey: Rutgers UP, 1986. Print.

Lasch, Christopher. *The New Radicalism in America, 1889–1963*. New York: Vintage, 1967. Print.

Lauter, Paul, *et al.*, ed. *The Heath Anthology of American Literature*, Vol. C, D. Boston: Houghton Mifflin, ongoing. Print.

Lavelle, John F. *Blue Collar, Theoretically*. Jefferson, North Carolina: McFarland, 2012. Print.

Lears, T. J. Jackson. *No Place of Grace: Antimodernism and the Transformation of American Culture, 1880–1920*. Chicago: U of Chicago P, 1994. Print.

Lenthall, Bruce. *Radio's America: the Great Depression and the Rise of Modern Mass Culture*. Chicago: U of Chicago P, 2007. Print.

Le Sueur, Meridel. *Ripening: Selected Work, 1927–1938*. New York: Harper, 1938. Print.

Levenson, Michael H., ed. *The Cambridge Companion to Modernism*. Cambridge, New York: Cambridge UP, 2011.

———. *Modernism*. New Haven, Connecticut: Yale UP, 2011. Print.

Levine, Lawrence W. *Highbrow/Lowbrow: The Emergence of Cultural Hierarchy in America*. Cambridge, Massachusetts: Harvard UP, 1988. Print.

Levitt, Morton P. *Modernist Survivors*. Columbus: Ohio State UP, 1987. Print.

Levy, Helen Fiddyment. *Fiction of the Home Place*. Jackson: UP of Mississippi, 1992. Print.

Lewis, R. W. B. *The American Adam*. Chicago: U of Chicago P, 1955. Print.

Lewis, Sinclair. *Main Street*. New York: Harcourt, Brace, 1920. Print.

Lipsitz, George. *The Possessive Investment in Whiteness: How White People Profit from Identity Politics*. Philadelphia, Pennsylvania: Temple UP, 2006. Print.

———. *Rainbow at Midnight: Labor and Culture in the 1940s*. Urbana: U of Illinois P, 1994. Print.

Livingston, James. *Pragmatism and the Political Economy of Cultural Revolution, 1850–1940*. Chapel Hill: U of North Carolina P, 1994. Print.

Locke, Alain. *The New Negro: An Interpretation*. New York: Touchstone, 1997 (1925). Print.

Lott, Eric. *Love and Theft: Blackface Minstrelsy and the American Working Class*. New York: Oxford UP, 1993. Print.

Lottman, Herbert R. *The Left Bank, Writers, Artists, and Politics from the Popular Front to the Cold War*. Boston: Houghton Mifflin, 1982. Print.

Lowney, John. *History, Memory, and the Literary Life: Modern American Poetry 1935–1968*. Iowa City: U of Iowa P, 2006.

Luccock, Halford E. *American Mirror: Social, Ethical and Religious Aspects of American Literature 1930–1940*. New York: Macmillan, 1941. Print.

McCabe, Susan. *Cinematic Modernism*. Cambridge: Cambridge UP, 2005. Print.

McCormick, John. *The Middle Distance: A Comparative History of American Imaginative Literature, 1919–1932*. New York: Free P, 1971. Print.

McCracken, Scott. *Masculinities, Modernist Fiction and the Urban Public Sphere*. Manchester: Manchester UP, 2007. Print.

McKenney, Ruth. *Industrial Valley.* New York: Harcourt, Brace, 1939.

Magny, Claude-Edmonde. *The Age of the American Novel: The Film Aesthetic of Fiction between the Two Wars,* trans. Eleanor Hochman. New York: Ungar, 1972 (1948). Print.

Maltz, Albert. "Man on the Road," *The Strenuous Decade.* Ed. Daniel Aaron and Robert Bendiner. Garden City, New York: Doubleday, 1970:245–6. Print.

Manganaro, Marc. *Culture, 1922: The Emergence of a Concept.* Princeton, New Jersey: Princeton UP, 2002. Print.

Mao, Douglas. *Solid Objects: Modernism and the Test of Production.* Princeton, New Jersey: Princeton UP, 1998. Print.

Marchand, Roland. *Advertising the American Dream: Making Way for Modernity, 1920–1940.* Berkeley: U of California P, 1985. Print.

Marcus, Greil and Werner Sollors, eds. *A New Literary History of America.* Cambridge, Massachusetts: Harvard UP, 2009. Print.

Marcus, Jane. "Corpus/Corps/Corpse: Writing the Body in/at War," *Arms and the Woman.* Ed. Helen M. Cooper, Adrienne Auslander Munich, Susan Merrill Squier. Chapel Hill: U of North Carolina P, 1989:124–67. Print.

Marling, William. *The American Roman Noir: Hammett, Cain, and Chandler.* Athens: U of Georgia P, 1995. Print.

Marsh, John. *Hog Butchers, Beggars, and Busboys.* Ann Arbor: U of Michigan P, 2011. Print.

Matthews, John T. "What Was High About Modernism? The American Novel and Modernity," *A Companion to the Modern American Novel 1900–1950.* Ed. John T. Matthews. Malden, Massachusetts: Wiley-Blackwell, 2009:282–305. Print.

Matthews, Steven. *Modernism: A Sourcebook.* New York: Palgrave Macmillan, 2008. Print.

Matthiessen, F. O. *The Responsibilities of the Critic.* New York: Oxford UP, 1952. Print.

Michaels, Walter Benn. *Our America: Nativism, Modernism, and Pluralism.* Durham, NC: Duke UP, 1995. Print.

Miller, J. Hillis. *Poets of Reality.* Cambridge, Massachusetts: Harvard UP, 1965. Print.

Miller, Joshua L. *Accented America: The Cultural Politics of Multilingual Modernism.* New York: Oxford UP, 2011. Print.

Minter, David. *A Cultural History of the American Novel.* New York: Cambridge UP, 1994. Print.

——. *A Cultural History of the Modern American Novel* in *The Cambridge History of American Literature* VI. Ed. Sacvan Bercovitch. Cambridge: Cambridge UP, 2002:1–282. Print.

Mitchell, Verner D. and Cynthia Davis. *Literary Sisters: Dorothy West and Her Circle,* A Biography of the Harlem Renaissance. New Brunswick, New Jersey: Rutgers UP, 2012. Print.

Morrison, Toni. *Playing in the Dark, Whiteness and the Literary Imagination.* New York: Vintage, 1992. Print.

Moses, Omri. *Out of Character: Modernism, Vitalism, Psychic Life.* Stanford, California: Stanford UP, 2014. Print.

Murphy, Brenda. *American Realism and American Drama, 1880–1940.* Cambridge: Cambridge UP, 1987. Print.

Murphy, James. *The Proletarian Moment: The Controversy over Leftism in Literature.* Chicago: U of Illinois P, 1991. Print.

Nelson, Cary. ed. *Anthology of Modern American Poetry.* New York: Oxford UP, 2000. Print.

——. *Repression and Recovery, Modern American Poetry and the Politics of Cultural Memory, 1910–1945.* Madison: U of Wisconsin P, 1989. Print.

Nicholls, Peter. *Modernism: A Literary Guide.* Berkeley: U of California P, 1995. Print.

Nickels, Joel. *Poetry of the Possible: Spontaneity, Modernism, and the Multitude.* Minneapolis: U of Minnesota P, 2012. Print.

Nielson, Aldon Lynn. *Reading Race: White American Poets and the Racial Discourse in the Twentieth Century.* Athens: U of Georgia P, 1988. Print.

North, Michael. *The Dialect of Modernism: Race, Language, and Twentieth-Century Literature.* New York: Oxford UP, 1994.

———. *Reading 1922: A Return to the Scene of the Modern.* New York: Oxford UP, 1999. Print.

O'Brien, Sharon. "Combat Envy and Survivor Guilt: Willa Cather's 'Manly Battle Yarn,'" *Arms and the Woman.* Ed. Helen M. Cooper, Adrienne Auslander Munich, Susan Merrill Squier. Chapel Hill: U of North Carolina P, 1989:184–204. Print.

Olson, Liesl. *Modernism and the Ordinary.* New York: Oxford UP, 2009. Print.

Orvell, Miles. *The Death and Life of Main Street.* Chapel Hill: U of North Carolina P, 2012. Print.

Parrish, Michael. *Anxious Decades: America in Prosperity and Depression, 1920–1941.* New York: Norton, 1992. Print.

Patterson, Anita. *Race, American Literature and Transnational Modernisms.* New York: Cambridge UP, 2008. Print.

Pearce, Roy Harvey. *The Continuity of American Poetry.* Princeton, New Jersey: Princeton UP, 1961. Print.

Pearson, Carol and Katherine Pope. *The Female Hero in American and British Literature.* New York: Bowker, 1981. Print.

Peeler, David P. *Hope Among Us Yet: Social Criticism and Social Solace in Depression America.* Athens: U of Georgia P, 1987. Print.

Pells, Richard H. *Radical Visions and American Dreams.* New York: Harper, 1973. Print.

Peppis, Paul. *Sciences of Modernism: Ethnography, Sexology, and Psychology.* Cambridge: Cambridge UP, 2013. Print.

Perloff, Marjorie. *The Poetics of Indeterminacy: Rimbaud to Cage.* Princeton, New Jersey: Princeton UP, 1981. Print.

Pfister, Joel. *Individuality Incorporated: Indians and the Multicultural Modern.* Durham, NC: Duke UP, 2004. Print.

Poirier, Richard. *Poetry and Pragmatism.* Cambridge, Massachusetts: Harvard UP, 1992. Print.

———. *A World Elsewhere.* New York: Oxford UP, 1966. Print.

Posnock, Ross. *Color and Culture: Black Writers and the Making of the Modern Intellectual.* Cambridge, Massachusetts: Harvard UP, 1998. Print.

Potter, Rachel. *Obscene Modernism: Literary Censorship and Experiment 1900–1940.* New York: Oxford UP, 2013. Print.

Poulantzas, Nicos. *Political Power and Social Classes.* London: Verso, 1982. Print.

Pound, Ezra. "A Few Don'ts by an Imagiste," *Poetry* 1.6 (March 1913):200–1. Print.

———. "Imagism," *Poetry* 1.6 (March 1913):199–201. Print.

———. *Literary Essays of Ezra Pound.* Norfolk, Connecticut: New Directions, 1935. Print.

———. "Small Magazines," *English Journal* 19.9 (November 1930):700. Print.

———. "Vorticism," *Fortnightly Review* (September 1, 1914):469. Print.

——— and Marcella Spann, ed. *Confucius to Cummings.* Norfolk, Connecticut: New Directions, 1964. Print.

Pratt, Annis. *Archetypal Patterns in Women's Fiction.* Bloomington: Indiana UP, 1981. Print.

Pressman, Jessica. *Digital Modernism.* New York: Oxford UP, 2014. Print.

Rabinowitz, Paula. *Labor and Desire: Women's Revolutionary Fiction in Depression America.* Chapel Hill: U of North Carolina P, 1991. Print.

Rauchway, Eric. "An Economic History of the United States 1900–1950," *A Companion to the Modern American Novel 1900–1950.* Ed. John T. Matthews. Malden, Massachusetts: Wiley-Blackwell, 2009:1–12. Print.

Reynolds, Michael. "Ernest Hemingway, 1899–1961: A Brief Biography," *A Historical Guide to Ernest Hemingway.* Ed. Linda Wagner-Martin. New York: Oxford UP, 2000:15–50. Print.

Rich, Adrienne. *Of Woman Born, Motherhood as Experience and Institution*. New York: Norton, 1976. Print.

Rideout, Walter. *The Radical Novel in the United States, 1900–1954*. Cambridge, Massachusetts: Harvard UP, 1956. Print.

Roediger, David. *The Wages of Whiteness: Race and the Making of the American Working Class*. London: Verso, 1991. Print.

Rosenthal, M. L. *The Modern Poets: A Critical Introduction*. New York: Oxford UP, 1960. Print.

Ross, Andrew. *The Failure of Modernism: Symptoms of American Poetry*. New York: Columbia UP, 1986. Print.

Sanders, Gerald DeWitt, John Herbert Nelson, M. L. Rosenthal, eds. *Chief Modern Poets of England and America*, Vol. 2. New York: Macmillan, 1962. Print.

Sartre, Jean Paul. "John Dos Passos and *1919*." *Literary Essays*. trans. Annette Michelson. New York: Philosophical Library, 1957:88–96. Print.

Schocket, Eric. *Vanishing Moments: Class and American Literature*. Ann Arbor: U of Michigan P, 2006. Print.

Schoenbach, Lisi. *Pragmatic Modernism*. New York: Oxford UP, 2012. Print.

Scholes, Robert. *Paradoxy of Modernism*. New Haven, Connecticut: Yale UP, 2006. Print.

Scott, Darieck. *Extravagant Abjection: Blackness, Power, and Sexuality in the African American Literary Imagination*. New York: New York UP, 2010. Print.

Scruggs, Charles. *Sweet Home: Invisible Cities in the Afro-American Novel*. Baltimore, Maryland: Johns Hopkins UP, 1993. Print.

Seed, David. *Cinematic Fictions*. Liverpool: Liverpool UP, 2009. Print.

Sensibar, Judith. *Faulkner and Love*. New Haven, Connecticut: Yale UP, 2009. Print.

Sherman, David. *In a Strange Room: Modernism's Corpses and Mortal Obligation*. New York: Oxford UP, 2014.

Sherry, Vincent B. *Modernism and the Reinvention of Decadence*. New York: Cambridge UP, 2015. Print.

Showalter, Elaine. *A Jury of Her Peers: American Women Writers from Anne Bradstreet to Annie Proulx*. New York: Knopf, 2009. Print.

Shulman, Robert. *The Power of Political Art: The 1930s Literary Left Reconsidered*. Chapel Hill: U of North Carolina P, 2000. Print.

Smethurst, James. *The African American Roots of Modernism*. Chapel Hill: U of North Carolina P, 2011. Print.

Smith, Henry Nash. *Virgin Land*. Cambridge, Massachusetts: Harvard UP, 1950. Print.

Smith-Rosenberg, Carroll. *Disorderly Conduct: Visions of Gender in Victorian America*. New York: Oxford UP, 1985. Print.

Sollors, Werner. *Ethnic Modernism* in *The Cambridge History of American Literature* VI. Ed. Sacvan Bercovitch. Cambridge, Massachusetts: Harvard UP, 2002:355–556. Print.

Solomon, William. *Literature, Amusement, and Technology in the Great Depression*. Cambridge: Cambridge UP, 2002. Print.

Somerville, Siobhan B. *Queering the Color Line: Race and the Invention of Homosexuality in American Culture*. Durham, NC: Duke UP, 2000. Print.

Spariosu, Mihai. *Modernism and Exile: Play, Liminality, and the Exilic-Utopian Imagination*. New York: Palgrave Macmillan, 2015. Print.

Spencer, Jon Michael. "Modernism and the Negro Renaissance." *A Modern Mosaic, Art and Modernism in the United States*. Ed. Townsend Ludington. Chapel Hill: U of North Carolina P, 2000:47–66, Print.

Spilka, Mark. *Hemingway's Quarrel with Androgyny*. Lincoln: U of Nebraska P, 1990. Print.

Spiller, Robert E. *Literary History of the United States*. New York: Macmillan, 1948. Print.

Staub, Michael. E. *Voices of Persuasion: Politics of Representation in 1930s America.* Cambridge, UK: Cambridge UP, 1994. Print.

Stepto, Robert B. *From Behind the Veil: A Study of Afro-American Narrative.* Urbana: U of Illinois P, 1979. Print.

Stewart, Grace. *A New Mythos, The Novel of the Artist as Heroine 1877–1977.* Montreal: Eden P, 1981. Print.

Straganian, Lisa. *Modernism's Other Work: The Art Object's Political Life.* New York: Oxford UP, 2012. Print.

Stratton, Matthew. *The Politics of Irony in American Modernism.* New York: Fordham UP, 2014. Print.

Strychacz, Thomas. *Modernism, Mass Culture, and Professionalism.* Cambridge: Cambridge UP, 1993. Print.

Suarez, Juan A. *Pop Modernism: Noise and the Reinvention of the Everyday.* Urbana: U of Illinois P, 2007. Print.

Sundquist, Eric. *To Wake the Nations: Race in the Making of American Literature.* Cambridge, Massachusetts: Harvard UP, 1992. Print.

Susman, Warren I. *Culture as History: The Transformation of American Society in the Twentieth Century.* Washington, D.C.: Smithsonian Institution P, 2003. Print.

Sussman, Henry. *Afterimages of Modernity: Structure and Indifference in Twentieth-Century Literature.* Baltimore, Maryland: Johns Hopkins UP, 1990. Print.

Swirski, Peter. *From Lowbrow to Nobrow.* Montreal: McGill-Queen's University P, 2005. Print.

Szalay, Michael. *New Deal Modernism: American Literature and the Invention of the Welfare State.* Durham, NC: Duke UP, 2000. Print.

Terkel, Studs. *The Studs Terkel Reader.* New York: New P, 1997. Print.

Thrailkill, Jane. *Affecting Fictions: Mind, Body and Emotion in American Literary Realism.* Cambridge, Massachusetts: Harvard UP, 2007. Print.

Thurman, Wallace. *The Blacker the Berry . . . .* New York: Macaulay, 1929. Print.

Tichi, Cecelia. *Shifting Gears: Technology, Literature, Culture in Modernist America.* Chapel Hill: U of North Carolina P, 1987. Print.

Tonning, Erik. *Modernism and Christianity.* New York: Palgrave Macmillan, 2014. Print.

Toomer, Jean. *Cane.* New York: Boni & Liveright, 1923. Print.

——. "Outline of an Autobiography," *The Wayward and the Seeking, A Collection of Writings by Jean Toomer.* Ed. Darwin Turner. Washington, D.C.: Howard UP, 1980. Print.

Trask, Michael. *Cruising Modernism: Class and Sexuality in American Literature and Social Thought.* Ithaca, New York: Cornell UP, 2003. Print.

Turner, Catherine. *Marketing Modernism between the Two World Wars.* Amherst: U of Massachusetts P, 2003. Print.

Tylee, Claire M. *The Great War and Women's Consciousness: Images of Militarism and Womanhood in Women's Writings, 1914–1964.* Iowa City: U of Iowa P, 1990. Print.

Van Vechten, Carl. *The Dance Writings of Carl Van Vechten.* Ed. Paul Padgette. New York: Dance Horizons, 1974. Print.

——. *Nigger Heaven.* New York: Knopf, 1926. Print.

Waddell, Nathan. "Modernist Coteries and Communities," *The Oxford Handbook of Modernisms.* Ed. Peter Brooker, Andrzej Gasiorek, Deborah Longworth, and Andrew Thacker. New York: Oxford UP, 2010:740–64. Print.

Waggoner, Hyatt. *American Poets from the Puritans to the Present.* Boston: Houghton Mifflin, 1968. Print.

Wagner-Martin, Linda. *A History of American Literature from 1950 to the Present.* Malden, Massachusetts: Wiley-Blackwell, 2013. Print.

———. "Toomer's *Cane* as Narrative Sequence," *Modern American Short Story Sequences*. Ed. J. Gerald Kennedy. New York: Cambridge UP, 1995:19–34. Print.

——— and Cathy N. Davidson, eds. *The Oxford Companion to Women's Writing in the United States*. New York: Oxford UP, 1995. Print.

Walcutt, Charles Child. *American Literary Naturalism, A Divided Stream*. Minneapolis: U of Minnesota P, 1956. Print.

Wald, Alan. *Exiles from a Future Time: The Forging of the Mid-Twentieth Century Literary Life*. Chapel Hill: U of North Carolina P, 2002. Print.

———. *Trinity of Passion: The Literary Left and the Antifascist Crusade*. Chapel Hill: U of North Carolina P, 2007. Print.

Wald, Priscilla. *Constituting Americans: Cultural Anxiety and Narrative Form*. Durham, NC: Duke UP, 1995. Print.

Waldmeir, Joseph J. *American Novels of the Second World War*. Amsterdam: Mouton, 1969. Print.

Wall, Cheryl A. *Women of the Harlem Renaissance*. Bloomington: Indiana UP, 1995. Print.

———. *Worrying the Line: Black Women Writers, Lineage, and Literary Tradition*. Chapel Hill: U of North Carolina P, 2005. Print.

Wallace, Rob. *Improvisation and the Making of American Literary Modernism*. New York: Continuum, 2010. Print.

Warren, Robert Penn. *All the King's Men*. New York: Random, 1946. Print.

Whalen-Bridge, John. *Political Fiction and the American Self*. Urbana: U of Illinois P, 1998. Print.

Wiesel, Elie. *Night*. trans. Marion Wiesel. New York: Hill and Wang, 2006. Print.

Wilde, Alan. *Horizons of Assent, Modernism, Postmodernism, and the Ironic Imagination*. Baltimore, Maryland: Johns Hopkins UP, 1981. Print.

Williams, William Carlos. *The Collected Poems, I*. Ed. A. Walton Litz and Christopher MacGowan. New York: New Directions, 1986. Print.

———. *Selected Essays*. New York: Random, 1954. Print.

———. *The Selected Letters of William Carlos Williams*. Ed. John C. Thirlwall. New York: McDowell, Obolensky, 1957. Print.

Williamson, Jennifer A. *Twentieth-Century Sentimentalism*. New Brunswick, New Jersey: Rutgers UP, 2014. Print.

Wilson, Edmund. *Axel's Castle*. New York: Scribner's, 1931. Print.

———. *The Shores of Light*. New York: Farrar, Straus, 1952. Print.

Wilson, Sarah. *Melting-Pot Modernism*. Ithaca, New York: Cornell UP, 2010. Print.

Wintz, Cary D. *Black Culture and the Harlem Renaissance*. Houston, Texas: Rice UP, 1988.

Wolfe, Thomas. *Look Homeward, Angel*. New York: Scribner's, 1929. Print.

———. *Thomas Wolfe's Letters to His Mother, Julia Elizabeth Wolfe*. Ed. John Skally Terry. New York: Scribner's, 1943. Print.

Yaeger, Patricia. *Dirt and Desire: Reconstructing Southern Women's Writing, 1930–1990*. Chicago: U of Chicago P, 2000. Print.

———. *Honey-Mad Women: Emancipatory Strategies in Women's Writing*. New York: Columbia UP, 1988. Print.

Zafar, Rafia. "Fictions of the Harlem Renaissance," *The Cambridge History of American Literature*, VI. Ed. Sacvan Berkovitch. Cambridge: Cambridge UP, 2002:285–352. Print.

Zox-Weaver, Annalisa. *Modernists and Fascism*. Cambridge: Cambridge UP, 2011. Print.

INDEX